STARMAKER

LIFE AS A HOLLYWOOD PUBLICIST WITH FARRAH, THE RAT PACK AND 600 MORE STARS WHO FIRED ME

JAY BERNSTEIN

AS TOLD TO LARRY CORTEZ HAMM WITH DAVID RUBINI

ECW Press

Published by ECW Press
2120 Queen Street East, Suite 200, Toronto, Ontario, Canada M4E 1E2
416-694-3348 / info@ecwpress.com

Library and Archives Canada Cataloguing in Publication

Bernstein, Jay, 1937-2006
Starmaker : life as a Hollywood publicist with Farrah,
the Rat Pack & 600 more stars who fired me / Jay Bernstein and Larry Cortez Hamm.

ISBN 978-1-77041-012-1
ALSO ISSUED AS: 978-1-77090-044-8 (PDF); 978-1-77090-043-1 (EPUB)

1. Bernstein, Jay, 1937-2006. 2. Public relations consultants—
United States—Biography. 3. Celebrities—Public relations—United
States. I. Hamm, Larry Cortez II. Title.

HM1226.B47 2011   659.2'092   C2011-902822-0

Cover and text design: Cyanotype
Front cover image: Image Source Photography
Back cover image: ©Merkuri2/Dreamstime.com
Typesetting: Troy Cunningham
Production: Rachel Ironstone
ECW PRESS
ecwpress.com
Printing: Thomson-Shore 1 2 3 4 5

PRINTED AND BOUND IN THE UNITED STATES

THIS BOOK IS DEDICATED TO MY CLIENTS—
actors, directors, entertainers, musicians, composers,
producers, singers and writers—friends all, that I
represented as a publicist, personal manager and/or
producer during a Hollywood career that spanned
almost five decades. Collectively they are my family, my
history and the people who have given my life meaning.

—JAY BERNSTEIN

"The only rule in Hollywood is there are no rules."

—JAY BERNSTEIN

"If the reader prefers, this book may be regarded as fiction. But there is always the chance that such a book of fiction may throw some light on what has been written as fact."

—ERNEST HEMINGWAY,
Preface, *A Moveable Feast*

"And who can tell where make-believe leaves off and reality begins when fantasy is your business."

—EVELYN KEYES,
(Suellen O'Hara, *Gone with the Wind*)

IF VANITY IS THE FIRST CRITERION FOR WRITING A MEMOIR, *then I qualify without argument. One cannot negotiate successfully through the Hollywood jungle for almost fifty years absent a large ego, healthy or not. Egotism, however, was not my sole motive for penning the following pages. Rather, and more important, I was provoked by the collective ignorance of people who observe the motion picture and television industry from afar, particularly the Washington, D.C., crowd, the politicians and pundits who blame Hollywood for every national shortcoming. Seldom do they have knowledge of what they speak and write about. I wanted to set them straight, if possible, by penning a story as seen from the inside of an industry looking out, rather than the opposite.*

What the world calls "Hollywood" is not a monolithic entity responsible for continual cultural change, good or bad. In fact, motion pictures and television shows generally reflect what society looks like rather than what we might want it to be. It was the great Sam Goldwyn who had it right: "If you want to send a message, go to Western Union." The making of motion pictures and television shows is a diverse industry, as competitive as any on earth, and that's why it's called show business, not show art. We are lucky indeed when every so often a motion picture transcends its producer's intent of making a profitable entertainment and sublimates itself to a real meaning, to art.

Most of the people in this story were stars at a given moment in their careers—actors, writers, directors, producers—yet the majority are now forgotten. But that's the nature of our collective memory. How many people know who the eighth president of the United States was? Or the eighteenth? Few indeed. It is the same in Hollywood. As with most histories, Hollywood's is generational; some people forget very quickly, and young people seem not to care about the past at all, which is a mistake. If you don't know where you've been, how do you know where you're going?

Of the first generation of Hollywood stars, only Chaplin comes quickly to mind, less frequently Fatty Arbuckle, and for a few people the Keystone Kops. Valentino remains in our collective memory because of his youthful death, and Jean Harlow for the same reason. Had James Dean not died tragically at twenty-four he might not be remembered either, with a resumé of only three movies. Had Ronald Reagan not become president of the United States, he, too, would probably be one of those actors lost somewhere in a dark alley off Hollywood's memory lane.

This book was written for young people, all those wannabes who migrate annually to the West Coast seeking fame and fortune in show business. I want them to know how difficult and dangerous the path is. With rare exception, success does not come overnight, and for most it never comes at all. Hollywood is a jungle, make no mistake about it, and my own experiences will shed some light on the pitfalls often encountered by the uninitiated. Remember this: in the shadows behind every spotlight, there lurks a predator.

So here is my story of Hollywood, the way I saw it and the way I lived it—the good, the bad and the ugly.

Chapter 1

INTRODUCTION TO THE HOLLYWOOD JUNGLE

A couple of years ago, I was in a clothing store across from Morton's Restaurant, the famous celebrity watering hole and eatery in West Hollywood. It was near dusk on a beautiful, Indian summer day. I was killing time before a dinner engagement, watching the pretty girls and shopping for nothing when a woman's voice called out, "Jay!"

I looked; it was Kathy Hilton of the hotel Hiltons.

Back in the nineties, when I was married, my wife and I used to double-date with Kathy and Rick. We'd meet them for dinner. My wife was a social climber and it meant everything to her to be able to tell her friends, "Oh, the Hiltons joined us last night at Spago," as if the Hiltons gave a damn.

The relationship between the Hiltons and the Bernsteins was brief. I was married for about thirty seconds. Meanwhile, Kathy and Rick, once a noted couple on the social circuit of Beverly Hills, Manhattan and other hotspots of media interest, had succumbed to age and maturity: they were known now as the parents of Paris and Nicky.

Kathy and I chatted a moment about old times, of which neither of us remembered much, and then she said, "Jay, why don't you manage Paris?"

I hardly knew who Paris was—this was before her sexploitation video—and what little I knew about her came from the scandal sheets, which meant I knew nothing. She and her sister were yellow-journalism fodder because they were rich and their name was Hilton.

"What's Paris up to?" I asked.

Kathy gave me an update. Paris had done this and she was going to do that. I was intrigued. My claim to fame was managing entertainment careers, optimizing the potentials of would-be stars. I had three criteria garnered from decades of experience: 1) a client had to have talent, 2) she had to have a physical quality that appealed to me personally, and 3) she had to have a vehicle, a platform from which a career could be launched.

Suddenly Kathy said, "Paris! Paris! Come here!"

Paris came. She was not a naturally beautiful girl, but she had exotic features that were somehow attractive.

"This is Jay Bernstein, the starmaker," explained Kathy. "He created Farrah Fawcett and—"

"I didn't create anyone," I interrupted. "I guided them through the showbiz jungle. I took them from a level six to a level ten." It was my pat explanation, partly true, partly false.

The truth was, in my prime I had a Midas touch. If I said to someone, "This one's gonna be a star!" they didn't argue with me.

What I said, however, was unimportant, because Paris was in her own world. I watched her. She puffed a cigarette like an automaton. Her blue eyes darted about, often to her own reflection in a big mirror on the wall, as her mother spoke.

I had no idea if Paris had talent, but talent is only one ingredient in the recipe for stardom. She was like a nervous bird fluttering her wings; not a beautifully plumed cardinal or blue jay, more like a sparrow. Her attention span was so short she could hardly finish a laugh. She had no redeeming quality that appealed to me. What she had was a television reality show, a vehicle. Unfortunately, reality shows seldom showcase star appeal; they are dumbing-down endeavors, reaching for the lowest common denominator of an audience.

Kathy kept talking. Paris kept smoking and looking at herself in the mirror. Her resumé sounded as empty as a vacuum. She reminded me of Zsa Zsa Gabor, whom I had represented many years before as her publicist. Zsa Zsa had been married to *the* Hilton, Conrad, Paris's great-grandfather. But Zsa Zsa had never been a star, only a celebrity famous for being famous.

While Kathy kept talking, Paris fluttered her wings and flew away. She wasn't interested in being managed; in her mind she was a star already. Just read the tabloids. Her name was Hilton, and that seemed enough, along with her inheritance, to sustain her image.

I bid Kathy adieu and went on my merry way. I never knew if she was just being friendly or if she was serious about my managing Paris's career, but it made no difference. I didn't think Paris had what stardom required. She was certainly no Farrah Fawcett. In her prime, Farrah had gained icon status—a role model recognized around the world. Through unbelievably hard work and self-sacrifice, Farrah had become a star fixed luminously in the firmament. I suspected Paris was more of a comet, coming and going from time to time, but still no more than a flash in the sky.

Farrah . . .

Her name always came up. At its birth, Farrah-mania swept over the entire world like nothing seen since Elvis or the Beatles. From her beautiful blue eyes to her long, golden feathered hair, pearly white smile and sweet demeanor. She had a drop-dead gorgeous figure and possessed the type of over-the-top sex appeal that was fresh, exciting and internationally contagious. Women wanted to be her, and men wanted to marry her, not just sleep with her. Even the young actors and wannabes of the nineties and beyond were aware of Farrah, and this in an era when the longevity of a star seemed to rarely exceed Andy Warhol's proverbial fifteen minutes.

As her personal manager, I put together all the things I had learned along the way to finally do what I had originally come out here for—to be involved in creating Hollywood heroes and heroines.

There had been a time when the names Farrah Fawcett and Jay Bernstein were synonymous. And Suzanne Somers was often mentioned in the same breath. Farrah and Suzanne. I had created them, so it was said. Those were tough days, halcyon only in retrospect—my clients and I seemingly pitted against the world.

But there were many others. William Holden and Susan Hayward. Nick Adams and Robert Conrad. Sammy Davis, Jr., and Aretha Franklin. Robert Culp, Gig Young, Dionne Warwick, Angie Dickinson, Tom Jones, Peter Fonda, Charlotte Rampling, Linda Evans, Catherine Hicks, Tatum O'Neal—six hundred in all, spanning four generations of show business. And ultimately all of them had fired me. My glib explanation for termination was simple but true: "I took them where the air was rarified, they became deified, and then I was nullified."

Fired six hundred times, but I'm still smiling. In most cases I accomplished what I set out to do. I did it by replacing an effete studio system that collapsed in the 1960s—when one man had to assume the role of two dozen specialists the studios no longer provided. For my clients, I became head of wardrobe, style and fashion. I took over publicity for them when the studio publicity departments switched from promoting stars to promoting movies. I guided careers as Harry Cohn, Louis Mayer and Darryl Zanuck had once done as moguls of their respective star factories. None of it was easy, but I did it, and no one can take away my accomplishments.

I was a maverick by necessity, not by choice. Had I not been, people never would have heard of Farrah Fawcett and dozens of other names. Some established stars would have continued to run in place, never advancing. To my clients I was Sir Lancelot; to studio and network executives I was Darth Vader. In the early years it was not easy to be a split personality. I wanted to be popular, loved by all. Then I realized that Hollywood was divided like any industry: it was management versus labor. In most cases, I took the side of labor, the actors and entertainers.

Stars represented glamour to me. They portrayed heroes that gave young people direction and made life meaningful. They were America's role models. When bottom-line corporations gobbled up the studios, I became determined to keep glamour in the industry and stars as heroes. Jay Bernstein—one man against the system.

When I was growing up in Oklahoma City, I was the fattest kid in my class. I had no coordination. I couldn't climb a fence because of my weight; I couldn't do a single chin-up at the bar. I was a total failure athletically, yet my parents thought I should participate in sports: football, basketball and baseball. After school I was supposed to go to practice. I didn't. I caught a bus and went to a movie. Not once did my parents question my whereabouts. They never asked me why I didn't have to show up for a game. I figured they thought my athletic prowess was so negligible that at practice I was nothing more than a punching bag for the real athletes.

Movies became my life. I found my heroes through stars on the big screen: Gary Cooper, Clark Gable, Robert Taylor, John Wayne, Tyrone Power, Gregory Peck, Henry Fonda, James Stewart and, most of all, Alan Ladd. I tried to look like Ladd, talk like him. I became a kid version of Alan Ladd. By the time I graduated high school I had seen *Shane* seventeen times. I could recite the lines of every actor in the movie as they were being spoken. Alan Ladd was not just an actor named Alan Ladd, he *was* Shane. And Clark Gable was Rhett Butler, Errol Flynn was Robin Hood, and Gary Cooper was Sergeant York.

Westerns were my favorite genre. When I was fourteen, I was still acting out hero roles in front of a mirror in my bedroom. I had two cowboy hats, a white one and a black one, and two holstered toy six-shooters. Wearing my white hat cocked at a rakish angle, I would say into the mirror, "I want you out of town by sundown," and then I would switch hats. "I ain't goin' nowhere, Sheriff."

When I got carried away in my fantasy, my mother would call up to my room, "Jay, who's up there with you?"

"Nobody, Mother!"

"Don't lie to me! I hear voices other than yours."

"I'm talking to myself!"

"It doesn't sound like you."

My mother was incapable of understanding my fixation on heroes. She thought celluloid idols were for suckers. I was too young to express what I perceived intuitively: heroes were necessary. Kids needed role models who stood for something good in society, who fought injustice and villains. The actions of my heroes caused me to forget the mundane aspects of my life. To me, movies were the new literature of the masses. They made me forget I was fat.

I first visited Hollywood when I was twelve. I was with my parents and my sister. For them it was a vacation; for me it was serious business.

Hollywood. The word stirred my imagination. It conjured images of glamour, ideas of gallantry and action, and a variety of abstractions, good, bad and sometimes confusing. Hollywood—the dream factory. It was everything . . . but it could be nothing.

In 1949, the real Hollywood, the suburb of Los Angeles from which the motion-picture industry derived its name, was a town already gone seedy. At one end of Hollywood Boulevard was Grauman's Chinese Theatre, where the handprints and footprints were; at the other end was the Brown Derby Restaurant, where stars still lunched and dined. Between the two points you might as well have been in Kansas City. In the minds of most people, Hollywood was no longer a town; it was an idea, an all-encompassing term that meant motion pictures. Hollywood was about images you saw on a screen in a darkened auditorium that you paid to enter. It was about American royalty, like Carole Lombard and Clark Gable.

My mother's sister was an advance press agent for road plays like *Don Juan in Hell* and *John Brown's Body.* She had enough clout to get passes for my family to Paramount Studios, where we watched Alan Ladd flub twenty takes before he got it right in a scene for *Appointment with Danger.* Jack Webb and Henry Morgan played the villains, a turnabout from their later roles as two of television's most famous cops in *Dragnet.*

Watching Alan Ladd walk up to a water cooler and say one line the wrong way nineteen times was startling. Movies were not easy to make, and there were all those specialists on the set—cameramen, gaffers, grips, makeup people—it was mind-boggling for an impressionable youth, but magical, too.

Once my sister Jan and I were walking down one of the near-empty studio streets. A man rode toward us on a bicycle. He pulled up and stopped. "Hi, kids, I saw you on my set."

My heart leaped to my throat. He was Alan Ladd. It was one of the few times in my life I was speechless. I was so thrilled that I don't remember the ensuing conversation, but it had to be good, for Alan Ladd could do no wrong; he could flub *fifty* takes for all I cared! He gave me his autograph. My mind was made up: I wanted to be Alan Ladd, King of Paramount.

By the time I made my second trip to Hollywood, in 1953, I had suffered appendicitis, had an operation and lost weight. I could see my ribs for the first time. I could do one hundred chin-ups. I was Shane.

Then something happened. We went to Twentieth Century-Fox, where we saw a very young Robert Wagner in period tights acting in the title role of *Prince Valiant*. I got his autograph and those of other members of the cast—James Mason, Sterling Hayden and Victor McLaglen. I now had over one hundred star signatures in my autograph book, but something significant had happened: I didn't think I would like wearing tights.

Almost every young person who goes to Hollywood to pursue a career is running away from something; usually it's either a dysfunctional family or poverty. For me it was the threat of living a simple life of boredom in Oklahoma. It was also my mother. My problems with her were congenital. They reached the first of many peaks when I was in the fourth grade. Someone at school explained to me what the middle-finger sign meant. Fascinated with this newfound knowledge, I told my sister, who was three years younger than me. She told my mother, who slipped a note under my bedroom door telling me to leave and never come back. I was ten years old. I went downstairs, got a handful of kitchen matches, went back upstairs, and burned up my bedroom.

Fastidious was my mother's modus operandi; everything had to be perfect. While my room was going up in flames, she went to the kitchen and washed the dishes before calling the fire department. She didn't want firemen seeing dirty dishes when they arrived. Everything in the house had to be in an exact position, from pictures to chairs. She was a perfectionist, the gene of which I inherited. Her father had been extremely wealthy when she was young, but he lost his fortune during the Depression. In the time of plenty my mother spent two years in a finishing school at Lausanne, Switzerland, where the students were trained to marry French nobility. She beat into me the princess training etiquette she had learned abroad, like which of fourteen forks you use to eat spinach or what knife you use to cut asparagus. I resented the training, but it came in handy later down the road when I began to manage female stars.

When I moved permanently to Hollywood in 1960, I had no idea how my life would unfold. I knew nothing about movies except what I saw on the screen and read in magazines. I was a fish out of water, looking for someplace to swim. I was twenty-two, a college graduate, and a "six-month wonder" as a recently separated junior officer from the United States Army. I considered myself the Playboy of the Western World. My major had been history, from which I learned one truth: history *does* repeat itself. If an unknown John Doe could be successful in Hollywood, then so, too, could Jay Bernstein.

From Fort Benjamin Harrison in Indiana I went home to Oklahoma City. I had a scattered knowledge of literature, and after two weeks I realized Thomas Wolfe was right: "You can't go home again." Fourteen days in Indian Territory seemed an eternity of nothingness. I didn't even see an Indian; I suspected they were all in Hollywood.

I packed my bags and took off. I wanted to befriend Alan Ladd and find my niche in show business. I didn't know what I was going to do— only that I was not going to pursue an acting career. My thoughts had transcended the embarrassment of wearing tights. The male lead in a motion picture was always handsome; he received first screen credit. The female lead got second credit. The second male lead got third credit. I didn't think I was handsome enough to become a top star and I wasn't going to be third in anything.

I had a sky blue '48 Dodge passed down to me by my uncle Irwin; I had $1,000 cash in my pocket, a gift from my father, and an attitude full of piss and vinegar. Somewhere around Kingman, Arizona, I decided to veer north and go to Las Vegas. It was my first of many mistakes. Two days later I pulled off the Santa Monica Freeway into the heart of Los Angeles. My stake had been reduced to $400. The playboy was deflated but not defeated. I stopped at the first apartment building with a sign: Furnished Single Units, Ninety Dollars per Month. I had no idea where I was, but I didn't care. I already knew that Hollywood was a state of mind.

The apartment manager was an emaciated Hispanic wearing a muscle shirt and twenty-one tattoos I could actually count. I had left Oklahoma behind, but brought with me a bundle of southwestern prejudices. I rented a furnished apartment and by the time I finished two dozen trips from my room to the street and back, dusk had fallen to darkness. I lay down. My thoughts were racing at full speed.

Then a sharp, booming report blasted from the street, followed by a crash. I lurched and sat up. A second blast issued. I went to a window. A car straddled the curb in front of the building; a crowd was gathering. I went down the stairs again. People encircled the body of a bleeding, moaning man; no one was offering assistance. In the glow of a streetlight I could see where bullets had twice penetrated the man's body. The crowd grew with a mumble of voices, all speaking Spanish, whispers at first, and then rising.

A police car glided to a stop, its cherry lights blinking as if it were a spaceship from Mars. Two cops got out lackadaisically. A siren sounded. Everybody looked. An ambulance pulled up; paramedics hopped out and jockeyed through the crowd. I felt like an extra in a Raymond Chandler movie. I slipped into the shadows and escaped to my room. I was alone and lonely; I knew not a soul. I remember thinking, "Everybody is a nobody until they become a somebody. Welcome to Hollywood, Bernstein. The movie of your life has begun!"

I woke at first light of day. The boulevard was bustling with traffic; the air was crisp; pedestrians were in good cheer. My landlord was washing down the sidewalk with a hose. The night seemed remote, like a candle flickering its last breath, and suddenly it was out. It was time for me to get a job. Except I didn't—nor did I try.

I had breakfast at a corner café and perused the classified ads in the *Los Angeles Times*. Not a single studio executive needed an assistant. I got in my Dodge and drove up and down Sunset Boulevard, east to downtown Los Angeles and west to the Pacific Ocean. This became my daily routine: breakfast at the hash house, then a long, long drive.

I drove through Beverly Hills, Holmby Hills and Bel Air, down to the Malibu Colony, through the canyons of the Santa Monica Mountains and into the San Fernando Valley, past the famous Hollywood sign from which a frustrated, would-be starlet had once leaped to her death, an omen of what Hollywood could do. Like most young people who go to Hollywood in pursuit of a dream, I didn't know how to go about accomplishing it.

The studios were huge, walled-in complexes with guards hovering at their gates. Ditto for the three television networks. Nobody outside the walls seemed to know what was going on inside the walls, except for what they read in the trade papers. I had to figure out a way to break the barrier. I decided to use bullshit.

The Paramount gate hadn't changed since 1950, when Billy Wilder and Charles Brackett had made *Sunset Boulevard* with Gloria Swanson and William Holden. After my pitch, I expected to be passed through with the same courtesy extended to Norma Desmond, and then escorted to the office of the president, where, of course, my genius would be recognized. I pulled up to the guardhouse.

"Name?" asked the guard.

"Jay Bernstein."

He ran his finger down a list on a clipboard. "Who you got an appointment with?"

"Cecil B. DeMille."

He waved an arm in a brusque, twirling fashion. "You can turn around over there."

"But—"

"Mr. DeMille died a year ago. Now move it! You're blocking the driveway."

If I was naïve, I wasn't stupid. I headed next to Warner Bros., a drive sufficiently long for me to glean a name from *Daily Variety* and piece together a plan. This time I didn't try to drive through the gate. I parked down the street at a restaurant called the Smoke House and sauntered casually to the guardhouse, as if I owned the world.

"What can I do for you?" asked the guard.

"Nothing," I told him. "I forgot to tell my uncle to get me a pass. I'll wait for him. We're having lunch at the Smoke House."

"Who's your uncle?"

"Fred Zinnemann."

The guard snapped to. Zinnemann was one of Hollywood's top directors. *High Noon*, *From Here to Eternity*, *The Nun's Story*. Now he was doing postproduction at Warner's on *The Sundowners*.

"Want me to call his office?" asked the guard.

"No, he's probably tied up. You know how it is. Uncle Freddie's always running late. I don't want to bother him."

I waited, chatting amiably. After ten minutes I knew the guard's name, rank and serial number. He was calling me Jay. "I'd better go back and wait at the restaurant," I said.

"Okay, Jay. Have a good day."

"You too, Waldo."

Three days later I went back to Warner Bros. in a taxi. I got out at the gate. Same guard. "Morning, Jay."

"Has Uncle Freddie arrived yet?"

"Yeah, he came through about twenty minutes ago."

"Damn," I muttered. I looked at my watch. "I'm late. He's gonna be pissed off."

"Tell him you had a flat tire."

"Good idea." I began walking, wondering if Waldo was going to stop me. When I was thirty feet down the driveway, actually on the grounds of the studio proper, he called after me, "Have a good day, Jay."

That's how I got onto the Warner Bros. lot, and with similar chicanery, into Universal, Paramount, MGM, Disney, Columbia and Twentieth Century-Fox—the seven major studios.

Not knowing a soul was no deterrent. People thought I was somebody important. I watched scenes being filmed as if I were present at the request of an executive. I became a fixture, like a piece of furniture. I ate in the commissaries, eavesdropping on adjacent tables, piecing together a who's who of studio clientele. I was a phantom junior executive, dropping names incessantly. "Mr. Warner told me . . ." or "I was talking to Alan Ladd . . ."

Unfortunately, no one of significance recognized my talent. My rent was coming due, and I was forced to seek a job in earnest. Through my mother I had a remote connection to the Music Corporation of America, the giant talent agency that was on the verge of gobbling up Universal Studios.

I did some homework. MCA's roster of star clients included Marlon Brando, Gregory Peck, Clark Gable, Jimmy Stewart, Marilyn Monroe, Shirley MacLaine, Tony Curtis and Janet Leigh. I decided I wanted to be an agent, the guy who got 10 percent of their paychecks.

The agency's offices were in the heart of Beverly Hills. I was impressed. The headquarters looked like an antebellum mansion in Alabama. Inside, a huge crystal chandelier hung above a sweeping double circular staircase. I looked around, hoping to see Rhett Butler; then a receptionist sent me to the personnel office.

When I turned in my questionnaire, I said confidentially, "My mother was engaged to Bob Beckerman before she married my father. Beckerman is Edie Wasserman's brother." Edie Wasserman was the wife of Lew Wasserman, MCA's president and maybe the most powerful man in Hollywood.

The personnel guy shrugged. My mother's vaunted connection and the fact I was a college graduate with my military duty behind me were only good enough to get me on the bottom of a yearlong waiting list, which would not impress my landlord.

Next I drove to the venerable William Morris Agency, the oldest and most prestigious of the talent agencies. Among its clients were Frank Sinatra, Kim Novak, Sammy Davis, Jr., Steve McQueen, Warren Beatty, Clint Eastwood, Paul Newman and Joanne Woodward, for the most part a decidedly younger group of actors that appealed to me. The agency was headquartered in a new but profoundly dismal three-story building that was less attractive than a post office.

The receptionist was an extroverted, would-be actress with a bright smile. After we flirted a few minutes she dispatched me to the personnel office, where I received the same curt welcome offered at MCA. I was placed on another waiting list, this time for only six months.

Back in the lobby, I chatted again with the receptionist. It was important to make inside connections; she might be the secret lover of one of the lords of the manor. She kept answering the telephone. Finally I blew her a kiss and started to leave.

"Wait, Jay!" She covered the transmitter. "Come back!" It was a *Shane* moment—she was Brandon De Wilde and I was Alan Ladd—then she resumed talking into the phone.

I listened. One of the mailroom drivers had been taken to a hospital following a car accident. The receptionist said into the phone, "The young man you just interviewed was leaving, but I caught him." She hung up. "Go back to personnel," she said. "I think you'll get the job."

I did—at forty dollars a week—because some unfortunate young mailroom clerk had the decency to crash a company car.

Chapter 2

FROM THE MAILROOM TO THE BEDROOM

I thought it was demeaning to be relegated to the mailroom of the William Morris Agency rather than to an executive suite. I told people I was an agent, while I was really a glorified errand boy. Most of the time I drove around in a stick-shift company car, delivering packages to studios and production companies. One day I spent four hours managing the purchase and delivery of a rare pipe tobacco—rare, because pipe smoking had pretty much gone out of fashion when General Douglas MacArthur retired to his five-star suite at the Waldorf-Astoria in New York City.

Forty dollars a week wasn't enough money to cut the mustard of my hotdog life. My rent was more than half of my total income. I was nervous. My parents had reared me with few restrictions and given me a good education, including college, but now that I had reached my maturity they felt that parental obligations were finished. The thousand dollars my father had given me when I left Oklahoma was a final contribution to my welfare, with a tacit agreement between us that I should expect no more financial aid. Furthermore, my mother had been vociferously opposed to my going to Hollywood to seek fame and fortune. For me to come begging for more money would have delighted her, almost as much as turning down my request.

Thus I was truly on my own, and there was no turning back. I got a second job working the early night shift at a ball-bearing factory in beautiful downtown Burbank, but I still didn't have enough money. I took a third job parking cars on weekends at Lawry's, the famous prime-rib steakhouse on La Cienega Boulevard's Restaurant Row. It wasn't easy, but I kept up the pace, always reminding myself that things could be worse. And sure enough, that's what they became.

I had been at the agency three months and was en route to CBS to deliver a script. A sexy girl wiggling down the sidewalk distracted me. Wham! I was only driving ten miles an hour, but when you rear-end another car, even at a snail's crawl, it brings your thoughts back into focus. I leaped out. The driver of the other car was a nondescript man with a nonchalant attitude.

"I am so sorry," I gushed with Oklahoma innocence. "It was my fault. Are you okay?"

"Don't worry about it." He inspected my car. "Don't see no damage."

"It's a company car," I said. "I work for William Morris."

"Who's he?"

"It's the big talent agency."

He looked at the rear of his car. It didn't have a scratch.

"I'm terribly sorry," I repeated.

"Don't worry about it. What was the name of that company?"

The next day I was summoned to my superior's office. Overnight the guy I bumped into had suffered post-accident whiplash, although he wasn't so disabled that he couldn't file a six-figure damage suit against William Morris. "Today is your last day, Bernstein," said my boss.

I went to the mailroom and suffered through the day. Most devastating was the realization I was out of show business. Manufacturing ball bearings and parking cars was not remotely as satisfying as cleaning out the William Morris elephant cages. It was ironic: I got the job because of a car accident; now I was losing it ditto.

One of my mailroom colleagues was Steve Bershad, whose father was Sheldon Leonard, a successful television producer. Apparently my remorse over having had the accident and my sheer, absolute melancholy at having been fired touched Steve's soul where it counted. "I'm dining with my parents tonight at their home," he said. "Why don't you join us?"

Sheldon Leonard was not just another face in a cloudy montage of Hollywood personalities. He was legendary, not only as a TV producer and director but as a first-echelon character actor in movies. No serious buff was unaware of his face and his voice; his signature character was a Damon Runyon–like tough guy with a Brooklyn accent. More recently he had teamed with Danny Thomas to produce *The Danny Thomas Show* (formerly *Make Room for Daddy*) and *The Real McCoys*, television sitcom hits.

At five o'clock, I left the William Morris Agency for the last time as an employee, drove to my cracker-box apartment in the hood and got ready for dinner at seven thirty. My imagination was running rampant. I didn't know what I was going to do, but I knew I had to do something dramatic at the Leonard home; otherwise it was "Goodbye, Mr. Chips."

Steve and his parents met me at the front door. No doubt Steve had told his mother and father how depressed I was over being fired, but I took an upbeat attitude. I was good at social charm, and I wanted to impress Sheldon.

We were drinking cocktails on the terrace, talking about nothing in particular, when Sheldon said, "Steve told me you lost your job today."

I shifted gears and went from Jay Glad to Jay Sad, taking on a hangdog expression and staring at my shoes. "I'm not going to let it defeat me, Mr. Leonard."

"It's Sheldon, please."

"Thank you, but it's difficult not to call you Mr. Leonard. That's how much respect I have for you. You're one of my Hollywood idols."

Over dinner I went back to Jay Glad. When dessert was served, I switched again to Jay Sad, assuming the most god-awful look of depression I could muster. I stumbled through the remaining conversation, waiting for an opportunity to show my stuff. Finally Sheldon gave it to me.

"Are you okay, Jay?" he asked.

"Yes, sir. It's just that I . . . I . . ." And my story erupted like Old Faithful, spewing forth all the unlucky heartache a guy could get by losing the only job he'd ever wanted, the job that had been the stepping stone to attaining his lifelong dream. I laid it on as thick as tar, telling how I would have worked for William Morris for free, just for the experience of learning, how I had dedicated my life to the opportunity, and now, just because I bumped a fender while trying to do my dead-level best for the company, a company whose executives I would have died for, well . . .

I sighed and looked around the table. They were staring at me with sad, pensive eyes. In Oklahoma, where Southern sensibilities were de rigueur, I had been taught that a man never cried in front of other people, but I felt I had to do something drastic; otherwise I was out of show business and the elephant cages would fill up with dung. I broke into tears. I didn't just cry—I sobbed. "I'm sorry," I moaned. "I can't help myself."

Sheldon was sympathetic. After I cleared my eyes and blew my nose and stared into space like a stricken zombie, he said, "You really love this business, don't you, Jay?"

"I do!" I cried, and burst into tears again. "But I'm not giving up. I won't! I can't!"

Driving home, what guilt I felt at deceiving my hosts was shoved into a dark recess of my mind. The entire family had been compassionate about my plight, although Sheldon, the only one who could really do anything about it, had made no promises. But I had a gut feeling . . .

The next morning I put on my only suit, a double-breasted blue serge, with a matching silk tie and a white shirt. At nine, I sat down beside my telephone and waited for somebody to call—Steve, Sheldon, maybe Sheldon's secretary. Ten o'clock came without a ring, then eleven and finally noon. I did not move. When two p.m. came, my hopes began to falter. When three came, I decided to call it quits. I sighed and stood up for the first time in hours. That's when the telephone rang.

"Mr. Bernstein?" asked a mature woman's voice.

"Yes, this is he."

"I'm calling for Mr. Leonard. He wants you to go to Rogers, Cowan & Brenner for a job interview at ten o'clock tomorrow morning."

I caught my breath. Rogers, Cowan and who?

The woman gave me the address: 250 North Canon Drive in Beverly Hills. She explained that Rogers, Cowan & Brenner was an important public-relations firm. It was the first time I'd heard the phrase "public relations," something they didn't teach at Casady Prep School or Pomona College. I had no idea what it was, but if it was good enough for Sheldon Leonard, it was good enough for Jay Bernstein.

We hung up. My suit was dripping sweat. I hung the trousers on one hanger and the coat on another to let them air out and dry before my fateful interview the next morning. Then I relaxed. Perhaps I wasn't out of show business after all.

At nine thirty the next morning, I arrived at Rogers, Cowan & Brenner. I was impressed. The company was big, with dozens of employees scattered through dozens of offices on the entire second floor of a three story building. The first floor belonged to Doris Day's company, Martin Melcher Productions; the third floor housed Creative Management Associates, a talent agency run by David Begelman and Freddie Fields.

Teme Brenner, one of the Rogers, Cowan & Brenner partners, interviewed me. She had a Billy Wilder meet-cute attitude, as if she thought we were required to go through an interview ritual out of convention, which led me to believe I had a job regardless. At last she directed me to a small office with a desk, a typewriter and some paper.

"Write two pages, double-spaced, on what Sheldon Leonard thinks of comedy," she said, and winked.

I began typing clickety-clack with my index fingers. I hardly knew what I was writing, but I doubted if it would be read. When I handed it in like a schoolboy, Teme gave me the details of my new job as a publicist. My pay would be fifty-five dollars per week, fifteen dollars more than at William Morris.

Rogers, Cowan & Brenner was to talent publicity what William Morris was to talent representation, with one exception. While Morris had heavy-duty competition—especially from MCA—Rogers, Cowan & Brenner was number one in its field with no other company remotely close to it. It was the largest and most important public-relations firm in show business.

After Teme explained to me the company's function in the entertainment world, I knew I'd found my niche, if only temporarily. Public relations was a cousin of advertising. Advertisers bought space and time in newspapers, magazines and electronic outlets, while PR agents sought the same space and time for free, from the editors of the same media. "You have to be creative," said Teme.

It was right up my alley. During high school and college I had summer jobs, literally dozens of them because I always got fired. I even got fired from my father's popular ladies' apparel store. The manager said I spent too much time flirting with the customers, and my father backed him. I then got a job working for a livestock feed store. They sent me to the boondocks with a trunk full of small signs. I was supposed to tack a sign to a fencepost every hundred yards. I got tired fast. I had enough signs to post all the way to Chicago. My boss apparently thought we were selling Burma-Shave when we were just selling hay to local ranchers and farmers. I nailed the rest of the signs to one huge tree on the outskirts of town. My scheme turned out to be against the law, defacing nature or some such charge. I got fired, although the feed store got more publicity than ever before, and free.

Teme assigned me to the television department, one of five divisions, the gem being the personality department where stars were represented. I was an assistant to publicist Vic Heutschy, who was charged with promoting and publicizing several series, including *The June Allyson Show*, a weekly anthology hosted by Ms. Allyson; *The Rebel*, an offbeat Western series starring Nick Adams; *The Rifleman*, another Western, with Chuck Connors; and Sheldon Leonard's *The Danny Thomas Show*, with comedian Danny Thomas. My job was to come up with ideas to promote each week's shows. I was to report for duty the next morning. As I left the building, I felt a surge of happiness. I was back in show business and already plotting my future. My first goal was to get switched from the television department to the personality department.

My job gave me the freedom to hang out at studio soundstages without the use of chicanery and to act like a big shot with a small portfolio. I made friends with the actors in my assigned shows and flirted mercilessly with the actresses. I moved out of the barrio and into an apartment on Larabee

Street above the Sunset Strip in West Hollywood. I split the rent with Stan Moress, another young publicist. Stan, who would become my lifelong best friend, was related to Henry Rogers, one of the company owners. I gave up my executive positions at the ball-bearing plant and Lawry's parking lot.

I began a work ethic at Rogers & Cowan (Brenner eventually was bought out) that stayed with me for the next forty years. I figured if I worked twice as hard as others, I would go twice as far. Henry Rogers was at the office each morning at seven sharp, so I was there at six thirty. Warren Cowan did not show up until nine, but he stayed until seven, so I stayed until seven thirty. I did a thirteen-hour day shift at the office and on the sets of shows I was assigned to and another six-hour shift at night, making the rounds of parties, bars and restaurants where I might bump into important stars, producers and directors—"Hi! I'm Jay Bernstein with Rogers & Cowan!" I was at odds with the old-fashioned idea of working from the bottom up. I thought it was better to work from the top down.

I was a sponge, absorbing everything I saw and heard. The industry had an adage: "Be nice to the people coming down the ladder as you pass them on your way up." The implication was that everybody who gets to the top eventually goes back down. Another saying was "Hollywood devours its young and forgets its old." I didn't know what that meant, but I began to get an idea one night when I joined Henry Rogers backstage at comedian Milton Berle's current show, which was telecast live at NBC.

Berle, who had once been billed as "Mr. Television," was no longer at the height of his career. As host of the *Texaco Star Theater* (later *The Milton Berle Show*) in the late forties and early fifties, he had pioneered early television history. By 1960, however, at fifty-three, Milton was no longer deemed a viable commodity. He had a thirty-year contract with NBC, based on his earlier success, but essentially he was considered old hat. The network had made him host of a game show called *Jackpot Bowling*. At this point in my own burgeoning career, I was unaware of how brutal the industry could be to so-called has-beens. To me, Milton Berle was still a champion of comedy.

Henry and I were standing on the wing of the stage at showtime when Milton emerged from his dressing room and stopped to chat. I was excited to meet the guy, but after we were introduced I moved closer to the stage so Henry could speak to him privately. I was standing there alone, the only person between the stage proper and the curtained wing, when someone yelled, "Milton, dammit, you're on!"

Suddenly Milton made a headlong burst toward the stage. He easily could have gone around me, but rather he caught me with a kidney chop so hard it knocked me out of his way and off my feet. As I hit the ground, Milton gave me a quick look, as if to say, "Don't block my path, kid—I'm not defeated yet!" and continued his dash to the stage. Embarrassed, I got to my feet and brushed myself off, telling everyone who was interested that I was okay. Actually I suffered a severe kidney bruise, which prompted me to think Milton Berle was a first-class asshole. It turned out to be my first but not last collision with Milton.

Late at night, after nursing a drink at one of the elite spots in Beverly Hills that stars patronized, I usually ended up at one of the joints on the Sunset Strip or nearby Santa Monica Boulevard, where young people my age hung out. I was always looking for a girlfriend. The waitresses were actresses; the bartenders were actors; the customers were Xerox copies. There were thousands of them—everybody was a would-be actor. Something was amiss. They all did the same thing. They paid for a composite set of photographs; they went to auditions; some went to acting classes. They were broke, always. Most of them worked at menial jobs. Only a small percentage ever wound up on the set of a movie or television show. Those who did seemed to have a star friend: "Jimmy liked me. He gave me tips before my scene was shot. Nice man. I worked with him in . . ." or "Marilyn? She's wonderful. We grew really close when I had a part with her in . . ."

I did not doubt the truth of the stories, but did Jimmy Stewart or Marilyn Monroe remember the storytellers? I learned a valuable lesson: it wasn't who you knew in Hollywood that was important; it was who knew you.

All the young actors were trapped in a catch-22. To get an acting part they needed a Screen Actors Guild membership card; to get a SAG card, they needed a role in a movie or television show. Usually it took an agent to find an actor a job, but agents wanted to handle proven actors. It was a mess, a vicious street with a dead end. I realized that upstart actors needed mentors, someone who could pull strings. They needed a guide through the Hollywood jungle, an experienced leader who knew how to avoid the quicksand, the alligators and the cannibals.

I did some research. The supply of actors was grossly larger than the demand for actors, even for those with Guild cards. At any given moment only a few hundred were actually gainfully employed as actors. Yet they were as ample as ants at a picnic. It became apparent to me that few of them would ever have a steady job as a professional actor. They were living in a dream world.

The star system was collapsing. Box-office revenues had fallen 50 percent from its 1947 high, when 90 million people saw a movie every week. The studios were tightening their belts. Contract players were diminishing. In the old days the studios hired an actor with potential and then guided his career. If a movie flopped, the actor was recast in a new project the next month. He was given another chance, and another, until he made it big or until it became evident he didn't have star appeal. That day was all but gone. The business was in a quandary—it was changing. Television was making a run for the money. Movie people hated television, because television was keeping customers at home, away from theaters. I was glad I had decided not to become an actor. The odds for success were unfavorable, no matter how talented you were. And in forty-five years, they've grown worse.

I enjoyed being a publicist immensely, except it was taxing. My task was to keep the shows I was assigned to in the news. With dozens of old but successful prime-time series airing every week and new ones premiering constantly, it was not easy to be consistently creative. But that was the prerequisite of a good PR man: you came up with new ideas or you were soon a teller at Union Bank.

I was a new kid on the block but with a talent for small talk and impeccable manners (an inheritance from my mother). I was a quick study and I was savvy. Many older people took a shine to me. I think they could see I wasn't afraid to take a risk, unlike my other young colleagues, who were overly cautious, weak and timid. It quickly became apparent to a young cat like me that to be really good in the Hollywood jungle would require intelligent risk-taking. I learned a lot about large payoffs and giant rewards simply by being fearless and taking heavily calculated risks.

For example, Paul Anka at this time was opening a nightclub act at the Ambassador Hotel's Cocoanut Grove. He wasn't old enough to legally buy a drink at the club's bar, but he was already a star. He was also a Rogers & Cowan client. I put two and two together and got an idea. Both Paul and Danny Thomas were Lebanese. If I could somehow get Danny onstage with Paul, I might get Danny to give Paul a cameo in *The Danny Thomas Show*. In the process each would reap huge dividends in publicity and I would get a healthy pat on the back. But after the Milton Berle episode, I had now become increasingly aware of the huge and brittle egos of stars, so I proceeded to engineer my idea with a modicum of delicacy. I didn't want Danny to think I saw Paul as a bigger star than him. I thought it over and approached Danny on his set, having learned that if you don't ask, the answer is already no. "Danny, why don't we go over and see this guy Paul Anka's show at the Ambassador?"

Danny's eyes lit up. "Let's do it," he said. "Make the arrangements."

The Grove was the last great showcase nightclub in Los Angeles. It was glamorous, studded with fake palm trees, papier-mâché monkeys and a ceiling littered with tiny glistening lights that gave the aura of a celestial sky above an open amphitheater. It was also expensive.

The place was packed. I reserved a table front and center, and our party, which included Danny and his wife, Rose Marie, and Danny's manager, accountant and sundry other members of his entourage, was received with über-celebrity treatment, including pictures taken by a photographer I had hired.

The purpose of the evening, of course, was to get Danny onstage with Paul, which happened as I predicted. Paul Anka was a great live entertainer with pizzazz and flair. When the electricity was really zipping, he recognized Danny as his Lebanese brother or cousin or father or whoever, and suddenly Danny was onstage with him doing a song, and my photographer was popping bulbs as if they were fireflies.

It was perfect. When Danny came back to the table he was in heaven. We had dinner, lobsters and filets mignon, wine and champagne, and then cocktails that cascaded like Niagara Falls. Every once in a while someone said, "Thanks, Jay, this is a great evening." After six thank-yous I began to get a sinking feeling in my stomach. I realized Danny thought it was a Rogers & Cowan invitation rather than a Jay Bernstein invitation.

At last the show was over, dinner and drinks were done, and the bill was passed respectfully to none other than me. I looked at it and gulped: $500-plus (probably $2,000 today). I had exactly $18.76 in my pocket. I did the only thing I could do; I signed two names on the bill, neither of them mine: Rogers and Cowan.

Once I got over the shock of forging my bosses' names on the bill and beyond the first question that entered my mind—namely, "What the fuck am I going to do now?"—I acted. If I could get some publicity out of the evening fast, like immediately, then I could possibly justify the expenditure the next day at the office. I had already dispatched the photographer to his darkroom. While I was getting my guests into their limousines and bidding them adieu, he returned holding a manila packet. As the limousine pulled away, I asked, "Did you get anything?"

"Yeah, I think so."

I looked at the photographs—one of Danny and Paul onstage at the microphone was perfect. I jumped into my car and raced to the Associated Press office. The deskman reminded me of a hit man in a Warner Bros. film noir. "Sorry, pal. Can't do it."

I explained my desperation. "If I don't get this photograph on a wire, I'll get fired."

"Sorry, pal. Can't do it."

I went to United Press International, where I got the same reception, with only a slight improvement in courtesy. My days as a publicist were running short.

"When does your shift change?" I asked the receptionist.

"Four a.m."

It was midnight. I had to kill four hours. I drove to Hollywood Boulevard and went to an all-night movie house with a double feature, *Exodus*, with Paul Newman, which I had seen, and *Esther and the King*, with Joan Collins, which sent me dozing a half-dozen times. When I left the theater at 3:45 a.m., I didn't know who was Esther and who was the king.

The new man at UPI was a young guy about my age. I told him my story and handed him the glossy.

"Thomas and Anka, huh? Okay, let's get it on the wire."

Where there was a will, there was a way. By the time I got home, a photograph of Danny Thomas and Paul Anka was whizzing around the world. From that point forward, I made sure I was on a first-name basis with all wire-service personnel.

I got a raise and went to the Polo Lounge to celebrate. Stars had been hanging out at the Beverly Hills Hotel since the 1920s. Its cocktail lounge got its name because Will Rogers, and later Darryl Zanuck, went there with their cronies after they played polo. Usually I parked on a side street and walked across the hotel's great lawn and through the gardens, but now, with a nice, healthy raise, I decided I could afford valet parking.

I drove up the carriageway in my '48 Dodge and stopped at the curb near the red-carpet entrance. None of the valet boys came to open my door. I waited; if I was going to pay for the service, I wanted it. I waited longer. Cars stacked up behind me, Rolls-Royces and Cadillacs. The valets tended to them. I was getting antsy and angry. Finally the chief valet came to my window. "Deliveries are made in the back of the hotel," he said.

I opened my door and got out. "The only thing I'm delivering is me," I told him. I handed him my keys. He shrugged.

The next day I bought a new car, a persimmon-and-white Sunbeam Alpine convertible. I couldn't afford it, but I didn't want to be embarrassed again. The next time I went to the Polo Lounge the valets swarmed at my door like flies. Hollywood was a status town, like it or not.

Sheldon Leonard started a new television sitcom. Vic Heutschy assigned me to publicize it, not because I was the hotshot I thought I was, but because everybody said it was going to bomb. The star was a tall, lanky fellow named Dick Van Dyke. I set up an interview for him with the *Saturday Evening Post*. Dick said it was the first major interview he'd ever had. Richard Lewis, the *Post* writer, said Dick was the most boring person he'd ever interviewed. The show became a hit anyway.

"Hey, Jay," said Dick. "Why don't you meet me for a drink tonight at Frascati's."

I did, and the next night also, and the next. Dick and I began to meet for drinks three or four times a week. Frascati's was a popular Sunset Strip restaurant-bar, but it was just the starting place for us. We barhopped the Strip, and then moved to Melrose Avenue. Dick always started in a mellow mood, but with each drink he perked up—he got funnier and nuttier. Between bars we'd hit the streets and freeways like Grand Prix race drivers, playing games in our convertibles. Dick had an XK-E Jaguar and I had my new Sunbeam Alpine. We'd race side by side with our tops down, tossing cocktail glasses back and forth from one car to the other. It was crazy. We were heading for trouble, but booze never lets you in on secrets that lie in the future.

Dick should have been on top of the world, but there was something amiss in his life. He was an unhappy man. His show wrapped each day at six p.m., but he told his wife he had to work until ten. He cut Sunday school, so to say. We played the Hollywood nightlife into the second season of his show. After a few drinks, Dick always changed to happy. I was too naïve to put two and two together, the sum total of which was booze. I was young, hardworking and happy-go-lucky. Fortunately I handled alcohol well and never considered that some of the people who hit the bars at the end of the day had a problem other than the joy of living. Dick had myriad problems, and alcohol was his means to escape them. Later, it became *the* problem.

Like almost every major star I've known, Dick came up the hard way. It had taken him the standard decade to be recognized. He and his wife, Margie, had been married on the radio show *Bride and Groom* back in 1948 because the show paid for their wedding rings and a honeymoon. They had been unable to marry otherwise, as Dick was broke. After all, he was an actor. In fact, even after their marriage, they were so poor they lived in their car for a while.

Twelve years elapsed between their marriage and the Broadway musical *Bye Bye Birdie*, which finally launched Dick's career and earned him a Tony. In the interim the Van Dyke family had grown from two to six, a nuclear unit large enough to be nerve-wracking for a struggling actor and a catalyst for alcoholism. Dick said Margie reminded him of his mother.

One night we went to the Steak Pit on Melrose. It was an exclusive place, and it made me feel like I was at last in the big time. You knocked on the door like it was a speakeasy. A little aperture opened and two eyes checked you out. We got in because of Dick. After eating rare steaks and getting sufficiently tanked up, we hit the street, racing our cars down Melrose toward La Cienega Boulevard. Dick was in front of me, zooming at high speed. I decided to pass him, even though traffic was coming from the opposite direction. I zipped out of my lane and was racing parallel to Dick. He glanced, smiling; then he floored his car. We were near the intersection now, with a traffic light looming, its red stoplight glowing bigger and brighter by the second, with a car coming toward us—me, since I was in the wrong lane. I slammed on my brakes, veered, missed the oncoming car, flipped and skidded into the intersection like a puck on ice. The only good thing about it was that I lived to drive another day. I wasn't injured, but my nervous system was shaken abruptly into sobriety. I climbed out of the car and looked around. Dick had pulled to the curb. He didn't ask if I was okay; he laughed his ass off.

Two weeks later, Dick flipped his Jaguar coming around a curve near ucla. Had he not been wearing a seat belt, he would have died. He got rid of his xk-e and bought a Studebaker Avanti, which was supposed to be one of the safest cars on the road because of its interior padding, a novelty in those days. I capitalized on the accident by getting Dick a "buckle up" public-service commercial.

After our accidents, Dick and I continued meeting for cocktails. For me it was fun, the expenditure of youthful exuberance; for Dick it was something else. He was tired of what he called "boring." After years of struggling, he wanted some Tabasco in his life. What he eventually got was salsa picante in the person of Michelle Triola, the sexy dancer-actress who invented "palimony." Lee Marvin told me, "There are forty positions for coitus and Michelle knows fifty of them." Michelle was the last person anyone thought could straighten Dick Van Dyke out. She fooled everyone.

Eventually I recognized that the biggest fraternity in Hollywood was not Sigma Chi but Alcoholics Anonymous. I used alcoholism as an entrée to befriending and representing some of the most legendary stars in the business. Judy Garland would call me at three in the morning and slur her way through hours of babble. I was the only person who would talk to her. She was thirty-nine, but her movie career was virtually over. Gravity had taken its toll, and booze was her only elixir. It was a learning experience for me, and I finally understood the maxim "Hollywood devours its young and forgets its old." Dick was only three years younger than Judy, but he was new to screen and tube. Through Michelle, he eventually saw the fork in the road: one way went high and the other went low. Dick chose the high road.

A few months after Dick flipped his xk-e, he stopped calling me. We no longer met for fun and drinks. When I saw him on his set, he averted his eyes. Twenty years after the fact, I ran into him at the funeral of Ruth Berle, Milton's first wife. We sat down on a bench outside the chapel.

"Why did you ignore me all those years?" I asked.

"I was embarrassed," he said. "I was an alcoholic; you weren't. You were drinking for fun; I was drinking because I had to. I was living a double life. I couldn't face my friends after I sobered up. It was too embarrassing. After I wrecked my car, I began to realize my problem. I had to get clean—I had to stop trying to kill myself. It took years, but I did it."

He was one of the few who did. I've often wondered what happened to Margie.

"Old" Hollywood was dying in 1960. The system that had nurtured Alan Ladd and made him into a star no longer existed. Nick Adams was "new" Hollywood. Hollywood had always been a dog-eat-dog world, but by the early sixties it was dog-eat-anything. Today most of Ladd's contemporaries have forgotten him, and the younger generation has never heard of him. At least he was in the pantheon briefly; Nick Adams never was. If today you ask a literate person if he remembers Nick Adams, he's apt to say, "Wasn't he a character in Hemingway?"

Nick was one of those actors who never quite made it, but one who should be remembered, not so much for his talent but for his perseverance. He had some minor roles in big movies—*Mr. Roberts, Picnic* and *Rebel Without a Cause*. He had been a good friend of James Dean, which appealed to me. Nick was a case study in attitude and guts. He was fearless, much like his character Johnny Yuma in *The Rebel*, the CBS Western he starred in. I hung around his set a lot. Nick and I became friends, because Nick needed adulation, which I was willing to give, and because I was always in need of a hero.

I was in his dressing room telling him about my Danny Thomas–Paul Anka experience at the Cocoanut Grove. Nick laughed arrogantly. "Do you really believe Rogers & Cowan would have made you pay the bill had you not scored a publicity hit?"

"Yes," I told him.

"You got a lot to learn, Jay. Out here you're playing with the banker's money. We're just a bunch of serfs working for the manor, and the manor is the banker, and the banker is making tons of money off your elbow grease. Do you think Rogers & Cowan absorbed that bill? Don't kid yourself. They sloughed it off on Thomas and Leonard Productions, and TL sloughed it off on the network. The network is the house, pal, and in television everybody's playing with their money."

I didn't totally agree with Nick, but what he said registered nevertheless. The system was one vast sum of money that started at the networks or the studios, and then was flushed down through the mechanism of production and talent and publicity and promotion and merchandising and distribution until it made the rounds of a vicious circle and ended back where it began, in the manor house, the casino bank.

"We're peons," Nick continued. "The profits from one hit show are so tremendous that twenty failures can be thrown aside like used toilet paper, after they've wiped your ass with it. Do you think I'm getting rich as Johnny Yuma? Hell, no! But the network is, so don't worry about blowing a little of their bread. Fuck 'em!"

That was Nick—cocky, arrogant, rebellious and analytical. He was a hustler by necessity, lacking the anchor the old studio system would have provided by guiding a contract player's career. He was out there all by his lonesome, making decisions by hunch and experience rather than by good judgment. He took what he could get and made up the rules as he went along, which ultimately proved to be his downfall, along with considerable help from me. But that comes later.

Nick was five years older than me, a span sufficient to make me look up to him, but short enough to make us contemporaries. Through Nick I met other people who became more than mere acquaintances. One of them was Robert Conrad, another rugged, he-man actor who also was trying to work up through the ranks. Bob was co-starring in a contemporary gumshoe series called *Hawaiian Eye*—for which he received a grandiose $300 per episode his first year—and reveling in his stardom after years of being ignored. If Nick Adams acted tough, Bob Conrad *was* tough. Like Nick he wasn't tall, but he was built like a linebacker. Bob was usually nursing an injury, a sprained ankle or a bruised shoulder, because he did most of his own stunts. He once gave me a supreme compliment: "If I was in a foxhole during combat and only one fellow soldier could be with me, I'd want him to be Jay Bernstein."

After Dick Van Dyke and I went our separate ways, I would often join Nick and Bob for midnight carousing. We'd make the bar rounds, tipping a few and having a jolly good time. Actually, it was Bob and I who did the tipping. After one drink Nick was usually sloshed; after two he was under the table. Sometimes John Ashley, an actor and fellow Oklahoman, joined us. The four of us thought we were the hottest items in town. Nick and Bob actually were, at least among young television actors, and John was coming up, co-starring in a slew of beach pictures with Frankie Avalon. I was the low man on the totem pole, but I had too much pride to admit it.

Nick and Bob had wives, but the sixties were difficult years for long-term relationships. Beginning May 9, 1960, every young woman had a new item in her drug cabinet. It was a little plastic compact obtained by prescription. Pharmacists called it Enovid; to the rest of the world it was "the Pill." For ten dollars a month, "nice girls" could now enjoy sex as freely as the boys, if they wanted to. And most of them did.

In his novel *On the Road*, Jack Kerouac wrote that the most beautiful girls in the world were in Des Moines, Iowa. I didn't finish the book. Tinseltown had, and still does, more female pulchritude per square block than any place on earth. For me, who had arrived with very Midwestern values regarding the sanctity of women, the Pill was a godsend. I no longer had to spend weeks, even months—not to mention untold dollars—courting a girl simply for the pleasure of her flesh. The Pill was a time-saver.

Not that I was promiscuous. I liked the idea of having a steady girlfriend. But I wasn't looking for love; I was looking for companionship, which was difficult to find when my job consumed most of every twenty-four hours. I was at Warner Bros. on the set of *Surfside 6*, a popular, campy private-eye television series starring Troy Donahue, Van Williams and Lee Patterson, when I fell in lust. She was a beautiful blonde, lithe and effervescent.

"Who's that?" I whispered.

She was Diane McBain, a contract starlet Warner's was promoting as the new Carroll Baker. She had been showcased in an Edna Ferber epic, *Ice Palace*, with Richard Burton. Now she was playing Daphne Dutton, the rich young landlady to the three *Surfside 6* detectives. She was eighteen years old and stunning. I got Troy Donahue to introduce us.

"Would you like to join me for a drink after work?" I asked her.

"Oh, thank you, but I can't."

"How about dinner?"

"It's sweet of you to ask, but I really can't."

"Breakfast in the morning?"

"Really, I—"

"High tea tomorrow afternoon at four?"

It was a measure of my persistence that within two weeks, up-and-coming starlet Diane McBain and publicist par excellence Jay Bernstein became a gossip-column item. The item ran exactly the way I planted it.

We were lovers, but not live-in lovers. Diane had her apartment; I had mine. We spent as much time as possible at one or the other. It was better at her place, because I lived with Stan Moress.

Aside from mutual sexual attraction, my compatibility with Diane lay in ambition: she wanted to be a star and I had an inkling that I wanted to be a starmaker. When she wasn't working, Diane usually joined me on my night shift. She loved my networking life and was encouraged by my devotion to her career. Picking up her Warner Bros. publicity line, I told people, "She's going to be the next Carroll Baker."

Chapter 3

THE
RAT PACK

Shortly after John F. Kennedy's inauguration, I received good news. I was being transferred to Rogers & Cowan's personality department under the supervision of Guy McElwaine, a new senior publicist. I was ecstatic. Personalities were people whose substance I could promote; the shows I had been promoting in the television department were abstract and ghostlike, ever changing from week to week.

McElwaine's major connection in 1961 was Frank Sinatra, no small link since Sinatra was the most influential and powerful star in the industry. Guy had been in charge of studio publicity for *Some Came Running*, the 1958 screen success starring Sinatra, Dean Martin and Shirley MacLaine, and now he brought Sinatra's next movie project with him to Rogers & Cowan.

He summoned me to his office. "Have you ever been to Kanab, Utah?"

I hadn't.

"Well, you're going, and for several weeks."

Frank Sinatra and Co. were producing a Western in the hinterlands of southern Utah. I was being assigned to *Sergeants 3*, a takeoff on Rudyard Kipling's poem "Gunga Din," now set in the 1880s West. My instructions were to stay with the company for the entire shoot, taking care of the needs of what the media were calling the "Rat Pack"—Sinatra,

Dean Martin, Sammy Davis, Jr., Peter Lawford and Joey Bishop—while coordinating publicity as an assistant to Chuck Moses, the unit publicist.

I was floored. This was a sign of amazing serendipity from up above. To me, the Rat Pack was the epitome of cool. Others could don sandals and chinos and shuffle about on the Venice boardwalk in search of Zen, karma and Kerouac, but not me. I dashed to pack my bags.

Naturally Diane would be upset. That night I took her to La Scala in Beverly Hills. We got a good table because of Diane, not me, but my time of recognition was on the horizon.

"Guess what?" I said. "I've been assigned to a Rat Pack movie."

She stared into space. "How nice."

"This is a big break for me," I continued, "but there's one problem. It's a location picture. It's going to be shot in Utah."

She looked at me, feigning teenage innocence. She was so gorgeous— I thought she was pushing toward an eleven on a scale of one to ten—but her silence baffled me. I took a bite of pasta.

"I won't be upset if you'll marry me," she finally said.

Chicken cacciatore hung in my throat. She was a teen, and for all my wheeling and dealing and acting like a big shot, I recognized that by Hollywood standards I was hardly out of short pants. Marriage? Was she out of her mind? My eyes watered. "Excuse me. I'll be back."

I went to the men's room, cleared my eyes, cleared my throat and cleared my brain. When I returned to the table I was no longer Jay Bernstein; I was Rhett Butler.

"Are you okay?" asked Diane.

I nodded and said, "How much money do you make?"

She stared at me with a hopeful, wistful look in her eyes, and then, to my surprise, she told me, to the very penny.

I said, "Do you realize I hardly make a tenth of that?"

Diane nodded and smiled.

"Maybe we're being premature," I continued. "Don't you think we should give marriage some serious thought before we jump into it?"

"Is that a no?" she asked.

"I'm just suggesting that we shouldn't rush into something. Maybe we should take some time to think it over." I lifted Diane's left hand, pulled it gently across the table and kissed it. She smiled appreciatively.

"Will you think about me every minute you're gone?" she asked.

"Every minute."

"Will you call me every night?"

"Every night."

We left and went to her apartment. I was out of cigarettes. I was always out because I puffed one after another; a pack lasted four hours. I needed to keep my cool, but I couldn't do it without nicotine coursing through my veins. "I'm out of cigarettes," I moaned.

"You're not," purred Diane. "I bought a carton for you. It's on top of the refrigerator."

That was Diane—an eleven!

I flew to Utah in a twin-engine charter with a half-dozen *Sergeants 3* production big shots, led by Howard Koch, the executive producer, and John Sturges, the director. It was early morning. The crew and the secondary cast were already there or en route by car and truck, with filming scheduled to begin the next morning, absent most of the stars. At Guy's suggestion I made an effort to meet and befriend Koch, whom he had described as a pleasant man.

"Hi, I'm Jay Bernstein, with Rogers & Cowan."

"Just take care of Frank," Koch answered, and waved me away.

Guy had said the same thing, with an addendum: "Frank's the boss, Jay. Remember that."

By the time the plane landed at Kanab I was sick—not stomach sick, but mind sick. Flying was my bête noire. It required me to place my life in somebody else's hands. I was a control freak; flying meant I had no control. I sucked in some dry, high-desert air. Inside the shack of a terminal, Koch called me aside. "If you have any problems, son, come to me."

"Thanks, Mr. Koch." Maybe he was a pleasant man after all.

Compared to L.A., Kanab didn't exist. It wasn't a city; it wasn't even a town—it was a hamlet. The surrounding countryside was breathtakingly beautiful: red rocks and sandstone bluffs, sand dunes and incongruent stands of Ponderosa pine trees. I could see why so many Westerns had been filmed in the area, dating back to the Tom Mix movies of the 1920s. I had done my homework.

The Parry Lodge didn't belong to the Ritz-Carlton chain. It was a motel, quaint and rustic, nestled in a copse. It had about sixty rooms, most extending off the main building in two wings. It was small enough to give the production company a fraternal feeling, a closeness I thought might help me engineer my way into the Rat Pack. I was full of myself, with enough gumption to think the clan would welcome me into its fold with open arms. After all, I thought I was pretty cool, too.

The Pack members were arriving separately on a staggered schedule. Frank would fly in at noon on his private plane, from Los Angeles. Dean would arrive later in the afternoon, from Las Vegas. Peter was coming in that night, from wherever, and Sammy two days later, after wrapping a nightclub engagement at the Cocoanut Grove. Guy had instructed me to be waiting at the curb when Frank arrived.

The lobby was frenetic with energy. And I loved it. I likened a motion-picture company to a circus—transient workers with no home, unhampered by social rules. Fleeting romances were already burgeoning, and the producers of the film had now morphed into carnival-like barkers giving orders to everyone, from the head grip to the assistant cameraman, everyone moving in a different direction. Only the teamsters stood in a corner, not moving a muscle, most wearing cowboy boots and Western hats. The real cowboys, the wranglers, were already at work, corralling horses and livestock at a big barn out back, or taking inventory of tack and saddles. There were wardrobe people, makeup artists, set designers, carpenters and prop men. Their energy was palpable; it flowed like electricity. They were an army of bees working on behalf of the queen, except in this case the queen was a king. His name was Frank Sinatra.

Until *Sergeants 3*, my experience had been in television, and television and motion-picture people were as segregated as the races. A tacit rule was a fact of life: motion-picture people could step "down" into television production, but few television people could step "up" into motion-picture production. A motion picture was the cat's meow; a television show was the cat's paw—depending, of course, on whom you were talking with. What was true, as I perceived it in 1961, was this: movie actors were stars and television actors were personalities. Sinatra went from movie to movie, playing a different character each time; Danny Thomas was always Daddy, with his television kids making room for him. Sinatra was stuck in a role for eight weeks; Thomas was stuck in a role for life.

At noon I was standing at the driveway curb. I had Sinatra's room key in my pocket. I was excited but doing my best to maintain a professional calm. I was good at that; it was an acting job. A station wagon pulled up and Sinatra hopped out, 150 pounds of energy, 100 percent dictator. I was struck by clairvoyance; I sensed immediately we would never be fast friends.

"Mr. Sinatra, I'm Jay Bernstein with Rogers & Cowan."

He measured me with penetrating blue eyes. "So you're McElwaine's man," he said. It wasn't a question—it was a statement.

"Yes," I answered, and then asked my first stupid question. "How was the ride from the airport?"

"Lousy," said Sinatra. "Next time, I want a chopper."

"A chopper?"

"A fucking helicopter."

His rudeness was shocking, but I tried to mask my feelings by being authoritative. "I'll talk to the production office."

"Fuck the office. Just get me a helicopter."

We stood watching for a few moments as a couple of country bellboys unloaded the wagon's baggage compartment, their eyes glancing back and forth from Sinatra to the suitcases. A member of Frank's entourage, a black man who turned out to be George Jacobs, Frank's man Friday, supervised.

At last Frank said, "Take care of them, George." He turned again to me. "Okay, Rogers & Cowan, let's you and me go look at my suite."

The Parry Lodge didn't have suites. It had a half-dozen bedrooms, slightly larger than average, on the second floor. They were reserved for the stars—Sinatra and the rest of the pack. As we passed through the lobby, a path opened in the crowd. A man said, "Hi, Frank," and another said, "Glad you could make it, Frank," as if to be funny. Frank ignored them. It wasn't that he was unfriendly, but he was in one of his moods, of which he had plenty.

Upstairs Sinatra and I stood in the center of a freshly carpeted room. Frank looked around, slowly turning on his heels until he clicked off a 360-degree pan shot. Then I asked my second stupid question. "Is this good enough for you, Mr. Sinatra?"

He fixed me with a glare. "No, it's not good enough." He pointed to his right. "I don't like that wall. I want a door in it, and I want Dean in the adjacent room." He pointed to the opposite wall. "And I want a door there, and I want Peter in that room." He looked at me. "Got it?"

"I've got it," I answered.

He barked off some more orders, primarily a dictate to stock his bar, notably with Jack Daniels, black label. Finished, he said, "What did you say your name was, kid?"

"Jay Bernstein."

"Well, say hello to Guy McElwaine for me."

"Yes, sir."

"And when Dean arrives, I want you waiting out front for him, just as you were for me. You're the only guy around here who seems to have any fucking class."

My first meeting with Sinatra was a study of arrogance and power—all Frank's. I found little to like about the man, but I gave him the benefit of the doubt. That's how badly I wanted to be "in." The saving grace was that he told me to be on hand for Dean Martin's arrival. I went to Howard Koch and told him Sinatra wanted a chopper and two new doors in his room.

"Tell the production manager," said Koch. "Tell him to get *two* choppers, in case one breaks down."

The difference between a television production and a motion-picture production was spectacular. Money was the factor. Television watchdogs had their eyes on every penny; they shot fast and moved forward, always looking for ways to save money. A chopper for Nick Adams? Forget it. Two? Don't be crazy! But this was Sinatra and Co., with each star pocketing more money up front than the entire cost of a weekly television episode.

In the afternoon I was back in front of the motel waiting for Dean Martin. I had dismissed Sinatra's arrogance. I kept telling myself, "Just play it cool." If I were to be accepted by the Pack, I would have to roll with the punches. Here I was, a kid from Oklahoma, having been in Hollywood for hardly more than a year, and already I was rubbing shoulders with the biggest stars in the business. It was breathtaking when I considered my luck, so it was easy to dismiss Frank's superciliousness. I would shadowbox until I saw an opening. Then I would punch into the sunlight and let the Chairman see how really important and endearing I truly was. But now I had to deal with Dino.

Forty-five years later I still recall vividly my excitement as the motel station wagon pulled to a halt. In my galaxy of star celebrities, Dean was only a slight notch below Sinatra when it came to cool. He had stolen Frank's thunder in *Some Came Running*, and onstage in Vegas the other Rat Packers seemed always a step behind him. It was exciting to meet a star in person, because they were never quite what you had gleaned of them from the screen. Look at my Sinatra experience. I was up close to him for the first time, and his flaws and idiosyncrasies were exposed without makeup or script. Dean, however, was precisely as he looked on the screen. The best adjective to describe him is "languorous." To Dean, everyone and every action—Kanab, the movie, Sinatra, Koch—were just part of the day's twenty-four hours. He took everything in stride with a maturity Sinatra lacked. Two men got out of the wagon with him.

I went through my ritual. "I'm Jay Bernstein, with Rogers & Cowan."

Dean's response was perfunctory, as if from a man who was tired of it all. "Hello, pally," he said without expression. "This is Mack."

Mack and I shook hands.

"And this is Jay, Jay."

Dean smiled. He was the first person who had actually remembered my name. Mack was Mack "Killer" Gray, Dean's primary factotum, whom he had inherited from George Raft after Mack's twenty years of service to him, and the other Jay was Jay Gerardi, Dean's movie double and wardrobe attendant. The two men served as buffers against the outside world for an ambiverted man who leaned heavily toward introversion.

As I shook their hands, I realized they had separated me from Dean like a wall. I wasn't so naïve as to miss what was happening. Martin wanted to be left alone, and after I gave my pitch—"If there's anything you need, just give me a call"—I left Dean in his own private world.

That night I hung around the lobby introducing myself to people I had not met. I was really doing it in hopes of running into Sinatra or Martin again. I didn't, and finally I went to my room to call Diane. I got her answering service. Rather than leave a message, I hung up. I waited an hour and called again. This time no one answered. I went to sleep, my imagination astir.

Sometime during the night my phone rang. It was the front desk. "Mr. Lawford is here," whispered the clerk. "Could you come to the lobby?"

Peter Lawford was no longer the lithe actor I remembered from his movies. He had evolved into a tall, fleshy man—with a paunch—whom I hardly recognized. When the clerk saw me, he sighed and pointed. "That's him, Mr. Lawford."

Lawford turned, extended his hand and said with slightly inebriated civility, "Peter Lawford. Sorry to wake you, but they don't seem to have a key to my room."

I looked at the baffled clerk. "You don't have a key to the room of Peter Lawford?"

"Mr. Koch took it."

"Jesus, don't you have a master key?"

Embarrassed, the clerk shook his head. He gave me Koch's room number, and Peter and I took off.

"I'm sorry, old man," said Peter, as if we were a couple of Brits leaving a pub. "I had to call somebody, and Rogers & Cowan was the only name I could come up with."

I knocked on Koch's door. No answer. I rapped again, harder. When I rapped a third time, a gruff voice said, "Who the hell is it?"

"It's Jay Bernstein of Rogers & Cowan, with Peter Lawford."

"Just a minute."

We waited.

"I'm really sorry, old man," repeated Peter.

Koch opened the door, sleepy-eyed. He was dressed in a robe. "Peter, good to see you," he said amicably. "When did you get in? What's up?"

"They don't have a key to my room," said Peter. "The kid at the desk said you have it."

"Damn!" said Koch. "Just a minute." He shut the door in our faces.

"I'm really sorry, old man," said Peter. His breath wafted with the sour stench of alcohol.

The door opened again. Koch handed Lawford the key. "I'm sorry about the mess-up, Peter. Get a good night's sleep. I'll see you tomorrow." He closed the door.

"Thanks, old man," Peter said to me. "I'm truly sorry about this."

I went back to my room, feeling good inside. Solving their problems was my entrée to the Pack. I wanted to be accepted by them so badly I could hardly hold it in.

It was after three o'clock. I called Los Angeles again. No one answered, neither Diane nor the service. I was bothered immensely.

My eyes popped open at the crack of dawn. It was the first day of filming. I went to the lobby. The crew were dashing helter-skelter. I saw Howard Koch. He wiggled a finger at me and I followed him into a corner, expecting a thank-you for taking care of Lawford.

"Listen, Bernstein, don't ever wake me again in the middle of the goddamned night, especially for a fucking actor! Do you understand?"

Taken aback, I mumbled, "Well, uh . . . yes, sir."

"Who the fuck does Peter think he is anyway?"

I protested meekly. "The clerk didn't have a key, and he said you—"

"Next time, get a fucking locksmith," growled Koch, "or you'll be thumbing your way back to Hollywood."

Shaken, I returned to my room. My telephone was ringing. I grabbed it, expecting Diane. It was one of Sinatra's henchmen. "Frank wants you in his suite, kid."

Carpenters were measuring the walls for the new doors. Peter Lawford was standing at a window, staring out over beautiful downtown

Kanab. Dean Martin was lazing in a chair with his feet propped on the end of the bed. Hangers-on were stationed about like props. Sinatra was under his bedcovers, sitting up in his pajama top. They were all sipping from cups of coffee.

Peter was the only one who greeted me. "Thanks again for the help last night, old man."

"Forget it," I said. "That's what I'm paid for."

"Sit down," said Sinatra.

Martin stood up. "I've gotta go," he said.

"Go where?" asked Frank.

"Outside."

"What are you gonna do outside?"

"Count the out-of-town license plates. What else?"

Frank and Peter laughed. The fixtures laughed like a soundtrack. Dean didn't; he left. I sat down in his chair.

"I want you to send a wire to Sammy in L.A.," said Frank. "It's from me." He waved a piece of paper in the air. Peter snatched it and handed it to me. "You can work it over, but that's the gist of it."

I looked at the paper. It was a couple of lines scribbled on Parry Lodge stationery. It read something to this effect: "Sources say Jerry Lewis onstage with you at Grove last night. Dean pissed. As punishment, you can't speak first 24 hours in Utah."

I looked at Sinatra. He was serious. I looked at Peter. He was the same. I thought they were nuts, like spoiled, mischievous children.

"Any questions?" asked Sinatra.

"Yes," I said, trying to be equally serious. "When is Sammy gonna be here?"

"Tomorrow about two, and I want you to meet him at the airport. If he utters a word, I'm gonna send him home. It won't be the first time I've fired him."

I nodded. "Anything else?"

Sinatra thought for a moment. "Yeah, tell the desk I want Sammy's room in the back of the building." He paused, his brain clicking, drumming up punishment for Sammy Davis, Jr. "Tell Sammy he can't come through the front door." He looked at Peter, his face excited. "How about that, Peter?"

"I like it."

Then, to me, Frank said, "I want him to have to walk to the back of the building to get in. I want his room to be as far away from here as they can get it. Got it?"

I got it.

"And listen," said Sinatra. He looked at Peter and grinned. "Listen to this." Having Peter's rapt attention, he looked at me and escalated Sammy's punishment with the assurance of a slave-master. "Get a watermelon, and get the kitchen to do up some fried chicken. Wings and gizzards. Put them in his room with a note from me. Not Sinatra—from Frank."

He laughed. Peter laughed. The others laughed. I laughed too; it seemed fashionable. Peter laughed so hard he was embarrassed at his own lack of composure. "I'm sorry," said Peter. "It's just too damned funny." He turned away and laughed into an empty corner of the room.

"Laugh, Peter," said Sinatra, laughing. "Maybe you'll laugh off some of that fat."

Everybody laughed.

"Is that it?" I asked, laughing.

"No," said Sinatra. "Cut the watermelon in half and leave the knife with it. Not a knife and fork, just a knife."

Peter laughed anew. Sinatra laughed. I laughed. Everybody laughed.

"Is that it?" I repeated.

"Don't you think that's enough?"

Guffaws all around.

I stood and began my exit. Sinatra called after me. "I forgot, kid. What's your name?"

"Jay Bernstein, Mr. Sinatra."

Sinatra rolled the words on his tongue. "Jay . . . Bernstein. I'll try to remember. And call me Frank."

"Thanks, Frank." As I shut the door, the entire room burst into new laughter.

Chapter 4

SINATRA THE TERRIBLE

I did not rush to send a telegram to Sammy Davis, Jr. I wanted to mull it over. Watermelon and chicken wings? Was Sinatra serious? I wondered if I was being set up. Was it going to be a joke on me or on Sammy? It didn't seem plausible that Frank would take advantage of a brother Rat Packer because of the color of his skin. Besides, I had my own baggage concerning racism and prejudice.

When I was growing up, Oklahoma City was segregated—it was two cities in one. The only blacks I saw were the servants in our home and those in the rear of the bus when I stole away to watch movies after school. I never thought much about it; it was the norm. I didn't shed tears over the plight of black Americans any more than I cried over the demise of American Indians. I did, however, have a sensitivity born of my own experience.

Between my junior and senior years at Casady Prep School, I accepted a summer scholarship to Presbyterian Westminster Choir College in Princeton, New Jersey. My sponsor was Professor Bayard Auchincloss, of the famous New England Auchincloss family, and my choirmaster was the first cousin of Ernest Hemingway.

Another student was Barbara Smith, who by coincidence was from Oklahoma City, where her father was the minister at the First Presbyterian Church. Barbara and I happily entered into a puppy-love relationship.

When we returned to Oklahoma at summer's end, her father wanted to meet me.

"Hey, that's neat!" I thought. It was an indication of the seriousness of the relationship Barbara and I had. Her old man wanted to check me out, see if I was of the same stock as my father, Jerry, the proprietor of Jerome's, Oklahoma City's finest women's clothing store.

I put my act together and duly went to see Barbara's father, chock-full of charm and good manners. But our meeting was not what I expected. The Reverend Smith first told me how he had grown up in Philadelphia, where "Jews weren't allowed to build."

I stood listening to him, thinking, "Build what?" I had not the foggiest idea that he was talking about ethnic restrictions in white Anglo-Saxon Protestant neighborhoods.

"Bernstein," he continued, "is a Jewish name."

It was the first time I'd heard that revelation with a negative connotation. All I knew was that my family's name was the only Bernstein in the phonebook. Reverend Smith wrapped up the conversation by inviting me to hear his sermon the following Sunday at his church.

I went. Barbara was up in the choir. She sang, her eyes pinned to me sitting alone in my pew. Then Reverend Smith began preaching: "Jews are a community within a community, and we as a Christian congregation should be nice to them." As he continued, I began to feel more like a caged animal in a zoo than like a Jew in a Christian congregation. Before the sermon was finished, Barbara began to cry, until at last she escaped in tears from the choir gallery.

The Reverend Smith's point was well taken by me. After the sermon he forbade Barbara and me from seeing each other. At sixteen, it was my first experience of prejudice, against me in particular because my name was Bernstein, and against Jews in general for no reason I could honestly discern.

Like Romeo and Juliet, Barbara and I didn't follow her father's injunction. We continued to see each other on the sly, but it was hard on Barbara; finally she succumbed to the stress and we broke up.

A few years later, when I was in college, my mother sent me a clipping about Reverend Smith's appointment as chairman of a Christian-Jewish conference in Oklahoma City. The purpose of the conference was to foster Christian-Judaic unity and eliminate prejudice. To me, appointing the Reverend Smith to head up the conference was like making Adolph Hitler a rabbi. It was ludicrous, and I vowed to exorcize hypocrisy from my being.

I wrestled with the telegram chore Sinatra had given me. Then Peter called. "Jay, can you get me an extra key to my room?"

"I'm sure I can," I told him.

"Did you send the telegram to Sammy?"

"Not yet."

"Better send it before you see Frank again."

Frank won out. I sent the telegram. My desire to ingratiate myself with the Chairman of the Board was too strong. Besides, I could call him Frank now. He had said so himself. I was making headway.

The next morning Sinatra cornered me in the lobby before he went to the set. "Did you get the melon and the chicken?"

"Yeah."

"Let me know if he breaks the rules." He was dead serious.

At two o'clock I was waiting on the tarmac at "Kanab International," the name Dean had given to the two intersecting strips of hardtop. Sammy's puddle jumper taxied to a stop.

It was no secret that Sammy was a little guy physically. What surprised me was that he was tiny. He was like a shrew darting about, radiating energy. He could hardly keep still, even as I approached and stuck out my hand. "I'm Jay Bernstein with Rogers & Cowan. Frank asked me to meet you."

Sammy cocked his head, raised his sunglasses and looked at me with his one good eye. Then he lifted a finger in the air as if to give the moment pause, pulled a little notebook from his breast pocket and quickly scribbled a note. He handed it to me. It read: "Nice to meet you, Jay. I can't speak for 24 hours."

Obviously he had received the telegram. He grinned. I didn't; I was too flabbergasted. Here were grown men, some of the most important figures in show business, playing children's games in earnest. Finally I laughed. If Sammy was partaking, then I would, too.

We rode in silence to the Parry Lodge, Sammy's bodyguard in the front seat, the rest of his entourage following in a second car. Sammy squiggled in his seat, occasionally dashing off a note and handing it to me. One read: "I can outdraw Frank, Dean and Peter combined."

I didn't understand. Sammy wrote another note: "Like in *High Noon*."

"When I was a kid," I told him, "I used to go home after the movies and act out the gunfights. I did the good guys *and* the bad guys!"

Sammy stabbed his chest and mouthed the words "Me, too! Me, too!"

He was a fast-draw artist, and he was looking forward to using his talent in *Sergeants 3*. The script didn't have a fast-draw scene for his character, but Sinatra and Co. weren't following the script anyway, a predisposition to innovation Sammy was aware of. Sammy's character was a runaway slave with a bugle; unfortunately, it remained a runaway slave with a bugle.

Sammy followed Frank's order, never once uttering a word. When he was momentarily still, he was like a stick of dynamite ready to explode. The wagon pulled up to the motel. He hopped out before it had come to a complete stop, heading for the lobby. I caught up with him and tugged his arm. Sammy stopped and looked at me quizzically.

I mimed Frank's instructions as if we were two deaf mutes, shaking my head and pointing to the rear of the motel. Finally I got my senses back and said aloud, "Frank said you can't go through the lobby. You have to go around to the back, where your room is."

This was 1961; the civil-rights movement was incipient, not full-blown, and "coloreds," whether they were stars are not, were usually not welcome in so-called "white hotels." In fact, it was because of Sinatra that this time-honored segregation had been broken in Las Vegas, where Sammy and other black entertainers could now stay in the same hotels where they performed. Sammy looked at me and grinned. Then he jotted a note: "Do you have the room key?"

I nodded vigorously and mouthed the word "yes." We took off, walking around the motel to the rear entrance. It was nuts; we were playing charades. Yet Sammy was all but dancing with excitement.

When we found his room I thought it was time to excuse myself. I knew what hors d'oeuvres were waiting inside, since I had choreographed their delivery. I gave Sammy his key and said, "I'll see you later."

Sammy wouldn't have it. He mouthed, "No, no. Come in, come in."

We entered. An odor of grease struck our nostrils. The place smelled like a Kentucky Fried Chicken shop. The watermelon, chicken wings and gizzards were on plates on the dresser. Sammy stared, and then tugged my arm for attention. He mouthed the words "That . . . son . . . of . . . a . . . bitch! Si-*nah*-tra!"

I got along with Sammy better than I did with the others, although we seldom communicated directly. It was more of a mutual commiseration. We shared the role of Frank's whipping boys.

When we went to the set the next day, Sammy's first, Frank told him, "You're riding in the back with Bernstein, Charlie. It's punishment for being two days late."

Joey Bishop was not an outdoor person, and he complained constantly. He was a stand-up comic whose humor was sarcastic. Once, when a conversation drifted to Frank's amorous achievements—the press had recently made hay out of his affair with long-legged dancer Juliet Prowse—Joey said, "When Frank dies, they should retire his zipper to the Smithsonian."

Dean remained aloof, only appearing to be a consummate yes-man to Sinatra. *Sergeants 3* was a continual news story because it was the second Rat Pack movie with all five members in the cast. The press came to Kanab in droves, and it was my responsibility to set up interviews. Every time I asked Dean if he could be on hand, he answered, "When and where, pally?"

"Ten o'clock tomorrow morning in the lobby."

"I'll be there, pally."

Not once did he show up. After a while, I stopped asking him.

From a distance, however, I admired Dean. He wasn't communicative, but his taciturnity seemed derived from a sense of independence. I thought most of Frank's pranks were foolish; Dean did also. He didn't kiss ass with anyone; as a consequence nobody ribbed him.

Frank and Peter had the strongest bond, probably because of Peter's relationship with President Kennedy, whom Frank idolized. *Sergeants 3* was filmed a few months before Kennedy snubbed Frank by staying at Republican Bing Crosby's house in Palm Springs, instead of at Frank's place, a breach that ended the Sinatra-Lawford friendship. I got on with Peter, but I never felt close to him. In Frank's absence, he was in his own world.

Every chance I got, I called Diane, my girlfriend back home. During the day I got her service; at night she did not answer. I was more than suspicious; I was angry, antsy and horny. The Rat Pack apparently shared my mood because Frank decided to fly them to Vegas the second weekend. I was hoping they would ask me to go with them; when they didn't, I rented a car and drove all night to Los Angeles, smack through Las Vegas, five hundred grueling miles. It was stupid, but nature was calling.

It was evening when I arrived at Diane's apartment. I was so eager to get there that I didn't stop to buy cigarettes. I knocked; she didn't answer. I had a key, so I went in. She was in the shower. I didn't say anything. I took off my clothes and got in the shower. She was startled. "My God, Jay! What are you doing here? You scared me to death!"

I didn't answer; I just did my thing. By the time we were finished, the hot water was cold. We got out of the shower, and I put my clothes back on while she was toweling off. I said, "I'm out of here. I've got to get back to Kanab. They don't know I'm gone."

"Are you crazy? You came all that way just for—"

I kissed her again. When I finished, she began combing out her hair. "I've been calling every day," I said. "Why haven't you answered or returned my messages?"

"I've been soooo busy, Jay," she said. "When I come home from the set, I'm just beat. I've been turning the ringer off."

"Would you turn it back on for me?"

"I promise."

I kissed her again. She picked up a hairdryer and switched it on. I left, but as I was walking down the corridor I remembered the carton of cigarettes on top of her refrigerator. I went back, unlocked the door and went to the kitchen.

I hurriedly opened a pack and lighted a cigarette on the gas range. The front door opened. I froze. A handsome actor, whom I recognized from a television series, entered and walked by the kitchen door on his way to the bathroom. He did not see me. His mind was focused on something else. After a moment the hairdryer stopped.

"Darling!" I heard Diane say coolly. "You're early!"

I sneaked out the front door. I never called Diane McBain again.

Back in Kanab I went to the set every day. I was learning, listening and watching. I did gofer work for Frank. The other members of the Pack never asked me to do anything. The only one I really talked to was Sammy. He used me as a valve to release his energy.

The action at the motel was in Frank's suite. I wasn't there much, but when I was invited I tried to act as cool as the others. Frank was never alone. Fame doesn't eliminate insecurity, and Frank, like the others, had his entourage of backslappers, a coterie that constantly told him how great he was.

One night he was planning another weekender to Vegas, ordering Peter to call this person, Sammy that one. Dean sat drinking a cocktail, paying little attention. Factotums were hopping about trying to act important. I don't remember Joey Bishop being there; I hardly remember Joey Bishop being anywhere, except during the rides to the set.

Someone called Frank's pilot and told him to rev up the engines. I kept waiting to be invited; when I wasn't, I went to my room disappointed. I had done my best to ingratiate myself with Sinatra, and failed. He was hot and cold, kind and thoughtful one moment, frigidly inconsiderate the next. Stardom had given him the rare and royal authority to answer to no one.

Half an hour later my telephone rang. It was Peter. "If you're going to

Vegas with us, you better get with it. Frank's not holding the plane much longer."

I got with it. For the next thirty-six hours, I was going to play follow-the-leader. So was everybody else.

First stop in Vegas was the Sands Hotel, Jack Entratter's gambling emporium, where the Rat Pack had been born and where Frank owned 6 percent of the action. He was king there; indeed, he was king everywhere. In those days Sinatra was the personification of Vegas. Wherever he went, the high rollers followed; so too did Dean, Sammy, Peter and, of course, Jay Bernstein, the mascot kid. When Frank snapped his fingers, everybody followed his lead like puppies after their mother. I felt privileged to be part of his court.

After twelve hours of nonstop partying, I began to think I was hallucinating. The drug was Jack Daniels. We had another twenty-four hours to go. Nobody slept, at least in the conventional sense. Dean or Peter might take off to his room with a showgirl, but he would be back in the fold in an hour. Sammy, still in the throes of love for Mai Britt, whom he had married three months earlier, was the only one who stayed aloof. Not that he didn't flirt. He had great lines for the girls. We were at a craps table when a petite young beauty edged between us. Sammy took one look at her smiling face and said, "Hon, I've got cuff links bigger than you!"

It was an existential weekend, a sort of do what Frank wants to do . . . or die! Keeping up with him was debilitating to body and soul. Frank was energized by Vegas, the casino sounds, the swirl of people, the gawkers and adulators, the music. Life in Kanab was snail-like by comparison, a vacation for superannuated geeks trying their best to suppress the inevitable wheeze of death rattles.

It was four in the morning and I was zombified. Why weren't the others? They were not imbibing any less than I was. Then it came to me like a biblical revelation. Women were literally throwing themselves at them—at Frank first, of course, and then down the pecking order. It made no difference that I was at the bottom of the ladder; the ratio was fifty women to one, take your pick. Even Frank would sometimes be gone for an hour. Then I got it; it was a face-saving game. The bastards weren't fucking; they were napping! And even if they were fucking, they were spending more time napping.

By dusk I was on the verge of collapsing from exhaustion, or maybe just exhaust, because my breath smelled like napalm smoke. I had to get out of there, to my room, bed. Frank hadn't given me the time of day for hours anyway. I figured no one would miss me, and if anyone did, he wouldn't remember it the next day, if the next day came. I slipped away, went upstairs in an elevator and bounced off the walls until I found my room. I flopped down on my bed, asleep in thirty seconds.

My telephone woke me. It was Peter. "Frank asked me where you were. He doesn't like it when a guest skips his party, unless of course it's to satisfy a certain need."

"She just left," I lied. "I'll be downstairs in five."

"Hurry, because we're going up the road."

I was raised from the dead, touched by the hand of Sinatra. "Frank asked where you were." Wow! He had hardly acknowledged my presence, but that he had noticed my absence galvanized me. I was more than a peripheral figure now; I was part of the group, a member of the ensemble.

Mix booze and gambling and you get madness. Throw in some beautiful girls and you get macho madness, insanity at its worst. When the plane lifted off at McCarran Field in Vegas late Sunday afternoon, our passenger list had doubled. We had eight beautiful chorus girls for the return flight, "chorus" being a title that gave some of them undeserved status. The party atmosphere had not diminished a thermal unit; rather, it was reaching a fever pitch of lecherous molecular frenzy. Inhibitions were not at low ebb; they were gone. As the plane ascended into the clouds, the Pack descended into a hellish inferno of animal culture, no different from a bunch of rutting, ravenous wolves. Fornication was perversely public. Booze seemed not to have waylaid anyone's prowess. For me it was glorious madness.

A naked showgirl was sitting on Frank's lap, her legs parted over his thighs. He suddenly expended himself with a groan that woke the gods and made the sound of the engines a murmur. Everybody looked. He edged the disheveled girl into the aisle and with an imperial wave directed her to another seat. Holding her clothes against her naked body, she seemed as satisfied as he. Frank pulled up his trousers and settled in his seat. "George!" he called.

George Jacobs trotted forth. "Yes, boss?"

"Get me a couple of hardboiled eggs."

"You bet," answered George. He headed for the galley.

What possessed Frank to want two hardboiled eggs after a roll in the clouds, I never knew. But the yolk was about to hit the fans of both props at 12,000 feet. George brought the eggs. Frank cracked one hard on the top of his diamond ring. Slurp! White and yellow gook poured forth on his hand, down his shirt and on his lap. The egg was raw.

An infinitely fleeting moment of nothingness followed. Frank looked at the ooze of egg; George looked at the ooze of egg. Next Frank looked at George; George looked at Frank. Then Frank exploded with the lightning flash of an atom bomb in the desert. He wasn't just angry—he was insane. Booze had taken over. He leaped out of his seat like a jack-in-the-box, spun George 180 degrees, wrapped his arms around the man's shoulders and started shoving him down the aisle, screaming obscenities. "You sonuvabitch, you uncouth bastard! You're out of here! Somebody open the fuckin' door!"

Most of us sobered abruptly into glassy-eyed statues, but someone—I don't remember who, but he was a sycophant beyond extreme—actually tried to unlock the door, such was Frank's power of command. George was squirming like a trapped animal; Frank was pushing and shoving and screaming. "Open the fucking door! This stupid motherfucker's outta here!"

Collectively we were so stunned at the unreality of what was happening, by the nightmarish nature of Frank's insanity, that had the door actually opened we would have watched impassively as Frank shoved George to his death. We were frozen in place, like wax figures in a museum tableau—except for Dean.

Suddenly he was in the aisle blocking Frank's path, blocking George's.

He was an all-American linebacker. The opposing team was on the goal line, inches from paydirt with time running out, but no one was going through the hole Dean was defending. No one.

"Outta my way, Dino!" screamed Frank. "I'm throwing this mother-fucker outta here!"

Dean was calm but determined. "You're not throwing anybody out, Frank."

"Get outta my way! Somebody open the fuckin' door!"

Dean planted his feet and with a powerful surge shoved Frank and George down the aisle. "Help me part them!" he cried.

We did, suddenly catapulted from the grip of our comas. The girls were screaming. Dean and Killer Gray wrestled George from Frank's grasp, separated them, heaved Frank into a seat and held him down as someone fastened his seat belt. It was done then, finished. Frank melted into a blob, his hands trembling. For a few moments Dean and Killer hovered over him like hawks; then they retreated to their seats. The party was over. For the rest of the flight all we could hear was the roar of the engines.

No one said anything on the ride from the airport to the lodge. No one said anything in the lobby. Most of them just parted and went their separate ways. Sammy, seeing that I was still in a state of shock, gestured for me to follow him to his room. When we got there, he closed the door and said, "That's just Frank's way. Get used to it."

I didn't say anything.

"Under all that bravado, he's a good guy," Sammy continued.

Suddenly I felt a bond with Sammy. He was trying to soothe my feelings. "You know, Sammy. We're alike, sort of."

"How do you mean?"

"Well, the prejudice and all. You're a Negro and I'm a Jew."

He laughed under his breath. "Jay, the only time we're alike is when we look in a mirror at midnight and the electricity is off."

The dailies were shown nightly in the basement of Kanab High School. Few people went, except Koch, Sturges, his assistants and the camera crew. The only member of the Pack who had an interest in seeing what had been shot was Sammy. A couple of times he asked me to go with him. Later, as we walked back to the lodge, Sammy would critique his performance.

"I could have done better in that scene had Frank let Sturges do another take."

I wanted to say, "Sammy, this isn't Shakespeare. It's a farce of the old West, a comedy." But I didn't.

As the production neared its end, Frank, in one of his generous public-relations gestures, ordered a rough cut of the movie. He then invited the citizens of Kanab to see the picture in the makeshift screening room at the school. Joining the Pack as they walked over from the motel, I caught up with Frank. "Is it okay if I see the rough cut?"

Frank stopped, looked at me and said, "I think . . . not yet."

It was a low blow. My feelings were hurt, which was Frank's intention. Had I kept my mouth shut, no one would have stopped me from going. As the picture's assistant publicist, it was not only my right but also my duty to attend the screening. I was simply being courteous with my question, trying to make conversation. Now I felt insulted. I stopped dead in my tracks. I shrank from five-eleven to four-ten, from four-ten to three-three, and kept shrinking until I was a pool of jelly. Frank walked on. I stood there as the others passed, then went to my room to wallow in my misery.

The next morning Frank called me. "Meet me in front of the motel in five minutes."

I went outside. Frank was waiting alone behind the wheel of one of the station wagons. "Get in," he said.

We drove silently to the home of one of the Parry brothers, who owned the motel. It was a ranch-style house on the outskirts of Kanab. No one was home, but Frank entered anyway. I followed him. A baby-grand piano was in the living room with a big, framed photograph of Ava Gardner leaning on its music stand. Ava, as the world knew, had been the love of Frank's life.

"Sit down," said Frank.

I sat in an overstuffed chair. Frank sat down at the piano and began to play and sing, partly to Ava, partly to me. He sang for two hours. It was his way of apologizing for blackballing me from the rough-cut screening without having to say the words "I apologize." Frank never apologized to anyone.

It was a moment to remember, those two hours. I felt privileged, but when we returned to the lodge I had not forgiven Frank for anything. I hated the bastard. If it took the rest of my life, I would get back at Frank Sinatra.

A few days later we wrapped location filming and moved back to Los Angeles.

Chapter 5

PREPARING FOR BATTLE

When I was in the ninth grade I carried a briefcase to Casady Prep School. I was part of the A group, but my briefcase kept me organized and set me apart from my friends. Of us all, I was the only one who made exceptional grades.

Jealousy is a powerful emotion, and my good grades prompted certain students to steal my briefcase. Had I not had a bad temper, the thefts would have been a passing fad, but losing my temper was the whole point of the ploy. The incident almost always ended in a fistfight, with me being pushed into combat against a decidedly superior foe, usually an athlete. I'd get in a good punch or two, but the end result was always the same: defeat and its consequent bruises and abrasions.

After a dozen or so fights, I got fed up. It was ridiculous getting my brains beat out by bigger boys. I knew, however, the theft of my briefcase would not stop—absent a different tactic on my part. Thus, the next time it happened, I was prepared.

We were in class and someone began to edge my briefcase, which was under my chair, to the back of the room. It was a relay with several students involved, but the case always ended up in the hands of a bigger boy I would have to fight to get it back. This time I had a weapon, the leg from a broken chair, and when the last bully to receive the briefcase taunted me, I bypassed the preliminary tough-talk altercation and hit him in the head as hard as I could. He went down with a groan and a bloody gash. After that, nobody stole my briefcase.

The incident was a learning experience. When people have no idea how you will react to a given circumstance, their mind-set changes. Suddenly there are no rules. Stronger, bigger people become intimidated, since no one wants his head cracked open or a bullet in his heart. Physical size becomes irrelevant. A weapon is an equalizer, and that's why I often have a holstered handgun in the breast of my jacket. I want bullies to be afraid of me, and they are.

Before I arrived in Hollywood, Sammy Davis Jr.'s affair with Kim Novak was a cause célèbre. Never again was he out of the public eye. His marriage to Swedish actress Mai Britt was deemed in some quarters a defiance of American values. In thirty-seven states, interracial marriage was felonious. Sammy's hate mail was incredible. In public he was on constant alert for would-be assassins. He seldom ventured outside his home without a phalanx of bodyguards. One in particular, Joe Grant, was his closest companion. Sinatra had an entourage for the purpose of reminding him of how great he was; Sammy's was to save his life.

When Mai became pregnant, Sammy was bombarded with the same crude question: "What color do you think your child is going to be?"

"I don't care if it's polka-dot," answered Sammy honestly.

In November 1961, Mai gave birth to a beautiful baby girl, Tracey. Hate mail doubled overnight. Sammy provided more hospital security for mother and child than Jackie O had when John-John was born. The day Mai and Tracey were scheduled to go home, Sammy asked me to be on hand at the hospital to handle the press if any reporters showed up.

In those days journalism was still a profession rather than an industry. I foresaw no problems. Two legmen for gossip columnists were hanging out in the lobby when I arrived. I knew both of them. I answered their questions, and then went upstairs, where Sammy was waiting. Mai was in a wheelchair holding the baby. Joe Grant was standing by.

"Any reporters waiting for us?" asked Sammy.

"Just a couple of legmen."

"Good, let's go."

We trundled the wheelchair to an elevator and began our descent. The Davises were in good spirits; Mai was looking forward to being home with her new baby and Sammy was looking ahead to his opening at Ciro's nightclub on the Strip.

The door opened. A horde of photographers and reporters blocked our exit. Camera bulbs flashed. Questions flew like missiles. It was pandemonium. Mai turned away to protect her baby. Sammy was speechless. I tried to wave a path open. "Come on, guys!" I yelled. "Let us out!"

They didn't. *Flash! Flash!* I bodily pushed them. They began to back up, except for one lone photographer determined to get a shot of Tracey. I popped him in the nose with one hand and gave him a roundhouse with the other. He went reeling back with a moan, blood squirting from his nose like water from a toy pistol.

We surged forward, a nurse and Sammy pushing Mai and Tracey while Joe Grant and I led interference. The horde fell back silently, perhaps collectively realizing how intrusive they were. We went straight to Sammy's limousine, which was waiting at the curb outside the lobby. Nobody followed us, and then we were gone.

To me, the experience signaled the beginning of professional journalism's transition to a moneymaking industry interested solely in the bottom line. Most photographers and reporters were still thoughtful, giving quarter to human needs and emotions, but they were on the brink of change, and we saw an inkling of it that day. In a dozen years, with the collapse of the Nixon presidency, journalism as a profession would sigh its last breath. From that point forward, the ambition of Hollywood journalists would be personal celebrity, not honest reportage.

Back when I was at Rogers & Cowan, I came up with a publicity idea to celebrate Sammy's thirty-third anniversary in show business. He was performing at Mocambo, a popular Sunset Strip nightclub. My plan called for thirty-three different charities to join in giving him an award for his service to mankind. I gave Warren Cowan my pitch. He approved it with a smile and a complimentary pat on my back.

Finding thirty-three charities was easy, since Sammy was one of the most magnanimous entertainers in the world. I could have secured a hundred had I wanted to—that was not my problem. But I needed a dynamite emcee to handle the awards, someone who was contemporary and hot on television.

We represented the popular television series *Ben Casey*, as well as most of its stars. Vince Edwards, who played the title role of Doctor Casey, seemed a natural choice to make the presentations. I talked to Vince; he was delighted to perform the honors.

The thrust of the idea, of course, was to publicize the hell out of the event before it happened. For a solid month I barraged the media with press releases devoted to Sammy and the charities, the latter one by one, which sustained the campaign. Naturally, on the night the award was going to be presented, the club was packed like a can of sardines. That's when I ran into Milton Berle again, although this time it wasn't physical, like it had been on the stage of *Jackpot Bowling*.

"Why did you get Vince Edwards to give the award?" he asked with an intimidating tone.

"Because he's a television star in one of the most successful shows on the air," I told him, which Milton could have taken as a personal slur, since *Jackpot Bowling* had celebrated a lonely funeral at the end of its first year.

"Damn," said Milton. "*I* should be presenting this award. A year from now Vince Edwards' name won't mean shit!"

Vince gave the award, and Milton sat glumly with the rest of the stars. Later, he told Warren Cowan I was a rank amateur, with a few choice expletives thrown in for effect. After my second run-in with Milton, I really thought he was an asshole, although I kept my feelings to myself.

The truth is, I *was* an amateur. What I didn't understand at that stage of my career was the enormity of the ego that dwelled in the psyche of most entertainers. I took Milton's aggressiveness personally, which was a mistake. It would be a couple of years more before I learned that the bully ego of stars, past, present and future, had nothing to do with anyone except themselves and their audacious ambitions.

A few nights after Sammy's event, I was at Chasen's restaurant with a date. Milton came over to my table. "I got respect for you, kid," he said. "You're tougher than I thought."

I grew ten feet tall. Milton Berle had come to me . . . and with a compliment.

Sammy called me at my office. He wanted to come by "right now," which was unusual. Seldom did you meet with a star of Sammy's magnitude in your office. It was usually for lunch, if you were lucky, or dinner, if you were unlucky, because after hours an entourage of hangers-on was always close by and little business got done. I told Sammy I'd wait for him.

Within ten minutes he arrived, all excited, full of energy. He said he had been offered the honor of being the first Negro (the terms black and Afro-American had not come into vogue yet) to have the dramatic lead in a television show. "It's *The Dick Powell Show*," he told me, and he wanted it publicized to all known planets.

I read the script. Sammy would be playing an ex-prizefighter turned shoeshine boy. When I came across a scene in which three thugs physically beat him in an alley, my mind started clicking. Within minutes I had in idea. I called Sammy. "Are you using a double in your fight scene?"

"Hell no, man! I'm doing my own stunt!"

I called the studio and got the crew list; then I called Bob Conrad to see if he knew any of the stuntmen working the picture. Half of Bob's friends were stuntmen. I read him the list.

"I know them all," he said.

I explained to him the scene. "Can you set up a meeting for me with the stuntman who gives Sammy's character the coup de grace in the alley?"

He did, and I met with the stuntman. We talked about the scene. Then I popped my question: "How much would it cost me for you to accidentally hit Sammy in his bad eye at the climax of the scene?"

He thought I was kidding; I assured him I wasn't. He shrugged. "Three hundred bucks."

I only had three hundred to my name. "How about two-fifty?"

We settled on it; the deal was done.

My press connections were excellent, but I owed UPI a favor. I called the bureau chief. "Sammy Davis, Jr., is doing a dramatic episode for *The Dick Powell Show*." The service had been running the news releases I was filing, so he was aware of the episode and Sammy's role in it. "If you can send someone over to photograph the actual shooting of the fight scene, I'll give you an exclusive."

Another deal was done; this one for free.

Ernie Schworck was the UPI photographer. I made sure he got some shots of Sammy while the scene was being set up. Then I held him at ringside to make sure he didn't leave. Right before the take, the stuntman gave me a subtle thumbs-up signal. The actors were on their marks, the crew was ready, and the director yelled, "Action!"

Fight scenes are choreographed and well-rehearsed. This one went accordingly, until my stuntman gave Sammy a right punch that sent him to the floor.

"Shit! Cut!"

Sammy groaned; his face was bleeding from a small cut under his blind eye.

"Jesus, Sammy," said the stuntman. "I'm sorry!"

"It's nothing, it's nothing," muttered Sammy heroically.

As a crowd gathered, I whispered innocently to Ernie Schworck, "That was dramatic. Did you get anything?" Ernie was already leaving; he had something.

The story went out within an hour, with a photograph taken almost at the instant Sammy was hit. If it didn't go through the solar system, it went around the world more than once. It was a PR man's dream. It was on every wire, churning around the globe like whipped cream in the making: "Davis in Fight Accident!"

I drove through Laurel Canyon whistling under my breath. When I got to the office I had a message directing me to report to Warren Cowan immediately. I dashed to his office expecting high praise. Warren sat glumly behind his desk. "I just had a call from Aaron Spelling," he said. "They know what you did with Sammy Davis, Jr."

Spelling was Dick Powell's top man, just on the verge of entering the Hollywood jungle as an independent producer.

"What I *did*?" I asked, feigning naïveté.

"Yes, and I know, too," said Warren.

I stood like a statue wondering exactly *what* he knew. Had the stuntman confessed? I doubted it; he would have lost his union card. But something had gone awry. The question was: What?

"Rogers & Cowan is barred from Four Star as long as you are employed here," continued Warren.

Four Star Productions was the parent company of Dick Powell's mini-empire. It was big-time, so I understood the implication of Warren's words. "That's it?" I said. "I'm getting fired over an accident that happened on the set?"

"I think you know it's more than that, Jay," said Warren.

I had just pulled off the biggest publicity stunt of my young career, and I was getting canned for it. Something was wrong. What did Warren know that I didn't?

In those days the motion-picture television industry was far removed from what it is today. It was as segregated as the races, which is part of the irony of the story, since Sammy's role was an incipient effort at leveling the playing field for black actors. But in the early sixties television and movies were separate—as well as unfriendly—entities. Movie people thought television people were trying to destroy their industry, and television people resented the backseat role in which movie people tried to place them.

When I left Warren's office, however, I thought somehow word had leaked out about my role with the stuntman. That wasn't it at all. One of the wire stories sent around the world said Sammy had been hit during a stunt while making a movie. The key word was *movie*, as on the silver screen. Because I was Sammy's publicist, I was accused of defaming the television industry. Dick Powell, Aaron Spelling and other television bigwigs thought I was purposely putting their fledgling industry down. That's what Warren meant when he said it was more than Sammy being accidentally punched in the face: "I think you know it's more than that,

Jay." It was a television industry ego trip, and I hadn't even written the goddamned copy!

When the story came out the next day in the newspapers and trades, it had a different take, as it would later in the weeklies. The stories varied, but they had the same essential information: "Sammy Davis, Jr., failed to duck a stuntman's blow during a fight scene while filming an upcoming episode for television's *The Dick Powell Show*."

Television's *The Dick Powell Show*.

Warren called me. "Come back to work, Jay. The dailies have saved you."

I stayed in my office all day waiting for the call, namely the gracious thank-you from Sammy for my wonderful services rendered. He'd asked me to get him some worldwide publicity, and I had performed. The call came at five o'clock. I felt like lighting a victory cigar, but instead I propped my feet on my desk and picked up the phone. A feeling of pride in accomplishment swept my body; my voice literally sang, "Helloooo, Sammy!"

"We've got to get that son of a bitch!" he cried.

My heart sank. Did he know the stuntman had punched him on purpose? "What son of a bitch?" I asked.

"The one that wrote that fucking caption!"

"What caption?"

"The one that said 'Sammy Davis, Jr., failed to duck a blow.' Do you know how that makes me look? Do you know how fucking embarrassing that is? Like I can't handle myself in a fight! I want you to get that mother!" And he hung up.

When I was assigned Eddie Fisher's account, his career had been derailed by a series of romantic contretemps that had sent his popularity plunging. Eddie had dumped Debbie Reynolds, his wife, and married Elizabeth Taylor, whose third husband, Mike Todd, had been killed in a plane crash. Eddie had become Mr. Elizabeth Taylor, which was bad enough; but then Elizabeth had fallen in love with Richard Burton on the set of *Cleopatra* in Rome and sent Eddie scampering back to the States as the soon-to-be ex–Mr. Elizabeth Taylor, which was worse.

As in all cases of romantic intrigue and failure, the truth about the Debbie-Eddie-Elizabeth-Richard story was hidden somewhere between the lines of the gossip columnists and the words of the pundits. Eddie was devastated, but he was not defeated. He still had a huge following and, being a realist, he wanted to bring his fans back into the fold as quickly as possible.

I liked Eddie. For all of the adverse publicity that portrayed him as a doting wimp, he wasn't. At thirty-four, he was a seasoned professional in both work and romance, and his cool aplomb had not diminished a fraction. However, he was still obsessed with Elizabeth, who, when Eddie exited Rome, had given him a faint hope of reconciliation by trying to persuade him not to leave in the midst of her indiscretions with Burton. Given a choice between continued humiliation and sudden flight, Eddie chose the latter.

Before he opened at Cocoanut Grove, I was with Eddie almost every night. We were usually joined by Walter Winchell, who had moved to California after his decades-long heyday in New York as the most important—as well as the most merciless—gossip columnist in America. He was the prototype for the Burt Lancaster character J.J. Hunsacker in *The Sweet Smell of Success*, which gives an indication of how ruthless and brutal Winchell was.

Walter had been a mentor of Eddie's, and now that Eddie and Elizabeth had broken up, he gave Eddie his shoulder to lean on. I didn't particularly like Winchell; he was a heavy-duty drinker who became increasingly mean-spirited with each drink. He wanted to "get" people, particularly Burton, for having done injury to his protégé. It was the same every night—a convivial beginning and a hostile ending, with Walter in his cups. I didn't argue with Winchell's tactics, which for the most part were all talk anyway. Eddie was my friend, and as the publicist assigned to him, I wanted to help rejuvenate his career.

Warren Cowan came up with an idea. Eddie's two-week engagement at the Cocoanut Grove should be a "Back in My Own Backyard" sort of thing, where Eddie would sing to packed houses and the audiences could feel their heartstrings being pulled. Opening night, however, was not what we expected. A lot of stars were present, but the press, except for Winchell, was noticeably absent. It was probably for the best, because when Eddie sang "Danny Boy" to the tune of "Hava Nagila," a drunken Irish sailor got pissed off and began to heckle him. To top it off, the sailor stood on his chair and called Eddie a kike. Mickey Rooney leaped from his seat and punched the sailor before security guards rushed in. It was a bad start.

The next day Cowan cracked the whip. We had to devise something that would get the press interested in going to the Grove. Then he came up with an idea. "How about we bring the same sailor back? We'll get him a date, and we'll have a plainclothes cop there to supervise the situation. We'll show the warm side of Eddie."

My job was to make sure the press corps was present in toto. I called almost every columnist in town, from Louella Parsons to James Bacon. They all knew about the Rooney-sailor incident, so it wasn't difficult to get them there for the next performance. Fifteen minutes before curtain call, the showroom was full. I saw all the columnists—Hedda Hopper, Bacon, Parsons, Harrison Carroll and others—at their tables. The only one absent was Winchell. I went backstage to Eddie's dressing room; he told me Winchell was upstairs in Eddie's suite.

"I'll get him," I said.

"Be careful," answered Eddie.

Something strange was in the air, accentuated by Eddie's warning. I could not define it, but I could feel it.

I went up to Eddie's suite. Winchell had already imbibed a few drinks. I wasn't surprised because I had been out with him and Eddie almost every night for two weeks, and Winchell was an old-fashioned drinking machine. He had been knocking out coded columns with banner headlines through which Eddie was secretly trying to communicate with Elizabeth, an effort that indicated how much pain Eddie was suffering.

"Eddie's on in ten minutes," I told him.

"Okay," grunted Winchell, "let's go."

We got in the elevator and the door closed.

"You got press tonight?" he asked.

"Yeah, but they came because we invited the heckler back."

Winchell whipped a .45 from inside his suit jacket, cocked the hammer and placed the barrel between my eyes. His own eyes were glassy and his expression was maniacal. It was my moment of truth. It lasted for seconds; it seemed like minutes.

"I should kill you, you bastard! You're taking advantage of Eddie."

I stared at him without blinking. My fear factor was nil. I said nothing; I didn't want to push him over the edge. He pressed the barrel harder against my forehead. "I should kill you," he repeated. We stared at each other until he lowered the gun. The elevator door opened and I calmly stepped out. He remained inside. The door closed.

It is difficult to explain, but I did not feel frightened, even afterward which I'm told is often when fear surfaces. I had faced death and stared it down, because that crazy drunk bastard had been on the verge of shooting me. For the first time I realized what it was like to be Audie Murphy in combat or Ernest Hemingway facing a charging lion. Grace under pressure. It was a pivotal point in my life. I felt I had become a man.

Chapter 6

EVERY SOLDIER, EVERY SAILOR

One of my jobs at Rogers & Cowan, along with the other young publicists, was escorting female clients to social functions. We were like high-class gigolos without the promise of sex. The women were usually older, and some of them were widows. We were required to wear the Rogers & Cowan uniform, each of us in the same dark suit, as if it had been painted on our bodies. We were tagged the "Cufflink Cuties" or "Frankie's Flacks." At various times I escorted Kay Gable, Clark's widow; Greer Garson, the British actress and Oscar winner for *Mrs. Miniver*; Zsa Zsa Gabor (when her date canceled at the last minute); and Kathryn Grayson, the musical star.

I adored Ms. Grayson. In spite of her petite size (she was five-two), she had the most beautiful breasts I'd ever seen. I was always nervous when I was with her, because I kept staring at them. She thought they were beautiful, too, so we had that in common, along with Sinatra stories.

Kathryn had starred opposite Frank in the 1948 musical *The Kissing Bandit*. Frank played a Mexican who tried to outdo his father's reputation as a western Casanova. Kathryn played his potential inamorata. "Did you see the movie?" she asked me.

"Yes," I lied. "I loved it."

"Then you noticed that I kissed Frank only once, and very briefly. Do you know why?" She laughed at the memory. "Frank had a terrible cough that I decided was tuberculosis. It was probably smoker's cough, but I was young and terribly naïve. I wouldn't let him kiss me because I didn't want to catch the disease. The producer was angry, the director was angry, and Frank was angry, but I wasn't daunted. The kissing bandit only got to kiss the object of his affection once. I made them do it in one take!"

There was only one major problem with escorting these beautiful starlets. My dilemma was, back at home I already had a beautiful starlet. My new girlfriend was none other than the gorgeous and talented actress Leslie Parrish. She was also my client.

I had pursued Leslie with vigor immediately after *The Manchurian Candidate*, and I really didn't want to fuck up our good thing. Not for anyone. It had taken me a day to get to first base, but it took me a month to get to second, another month to land on third, and when I finally crossed home plate I was not only exhausted but also broke. It was worth it—I scored big. Leslie was my first true Hollywood love. I promptly moved into her rented house on Dorrington Street. It was Leslie, me and thirteen Persian cats. We kept our affair secret; office rules forbade flacks from sleeping with their clients.

Leslie didn't mind my escorting fading stars like Greer Garson or Kathryn Grayson, or even Sheila Graham, but when it came to Jayne Mansfield she grew livid. I had other female clients who were young, but they were involved with husbands or boyfriends and didn't require social chaperones. Jayne, however, had just separated from her husband, Hungarian muscleman-actor and former Mr. Universe Mickey Hargitay, and she didn't want to go out alone. I was twenty-five and she was twenty-eight.

Early in her career, when Jayne was auditioning for her first role, she had slipped a note to the show's producer. It was strictly numerical. She got the part, and rather than having her name printed on the back of her studio chair, which was the custom, her chair was emblazoned with the same message she had sent to the producer: 40-21-35.

The first time I escorted Jayne, Leslie threw a conniption fit. I didn't blame her. Had the roles been somehow reversed, I would have done the same.

Essentially Jayne and I had a date because she was lonely. She wanted to go to P.J.'s, a hot club on Santa Monica Boulevard in West Hollywood. The office provided me with a limousine and chauffeur, an indication that somebody high up thought Jayne still might go places in the industry. She wanted to see Eddie Cano perform, P.J.'s terrific jazz pianist.

I picked her up at her home on Sunset Boulevard, the Pink Palace, where everything was heart-shaped—the pool, the fireplace, the bed, the bathtub—everything except the house itself. The décor was pink pastel. I noticed all this because I had to wait interminably; Jayne was never on time for anything. When she finally slinked down the stairs, she wore a coal-black cocktail dress with deep décolletage, very sexy with the black against her pale skin and platinum hair.

"You look beautiful in black," I told her.

"I'm practicing to become a Catholic," she answered incongruously.

She must have seen my blank expression because in the limousine she said, "See, Enrico thinks I should become a Catholic before we get married."

"Enrico?"

"Bomba."

Enrico Bomba was an Italian producer Jayne had worked with recently in Italy, where she had made four spaghetti flicks of no importance. Nevertheless, Jayne was a true star. She had a dozen or so pictures behind her (some of them very big, including a co-starring role with Cary Grant) and a couple of *Playboy* centerfolds, but Twentieth Century-Fox had just declined to renew her contract. If Jayne was bothered by it, she didn't betray her feelings.

We were ushered to a front-and-center table, right by the piano. We had to sit through the interim performances to see Eddie's second show. A Mexican guitarist came out and strummed and sang a couple of songs, followed by the Scott Smith trio, the latter being college kids from Northwestern University—pianist, bassist and drummer. They were supposedly nobodies, of course, and the audience was more interested in watching Jayne than giving attention to the sets. Then an attractive female singer of Scandinavian heritage joined the trio. People perked up because she was so good. They were all good, but the showcase performer was Eddie Cano.

Finally Eddie came out for his second act and the room grew quiet. It was Eddie's gimmick to start at a cool level and work his way up a scale of heat. The audience usually followed his mood, growing hot with him as he played toward crescendo. People who had gone outside for a breath of fresh air returned; the room was packed. Smoke was thick and booze was flowing as Eddie's piano began to rattle heavy-duty jazz.

Jayne was composed. When Eddie reached the climax of his show and banged the last key, people leaped up and clapped boisterously. I looked at Jayne. She was clapping as if we were attending a chamber music concert, very delicately patting the palm of her left hand with the wrist of her right hand. I supposed she thought that was the way Catholics applauded.

As I look back from the perspective of almost forty-five years, I have no memory of what happened to Eddie Cano. Maybe he's still playing the small club circuit. The guitar player was a kid named Trini Lopez and the singer for the Scott Smith Trio was a girl named Ann-Margret.

After we left P.J.'s, I tried conversing with Jayne to get to know her better. She seemed restless, but I finally hit on a common chord. She had been reared in Texas and I in Oklahoma, so we had a remote, regional connection. Warming to the conversation, she suddenly said, "Can we go someplace else?"

"Sure. Where would you like to go?"

"The Pink Pussycat!"

I bit my lip. How would I explain all this shit to Leslie?

The Pink Pussycat was a strip joint featuring girls with names like Holly Come Lightly and Sugar For You. When we stepped out of the limo, Jayne grabbed my hand and pulled me close, smiling and cooing as if we were coming out of the closet of a clandestine relationship. Again we were ushered to a ringside table. If P.J.'s showroom had been smoke-laden, the Pink Pussycat appeared to be on fire. Jayne loved it; she had found her venue.

For two hours we drank martinis and watched girls in G-strings gyrate and grind. What Jayne had in common with them was 40-21-35. She was enchanted; I was bored. I had one of the most beautiful women in the world waiting for me at home, and I do mean waiting, for I knew Leslie wouldn't sleep until I gave her every detail of the Rogers & Cowan escort service.

At last the show was over. Jayne clung to my arm like a leech as we walked to the limousine, smiling and cooing at a couple of grave-shift photographers. As we drove back to the Pink Palace, I could see her face in and out of the streetlamps. She was leaning against me, staring up at me, her face suggestive. I averted my eyes.

"I want you to come in for a nightcap," she said.

"Not tonight, Jayne. It's late."

The limo driver parked in the circular driveway and I walked her to the door. She giggled as she fumbled for her key. "Just one more cocktail," she said.

"It's a little late, Jayne."

She looked at me. "It's never too late for that," she said suggestively.

"Really, I can't. It's three in the morning, and I've got to be at work at seven sharp."

"I thought you worked for me?" she said.

"Jayne, I've got a girlfriend waiting for me at home. We're very much in love."

She had the door open. I edged her across the threshold. She turned and leaned toward me, exposing her cleavage. "Every soldier, every sailor and every marine has my picture hanging over his bed, and you say you don't want me?"

"I have a girlfriend, Jayne."

"We'll see," she said, and closed the door in my face.

Leslie was waiting up, feigning reading a magazine in bed. "How did it go with Miss Mansfield?" she asked sarcastically.

"Pretty boring," I told her.

"I'll bet it was!"

I went into the bathroom. A *Playboy* centerfold of Jayne, circa 1955, was taped to the mirror.

Jayne began to demand my services with agonizing frequency. We went to the Chino Men's Prison, where she made a publicity appearance. Before we entered the compound, she signed an eight-by-ten glossy for every thief, rapist and murderer in the prison. Instead of dotting her i's, she drew little hearts. Bedlam was the response of the inmates when she entered. Jayne loved it. We had to stay until all the photographs were given away, something for the guys to jerk off to.

Afterward we went to a party at the Palladium in Hollywood. Mickey Hargitay, her estranged husband, was there, his eyes wistfully following her every move. I felt sorry for him. Jayne was downing martinis like they were made of water. She knew Mickey was watching. When the last vestige of her inhibitions was drained, she put her arm around my waist and pulled me close, a gesture calculated to make Mickey jealous. I was embarrassed. I took her arm away. "Don't do that, Jayne. Please."

She smiled. "Every soldier and sailor, Jay. Remember that. You're no different."

We drove to another engagement. We had more people now, including Charlie Goldring, Jayne's manager, and Mike Silverman, a local realtor notorious for having romanced Joan Crawford. ("She was like a Thomas Guide to sex," Mike told me. "She directed the fuck!") When we arrived at the curb, Jayne said, "You guys go ahead. I'm not getting out until I suck Jay's cock."

I literally choked on her words. Everyone except Jayne and me emptied the limousine, as if following the orders of Douglas MacArthur at Inchon. I was red-faced with embarrassment. "Don't ever do that again, Jayne!"

"Every soldier and sailor," she said, and she reached for my crotch.

I slapped her with an open hand, but hard. She wasn't fazed. We got out of the limousine and went inside. Of course, Silverman and Goldring thought I had gotten a blowjob.

That night Leslie was waiting up again. "I can't take this, Jay. It isn't right."

"It's part of my job," I complained.

We got into a heated argument. I left and went to my buddy Fabian's penthouse, which was becoming my second home. The former teenage heartthrob was wild and living the life. I felt badly, though, because in my heart I didn't disagree with Leslie.

A few nights later Jayne called me at home. It was one of the few times

I answered the phone. She told me she had granted a magazine reporter an interview at the Pink Palace. "You have to come over and supervise," she said.

"I can't."

"You'd better!"

I took a shower and put on a suit and tie.

"Where are you going?" asked Leslie.

I didn't say anything.

"It's Jayne!" said Leslie.

I drove to the Pink Palace and parked in the driveway. I rang the bell. No one answered. The door was unlocked; I went in. The house was quiet and empty. "Jayne?" I called.

"I'll be down in a minute," came Jayne's voice.

Ten minutes later she made her entrance. She was wearing a thin, see-through negligee and matching slippers with plumes on the tips that fanned the air with ostrich feathers. She had a martini in her hand and a sultry look on her face. "Every soldier, every sailor . . ." she began.

"Where's the reporter?" I asked.

"What we're going to do doesn't need to be reported," she said.

She chased me. I ran around in circles, staking a path around the couch. It was like an old silent-movie routine, but a farce that turned out to be real. Rounding the couch, I tripped on a footstool and fell. Jayne leaped on top of me. She was a predator, holding her martini glass in one hand and clawing me with the other. She tore my trousers, not in the crotch, but down the seam of my left leg. She was only five-foot-six, but topside she was a heavyweight. When she tossed her glass aside, sending it crashing in shards, I realized I had a choice to make—either fuck or fight. Later I told myself it was "consensual" rape.

By the time I left, I was a mess. I smelled like a perfume factory and my left pant leg was flopping like a flag. I drove home, praying that Leslie had fallen asleep. She hadn't. She was sitting on the curb in front of the house with a dead cat in her lap. It had been run over by a car. She said nothing; I said nothing. We went to the backyard. I dug a hole in the ground, and we buried the cat.

The next day I quit Rogers & Cowan. It was not my intention. I went to Warren, told him what had happened and asked him to remove me from Jayne's account. He nodded sympathetically, called Jayne and told her he was changing her PR representative.

"If Jay isn't my publicist," she told him, "then I'm changing firms."

I submitted my resignation, telling Warren I would not take any accounts with me (except Leslie's), or solicit any Rogers & Cowan clients for one year. I was Alan Ladd, playing out a heroic role of honor and integrity. Warren wished me well. Suddenly I was on the street, a publicist without anchor and with only one new client: Eartha Kitt.

Jim Mahoney, an old-line publicist with a touch of paranoia, gave me a job at $250 a week. He had some big clients, but I recognized from the outset that I couldn't work with Jim. He was afraid to let his reps meet his clients lest they steal them. I was relegated to dreaming up ideas and writing copy for people I would never meet and, in some cases, for people Jim kept anonymous for his own security reasons.

Although I was running scared, I enjoyed the freedom of being able to let people know Leslie and I were a couple. We no longer had to avoid spots where we were afraid we'd be found out and word of our relationship would get back to Henry Rogers or Warren Cowan.

One night at an alfresco party in Malibu, I saw Kirk Douglas meandering among the guests. "Come on," I said to Leslie, leading her across the garden.

"Kirk," I said, "have you ever met my girlfriend, Leslie Parrish?"

He stared at Leslie for a moment, then looked at me with a big Hollywood smile on his face. "You bastard!" he said.

Leslie and I thought we were happy. She was offered a part in *The Long Ships*, a costume movie about Vikings. The producer said it would be the next *Lawrence of Arabia*, which had been a blockbuster the year before. It was going to be filmed on location in Yugoslavia.

In truth, Leslie did not want to do the picture and I did not want her to go abroad. Her agent, however, said Robert Wagner had signed as the male lead, with Richard Widmark and Sidney Poitier in supporting roles.

He was sure the picture would make her a star. He told her it was the best script he'd ever read, just too fantastic to turn down.

"What do you think of it?" I asked Leslie.

"It's in London," she said. "They don't have a script available here."

The project smelled fishy, but Leslie gave in. When an actor is out of work for two weeks, it looks like the world is caving in. We had a sad parting. We stood at the airport gate embracing and kissing; then she flew away, first stop London. She still hadn't read the script.

I drove back to the house feeling sad, angry and jealous. I ate alone for the first time in months, Leslie's chair empty across from me, twelve Persian cats lapping at my feet.

The next day she called me six times from London. She was being fitted with wardrobe. She complained they were trying to dress her in cave-girl miniskirts with tops that barely covered her nipples. She kept asking to see a screenplay. "It's being rewritten" was the answer.

The second day she called me eight times, her voice cracking. Robert Wagner was not the male lead after all; it was Russ Tamblyn. Widmark and Poitier had arrived, but their main interests were settling their contracts with Columbia, the releasing studio.

The third day Leslie called me ten times, each call more hysterical than the one before. She had read the script. She had twenty lines and four nude scenes. This was before screen nudity was acceptable, and it would never have been acceptable to Leslie. On the eve of every battle— Vikings apparently spent 365 days a year fighting—some heathen character ripped off her clothes.

"Jay, get me out of this picture," she pleaded. "Get a lawyer! Do anything!" She was a basket case. The next day she left London for Yugoslavia.

I hired a lawyer to try to get her out of the contract, but I didn't hear from her. My alarm bell went off and my jealousy meter hit red. She was supposed to be in the mountains of Yugoslavia for three months. Diane McBain's infidelity colored my thinking. What I didn't know was that Leslie couldn't make long-distance calls out of Yugoslavia.

When she didn't call me the next day, I was ready to get on a plane. Then I got a call from the London office. Leslie had suffered a mental collapse; Richard Widmark was placing her on a flight back to the States. I speculated that she might have pulled off an acting job to get out of the picture, the kind of performance I had perfected.

My speculation was wasted imagination. When Leslie came out of customs, she passed me without blinking an eye; it was as if I no longer existed. She was bonkers.

"Leslie!"

She turned to face me, but she didn't recognize me.

"I'm Jay, Leslie, your boyfriend."

She stared dumbly through me. I got her luggage, coaxed her into the car and drove home, trying to explain to her who I was. I was talking to a statue. She never said a word.

The next day was a frustrating rehash of her arrival. I talked; she said nothing. This went on for days. Jim Mahoney was raising hell at the office because I was spending so much time with Leslie—feeding her breakfast, going home to make lunch and taking off early for dinner. She was totally out of it. When someone rang the doorbell, she would hide in the closet with the cats. Twelve cats and Leslie Parrish squeezed into a space the size of a refrigerator.

Gradually she began to speak, but her words made little sense. I persuaded her to go to a psychiatrist. The more she went, the more she spoke. It wasn't an improvement because what she said, which was nothing more than parroting her shrink, was that everything was my fault. "If you had not been jealous, I would have been able to get through it," she would say.

"Get through what?"

"*The Long Ships.*"

"You hated the movie, Leslie. They replaced you with a Yugoslavian actress named Beba Loncar. Doesn't that give you an idea of how unimportant your role was?"

"My doctor says—"

Mahoney fired me. Leslie said it was a blessing. It wasn't; I was broke and back at square one. It was Leslie, Eartha Kitt, a dozen cats and an unemployed Jay Bernstein.

I had to scramble fast. For two years I'd been selling hot air and fluff schemes for other people. I decided to become Warren Cowan, Henry Rogers, Jim Mahoney and a hundred others rolled into one. I didn't want to be equal to them; I wanted to be better.

Leslie's house had a spare bedroom that I turned into an office. For a fleeting moment I thought Leslie and I might make it. She was offered a new movie, an eight-week job that would give me the flexibility I needed to get Jay Bernstein Public Relations off the ground. I was already moving at Mach speed, while Leslie was still in her starting blocks. I needed to give the business 100 percent.

The movie was *Strait-Jacket*, starring Joan Crawford. Joan was no longer at the top of her form, but she still had a box-office calling card. The year before, she and Bette Davis had matched wits, talents and animosities making *Whatever Happened to Baby Jane?* The movie had revitalized their careers. It seemed a good idea for Leslie to take the part. *Strait-Jacket* might be the picture that would catapult her into the starry firmament.

The story was about a woman (Crawford) who had served twenty years in a penitentiary for a series of ax murders. Out of prison she begins living a peaceful life with her daughter (Leslie). Then murders begin anew, and Crawford is the suspect. The twist comes at the end when the murderer, who looks like Crawford, is unmasked, literally, and it's Leslie, the daughter.

Leslie signed on the dotted line, but when she put on the mask, one of those skin-tight, molded-rubber disguises that are commonplace today, she became claustrophobic. She went berserk and ripped off the mask in a mad frenzy. Goodbye *Strait-Jacket*, goodbye Joan Crawford and goodbye Harvey Lee Yeary, an unknown actor who was playing his first role. Leslie and I reverted to breaking up and making up as fast as ice melts and freezes again.

Chapter 7

JAY BERNSTEIN
PUBLIC RELATIONS

Word spread fast that I had left Rogers & Cowan and segued into my very own PR firm—Jay Bernstein Public Relations. One of the first people who called me was Sammy Davis, Jr.: "Jay, you're my man." When I told him of my promised moratorium to Warren, he said, "I hear you. I'll call you one year from today."

I started hustling accounts, knowing I wouldn't have Sammy Davis, Jr., for another nine months. My first client was Joel Grey, the actor, singer and dancer who later became famous in the Bob Fosse musical *Cabaret*. Warren Cowan helped me get a business account, a barbershop in Beverly Hills. I picked up Arthur O'Connell and Robert Blake, who was trying to break out of child-actor roles. Then Nick Adams and Bob Conrad came with me, followed by Mike Connors, all television actors who wanted to do movies. My selling point was dedication. I wasn't Rogers & Cowan yet, but I promised my clients I would work for them 24/7, and I did.

Though I was still in my twenties, it seemed like I had already worked an eternity in Hollywood, but I was just getting started. In practically no time, I had seventy-five clients. I was hot and on fire! Everyone in Hollywood, from the top to the bottom, took notice. I became an extremely powerful Hollywood PR force to be reckoned with, now competing with the big boys. I was a serious threat as I acquired an all-star cast of high-profile, celebrity clients. Everyone who was anyone in Hollywood wanted to work with Jay Bernstein. Practically overnight, I was feared, revered, respected and considered a major rival by my peers and mentors at firms like Rogers & Cowan and all of the biggest PR firms in Hollywood. I had finally arrived. Shit, I had finally fucking made it!

I opened offices in New York and London and had associates in Paris and Rome. I ran the business like a nuthouse with no medical practitioners. I was a terrible boss—I had no training in bossism. I was a perfectionist; I wanted my people to strive always for perfection. I didn't care about domesticity, holidays and having days off. I was married to my job; I expected my staff to be married to it also. They weren't, and they hated me for trying to make them into Jay Bernstein clones. Turnover was faster than a Ferris wheel.

I was with a doctor one day when something began to beep like a one-track roadrunner in the desert. "Excuse me," he said, and drew from his waist an instrument that looked like a sawed-off shotgun. It was in a holster that ran from his belt to his knee. He looked at a tiny window at the top of the gadget and said again, "Excuse me," adding, "I've got an emergency call." I was fascinated. After he took care of his emergency I wanted to know what the beeping thing was.

The next day I bought two-dozen pagers. Now our clients could reach us by telephone anytime, day or night. It was a revolutionary move for a PR agency. It was great, except my staff hated our beepers. And then they hated me, even more than before. I had beeper tests, sometimes on holidays, sometimes at three a.m. I would call and leave my number, then wait for everybody to call me back. I wanted them on the constant qui vive, ready to solve problems.

One year to the day after I left Rogers & Cowan, I signed Sammy Davis, Jr. I handled Sammy for several years, but we never became intimate friends. We were too much alike. Sammy needed to be entertained, both socially and intellectually. I was the same; when you have a business relationship, you don't sing to each other, you talk business. Yet Sammy and I shared the same chutzpah—we were go-getters.

I was a kid pitted against some very big men, and Sammy liked those odds. Through his influence I secured many members of the music industry. I represented Aretha Franklin, Dionne Warwick, Leslie Uggams, Isaac Hayes, Barry White, Diana Ross, the Temptations, Quincy Jones, Lou Rawls, Peggy Lee, Buddy Greco, Tony Martin, the Supremes, the Fifth Dimension, Al Martino, Rick Nelson and a dozen others.

In the early days, when Sammy opened, say, in Vegas, I would put an enormous effort into launching and publicizing his show. I would fly over to see his premier performance before a sellout crowd. I then would hang around the stage, always on the periphery of his entourage. He would come offstage and hardly notice my existence. Finally I said, "I'm not going to waste my time," and I didn't go back for his next opening.

Sammy, always observant, took my absence as a slight. One of his people called me: "Jay, Sammy's very upset that you weren't there last night."

"What are you talking about? He hardly recognizes my presence."

"Well, he's pissed."

I learned to be at Sammy's openings and closings, whether he noticed me or not. The fact is, he *did* notice me, although he seldom showed it. One time he came offstage and said, "Let's take a ride."

We cruised up and down the Strip in his limousine, sipping whiskeys. He told the chauffeur to open the sunroof: "I need air!" I understood his request, since he had just performed almost nonstop for two hours. He said, "If you want to, stick your head out the moon roof."

I laughed. "No, thanks, Sammy."

"Look," he continued, "I said that because I saw you looking up at the stars. Let me tell you, Jay, if you want to do something, then do it. Don't be afraid to be yourself with me. I ain't the Queen of England."

We rode in silence. I didn't know what to say.

Then he said, "I met her once, the Queen of England. It was *terrifying*."

We were drinking, but we were not yet at three sheets. We were at that stage where inhibitions fall aside. I was curious about his emphasis on the word *terrifying*.

"Why was that?" I asked.

"Shit, man, she was royalty! I grew up in Harlem. Nobody ever said,

'This is what you do when you meet the Queen of England!'" He looked at me. "Have you ever met a queen?"

"No," I said, "but I'm sure she got a kick out of you."

"Of course she did, but . . . Well, if she hadn't, then to hell with her! Right?"

Sammy looked off into space, thinking about the queen. I knew where he was coming from. Nobody in Oklahoma City had ever told me what to do if I met the Queen of England either, not even my mother, whose bible was Emily Post. It was too remote; the idea of the success we were sharing was alien to our backgrounds, whether from Harlem or Oklahoma City.

A few months after Sammy Davis, Jr., became my number one client he accepted the starring role in Clifford Odets' *Golden Boy*, which was scheduled to open on Broadway the following year. Before he left for New York to begin rehearsals he called me. "Meet me tonight at the Daisy," he said. "I've got some ideas."

The Daisy was Jack Hansen's private club located at the site of Michael Romanoff's original eponymous restaurant, on Rodeo Drive in the heart of Beverly Hills. It was the hottest spot in town, primarily because the Rat Pack hung out there. I became a member because Jack was a stickler for member-only clients. One night when he caught non-members Richard Harris and Peter O'Toole in the club, he kicked them out.

As usual, the Daisy was packed. I walked in and out of the shadows and smoke until I saw Sammy talking to some girls sitting in a booth. I hesitated; then he saw me and gestured for me to go to the bar. Peter Lawford was there, sipping a drink.

I approached Peter and offered my hand. He gave me a clenched fist in return, as if to brush me off. "Fuck you," I said, and walked away.

Sammy cut me off before I got to the door. "Hold up, Jay. Peter has arthritis. Sometimes his hand doesn't work the right way," he explained. "He can't help it."

It was true. Peter suffered from a childhood injury. I had worked an entire motion picture with him without realizing he was handicapped. I returned to the bar with Sammy and apologized. Peter laughed, taking it in stride.

We had a couple of drinks, and Sammy got down to business. He was excited and in a generous mood. He threw me two nuggets, one of fool's gold, the other genuine. I took the first one. While he was in New York, he wanted me to stay in his guesthouse, from where I could oversee his property as well as save the rent money I was paying my landlord at Doheny. I accepted his offer, not realizing the apartment would be in exchange for the $400 per month he was paying me as a publicist.

Second, knowing I was broke, he offered to invest $25,000 in my company. It was tempting. I needed the money, but Sammy wanted 50 percent of the action. He probably realized I was one of the few guys in Hollywood who would actually split my profits if I took the deal. Most agreements ended with the principal proprietor coming back at a later date and saying, "Here's your $25,000. I don't need it anymore." I thanked Sammy, but turned him down.

"The window is always open," he said. "If you ever need capital, just let me know."

It was ironic, because nobody I knew was more broke than Sammy Davis, Jr. He spent twice what he earned. When his income went up, so did his standard of living, which was always opulent. But that was Sammy. He lived on cash flow and spent a great deal of time dodging the IRS.

As for *Golden Boy*, he left the West Coast publicity campaign up to me. The only words he said were, "I want Hollywood to know I'm starring on Broadway."

Sammy's home was a thirty-two-room residence off Sunset Plaza, in the hills above the Strip. I took the guesthouse out back by the swimming pool. Sammy called it his "playroom." *TV Guide* thought I was living in the big house. After Sammy left for New York, it ran a blurb describing my new quarters: "The bedroom hangs over the living room on a balcony. It's got three baths, fireplace, piano, pool table, steam room, tape machine, stereo, 1,000 record albums, seventy-foot swimming pool, and a twenty-five-foot wet bar with beer on tap." One of the trade papers quoted me as saying, "My life is like a Hollywood movie set." I never said that, because living as Sammy's surrogate was a dangerous business.

Sammy was hardly out of town when some crazed racist expended a terrific amount of energy and money on decorating the grounds with about twenty cases of toilet tissue and accompanying crude, handwritten signs: Nigger Lover! Get Out!

I didn't bother reporting the lawn decorations, but when someone took a potshot at me with a rifle, I called the cops. They came out and inspected the place with the delicacy of a garbage collector in a hurry. It became obvious they weren't going to do anything.

"This happens pretty often," said one of the cops. "I don't think anyone is really trying to shoot you. It's just a scare tactic. They always shot over Mr. Davis's head."

When it happened the second time, I bought my first handgun, a .38-caliber pistol that I wore in a holster, either inside my coat or above my ankle. Sammy was afraid of would-be assassins; I wasn't. I was hoping it would happen a third time; I was going to charge the direction from where the shot came with my gun blazing. It didn't happen again, perhaps because I let it be known to any observer that I was armed.

I put 100 percent into my work. I signed everyone who was willing to give me a chance. I never had a plan beforehand. When I signed Nancy Sinatra, Jr., she was famous because her name was Sinatra. I signed her in order to sign her husband, Tommy Sands. I thought Tommy would become a superstar. Nancy decided she wanted to follow in her father's footsteps. I didn't think she was a very good singer, but I didn't tell her. I wanted to keep her account.

One night she wanted me to go with her to a recording studio in Hollywood. I felt obligated. It was a dingy place, low-rent and unkempt. I stood in the control booth while Nancy did her number. She flubbed it several times, and then several times more. We were there for hours. I had to call and cancel my date.

I had been with Sammy Davis, Jr., when he recorded. He did eight cuts and that was it. I thought it was normal. After several hours Nancy was still on the same song. She sang it all night long, one time after another. I was antsy, but I was afraid to say anything. By three in the morning, I was pissed—and Nancy was still singing the same song.

Frank Sinatra she was not. She was terrible. She couldn't sing. She was an amateur. If she ever got the song down, how was I going to promote it? I wanted to build stars, for God's sake. Nancy was just the daughter of someone I didn't like. She wasn't even a chip off the old block. She couldn't carry a tune.

The session went on and on. I was dozing. Nancy had to do multitracks to get it right. Finally they thought she had it. Everybody sighed with relief. Outside it was daylight. We'd been there all night. I told Nancy she was great and went home to shower and change clothes.

The recording was "These Boots Are Made for Walking."

"Frank Sinatra on line two, Mr. Bernstein."

Aha, my old nemesis.

I still held a serious grudge against Frank. I had been seething for years over the incident at Kanab, Utah, when he kept me from seeing the rough cut of *Sergeants 3*. His words, "I think . . . not yet," still rang in my ears like a sentence from a kangaroo court. Now I wondered what he wanted. It wasn't to say hello, because Frank didn't extend those kinds of courtesies. Obviously, he wanted a favor.

"Hi, Frank."

"Jay, how are you?"

"I'm good, Frank, thanks."

"I'm proud of you, kid. Sammy says you're rolling."

"Thanks. I'm keeping busy, that's for sure."

"Listen, aren't you handling this thing with Norman Rockwell for Marty Rackin?"

"I am, Frank."

"How well do you know the guy?"

"Rockwell? I got him to do the portraits, if that's what you're talking about."

Sinatra heard that Marty Rackin asked me to come up with a unique publicity idea for his forthcoming remake of John Ford's famous movie *Stagecoach*, and the news got out that I had hired the great Norman Rockwell for the project. Rockwell did twenty-one oil paintings for me in all, two portraits each of the ten actors, one preliminary and one final; and a huge action scene of the stagecoach fleeing an Indian war party on its perilous journey to Cheyenne. He thoroughly enjoyed the project and stayed with the company even when it went on location to Colorado. The portraits are invaluable today, capturing each actor and the essence of the role he or she played.

"That's it. I want him to do *my* portrait," Sinatra said.

I smiled. "Well, he's only commissioned to do portraits of the cast. I might have a problem there. Rockwell is a tough guy to deal with. Know what I mean?" I began doodling on a piece of paper, happy as a lark.

"Maybe you can ask him as a favor," said Frank. "After all, it would be a Frank Sinatra by Norman Rockwell."

"Like I said, Norman's a tough guy to deal with. But I'll give him a call."

"Thanks, Jay. I'll owe you one. When can you call me back?"

"Give me an hour," I said. I hung up, leaned back in my chair, propped my feet and lighted a cigarette. I killed an hour and called Frank.

"What did he say?" asked Frank eagerly.

"I'm sorry, Frank, but he said he just doesn't have time."

There was a pause. I pictured Frank silently cursing. Then he said, "Look, Jay, call him back and tell him I'll pay him fifty thousand dollars to do my portrait."

"Okay, but give me fifteen minutes," I said.

"I'll wait."

I killed another fifteen minutes and called Frank again.

"I'm sorry, Frank, but Rockwell said he just can't do it."

"Goddammit," said Frank. I could hear his teeth grinding. "Tell him I'll pay whatever he wants."

I smoked another cigarette and called Frank once more.

"What'd he say, Jay?"

"He said, 'No dice.'"

"Did you tell him I'm willing to pay whatever price he names?"

"Yes, I did. He's just not interested, Frank. I don't know what you want me to say."

"What did *he* say?"

"Frank, Frank . . . don't put me on a spot. It's just . . . he's just not interested, that's all."

"Goddammit, Jay. I want to know exactly what the man said!"

"Don't make me do this," I answered.

"What the fuck did the man say?" Frank demanded. "What were his *exact* words?"

"Okay, but for God's sake, don't hold it against me. He said, and I quote, 'Frank Sinatra doesn't have enough money to make me ever want to do his portrait.'"

"Shit!" cried Frank. He hung up.

I leaned back and propped my feet. How sweet it was!

By now I understood why Rogers & Cowan had corporate accounts. It was the big companies who sponsored television shows that brought in the revenues necessary to cover operating expenses. I made a list of the companies I wanted to represent. Then I went after them. My determination would pay off; within four years my two-room office would expand to include the entire floor, with forty-five employees.

When I got General Motors' Pontiac account, I felt I had made the big time. I flew to Detroit, where I was wined and dined at Pontiac headquarters. After the deal was consummated (I received about $25,000 for each sponsored television show), I was ushered into an elegant dining room for lunch and cocktails. One of the executives pulled me aside and said pompously, "Jay, I believe you are the first Jew who has ever been in this room."

Obviously General Motors needed a public-relations agency in Detroit as much as they did in Hollywood.

Another time, I went to Minneapolis in an effort to get the Betty Crocker account. I already had General Mills, so to sign Betty Crocker would be a feather. I had a steady, beautiful girlfriend who went with me. Lo! One of Ms. Crocker's executives charged me with immorality for staying in the same suite with an unmarried woman. I didn't get the account.

A couple of years later, it was different when I signed Motown, the biggest account I ever had—$250,000 annually. I dealt exclusively with Michael Roshkind, a Motown senior vice-president.

"Look," I told him before we signed. "I'm not married. My girlfriend is here with me. I left her at my hotel."

Mike look at me quizzically, as if I were some kind of a nut. "So? Do you want her here to see us sign this fucking contract?"

"No, I just want you to know that I'm not conventional, at least by Detroit standards."

"I don't give a shit if you're fucking a goat," said Roshkind. "Motown *is* Detroit's standard."

Chapter 8

MOTOWN, SAMMY AND BLACK HOLLYWOOD

Everything in the entertainment world ends up connecting—but sometimes the connection is a bad one. Motown was so important to me that I didn't want to meet Berry Gordy, the record label's president and founder, because I was afraid he wouldn't like me. When I was at Motown headquarters I was always nervous. One time Gordy and I were on the same elevator. I stared at the floor, trying to be obscure. I didn't want him to know I was his public-relations man. If he didn't like me, I might get fired. If he did like me, I might have to spend more time in Detroit. I didn't want either to happen.

Years later, after Motown moved to Hollywood, a good-looking guy named Bob Silverstein asked me for a job. He didn't care what he did—he just needed work. I wanted to help him, but I looked around and saw all my publicists with names like Rosenfield, Steinberg, Goldberg and Friedman. Jay Bernstein Public Relations was beginning to look like a refuge for Israeli transplants.

"What's your middle name?" I asked Silverstein.

"Ellis," he said.

I hired him as my chauffeur under the condition that henceforth he would be Bob Ellis.

Bob looked more like a movie star than a chauffeur, and girls were always flirting with him. One day he struck up a conversation with

Diana Ross when our cars were at a stoplight. Conversation evolved into romance and romance evolved into marriage.

I represented Diana as well as Motown. I was never around Diana much because she was always with Gordy. I wanted to protect both accounts, so I worked as a ghost. Even when I represented *Lady Sings the Blues*, I assigned a unit publicist to the picture. I didn't want to meet anybody.

When Berry Gordy found out Diana had married a chauffeur, he came unglued. He thought Diana was lowering herself socially. When he found out the chauffeur was in the employ of his public-relations man, he fired me. After giving me a quarter of a million dollars a year, Berry thought I should have been smart enough to put the quietus on the marriage. He didn't think Ellis would be accorded the dignity he deserved when people discovered what his job was. So much for Motown's liberal standards.

I was dancing as fast as I could, but I couldn't keep up with everyone. I assigned more and more of my clients to account executives. I kept the big stars for myself, primarily because I wanted to be seen in public with them, it sated my appetite for fame and it was the best advertising I could get.

For my money, Sammy was the greatest entertainer of his time, maybe ever. He was a phenomenon. No one had more drive and energy, and when he was onstage he radiated electricity. It wasn't a bolt, it was a constant surge. He was always moving—singing, dancing, mesmerizing—and when the curtain fell after two hours of nonstop performing, he would often collapse in his dressing room. For a minute—and then it was party time.

I never understood Sammy, but I understood his drive for excellence. He had no formal education, but somehow found time in his schedule to absorb books and magazines. Every time I went to New York, he would ask me to bring certain tomes to put in his suitcase library. It was an eclectic reading list—novels, philosophy, social sciences. I often wondered why he didn't go to a Manhattan bookstore to satisfy his curiosity, but I never asked him why. I secretly enjoyed the privilege of being his mobile library administrator.

What Sammy really wanted, I think, was to outdo Sinatra, his benefactor. In my judgment he did it, and against great odds, too, because he was black.

Sammy was also my most demanding client. He was responsible for my initial success, all the songsters. I couldn't relegate him to a junior member of my team (although I eventually did). I was always there for Sammy—many times when I didn't want to be. Often I served as his security blanket. We were characters in *Peanuts*.

"I'm flying to L.A. tonight," he said on the phone, "and you're flying out with me tomorrow."

"To where?"

"Tougaloo, Mississippi. Call Marlon Brando; he's got all the dope," said Sammy. "Then put out a press release. This is gonna be big but scary."

I didn't have to call Brando. A couple of weeks earlier, James Meredith, the first black student admitted to the University of Mississippi, began a solo civil rights march that was to span 220 miles from Memphis, Tennessee, to Jackson, Mississippi. The purpose was to show the world that Negroes were not afraid of southern whites. He was shot soon after he started, the moment he set foot on Mississippi soil, and was put in the hospital. Meanwhile, thousands of other protesters took up the cause to complete his march for him.

A few miles north of Tougaloo was Camden. That very day the march had reached an ignominious peak. A confrontation had occurred between blacks and whites; fisticuffs ensued, tear gas was used, but fortunately there were no fatal injuries. Thousands of people were now converging on Tougaloo for a last-minute rally before the final push to Jackson. Sammy wanted to perform for the troops; in this case, the invaders of Mississippi. Next to Vietnam, the heart of the old South was the last place on earth I wanted to visit.

I called my parents. My mother, who was not in sync with anything aside from her own self-inflated ego said, "Mississippi? How nice. Be sure and call the Levins!"

"This is not a social trip, Mother."

"Well, I don't want them to think you're rude. They're good, liberal Democrats."

"Yeah, and those liberal Democrats are the ones who are going to be shooting at us."

We flew to Jackson in a Lear jet, eight of us, including Marlon Brando and Tony Franciosa. Brando told jokes most of the flight, but few of us laughed. Sammy was quiet. Harry Belafonte had bamboozled him again. During *Golden Boy*, Harry had asked Sammy to go to Selma, Alabama. Sammy told his producer to tell Belafonte it would cost too much to close the show. "How much is too much?" Belafonte asked. "I'll pay for it."

The South frightened Sammy. His enemies shot and always missed in L.A., but in the old South—well, Sammy was afraid a Rebel sharpshooter would take a bead on him and shoot for the heart. His heart was a big target, bigger than his bank account.

From Jackson we motored in two cars to Tougaloo, where Sammy, Brando and Tony were scheduled to appear at a rally at the football field of the local college. I felt like Willie Stark's astutely observant PR man in *All the King's Men*, except my boss wasn't the white governor; he was an outsider who by genetic chance was black as the ace of spades.

As we approached Tougaloo, the crowds lining the road grew larger and increasingly hostile. Some carried shotguns, others clubs; sharecroppers held shovels and hoes. All of them were white. I suddenly realized the truth of Sammy's words that long-ago night in Kanab, Utah: "Jay, the only time we're alike is when we look in a mirror at midnight and the electricity is off."

We drove circuitously to a "black" motel "somewhere across the tracks." We were in a Negro shanty district, and my literary recollections shifted from Robert Penn Warren to the gothic depths of William Faulkner. Brando thought it was wonderful. He, too, was in a literary mood: "Tennessee would love this fucking town"—a reference to Tennessee Williams, his friend and favorite playwright. "It's so atmospheric!" he exclaimed.

Across from the motel, a horde of angry whites held banners, signs and weapons. On our side of the street was a mixed mob of freedom fighters, riders and kids crazy with energy they wanted to expend. The two groups were yelling at each other, mostly expletives. Before I got out of the car, I secretly unsnapped the strap that held my .38 in place above my ankle. I had no intention of starting anything, but I had every intention of defending our party, if necessary.

I waited in the lobby while Sammy and his fellow celebrities went to the "war room" to meet with Dr. Martin Luther King and other civil-rights leaders: Stokely Carmichael, Ralph Abernathy, Andrew Young and all the militants who ran the black spectrum of defiance from "civil disobedience" to "Let's kill whitey." I wondered what the hell I was doing there. Every network had camera crews on the scene and all the big newspapers had teams of correspondents. Public relations were out; the only news that could come out of this potential fiasco were hospital reports and obits, which were hard to put a good spin on. The heat was stifling. The humidity approached 100 percent. I sweated. An old-fashioned Coke box was in the corner, full of ice and soft drinks. A sign read: Pop, 10 Cents. I took a Coca-Cola from the ice and went to the desk to pay for it. The clerk, a burly black man, said, "That'll be a quarter."

"The sign says a dime," I told him.

"That was yesterday. Today it's a quarter."

We were supposed to be on the same side of the conflict that was brewing outside, but greed superseded principle. This was America, after all.

The afternoon waned. I was soaking wet. I'd drunk about two dollars worth of Cokes when Sammy and the others returned from their strategy meeting, which I knew had been a farce, since there was no strategy to strategize. Next on the schedule was the concert at Tougaloo College football stadium. When we went to our cars, some of the black kids on our side of the street yelled at Sammy. "Go back to Hollywood! We don't need no honky nigras!"

He ignored the taunts, but it wasn't easy. For years he had taken heat from both sides of the issue. Whites hated him for being successful in "their" world and blacks denigrated him for wanting to be white. The whites were right regarding his success; the blacks were wrong about what he wanted. Sammy was too smart to waste his time wishing he were white; what he wanted was to live like white people because his life's experience dictated it was a better way to live. I admired him because he put up with the name-calling and catcalling without comment. He was here for the "cause," as dedicated to civil rights as Martin Luther King was, but he wasn't going to change his lifestyle for anyone.

Outside the sports arena, which was the size of a high school football stadium, a few thousand whites were assembled, waiting and willing for action. Mississippi State Police cars cordoned off a pathway, but it didn't take a genius to know which side the police would be on if the crowd got out of hand. Inside the stadium the bleachers and field were packed with activists, both black and white, but mostly black. We parked near a makeshift stage in the center of the field. I kept my gun loose on my ankle.

The concert was an exercise in futility—a mob scene. Thousands of people were on hand for the warm-up session preliminary to the final march on Jackson the next day. It was a parody of entertainment. The sound system didn't work; there were no musicians. James Brown tried to sing; Sammy scatted a capella. Harry Belafonte and Sidney Poitier, who had flown in earlier, served as cheerleaders. Marlon gave a speech nobody could hear. He had a bumper sticker plastered across his forehead that read: We're the Greatest! It was loony tunes.

Part of the crowd started singing "We Shall Overcome," countered by Carmichael's supporters, who changed the lyrics to "We Shall Overrun." I watched, thinking how stupid they were. If violence got out of hand, they would be Switzerland against the Soviet Union. Those Mississippi crackers outside the stadium would slaughter them like pigs at an abattoir. James Meredith's purpose had been to show white America that Negroes weren't afraid to face white superiority in Mississippi. The truth was, everybody in the stadium was scared shitless, including me.

My group didn't stick around for the march into Jackson the next day. It was just as well; the end of the march was anticlimactic. King gave another stump speech, and then everybody went home, back to New York and other northern states. As far as I could see, the only beneficiaries of the march were soft-drink salesmen and the makers of over-the-counter blister ointments.

Strangely, flying back to Los Angeles was like having a victory party.

I understood Sammy's exuberance: he was still alive. But what had been accomplished? Brando still wore his bumper sticker like a mustard plaster. I didn't say anything. No logical reason existed for me to try to rain on their parade, but I saw hard times ahead for black folk. I saw violence, murder and mayhem.

Because of Sammy Davis, Jr., I had an elite list of black entertainers, ranging from Barry White to Leslie Uggams. By the early seventies, 65 percent of my performance clients were black. It had nothing to do with color—it was all about talent. My philosophy was always based on merit.

Chapter 9

SPIN-DOCTOR
MEDICINE

Most people consider Jane Fonda the outlaw of the Fonda acting
dynasty, but it was really her brother Peter who was the true black
sheep. Before *Easy Rider* created a motion-picture revolution in 1968,
Peter's name was already attached to a pocketful of low-budget, anti-
establishment pictures. Peter was a tall, lanky, bright young man, and a
rebel with a cause. He hated institutional authority (read motion-picture
studios) with a passion.

I became Peter's publicist in 1966 when independent producer-
director Roger Corman was wrapping principal photography on *The
Wild Angels*, an extremely low-budget bike picture that was a precursor to
Easy Rider but without the latter's vision. The movie starred Peter, Nancy
Sinatra, Bruce Dern and Diane Ladd. If you look at the film closely, you
can even glimpse Peter Bogdanovich as an extra in one of the rumble
scenes.

Peter Fonda and I became close friends, although our world perspec-
tives were at variance. The beatniks of the fifties had transmogrified into
the hippie movement, and Peter was a full-fledged member. Since beads
and marijuana were alien to my Oklahoma roots, I was not tempted to
join. It was a movement looking for its reason, dancing lightly on the
fringes of the Civil Rights movement, two years away from locking into

an antiwar stance. In 1966, pot smoking and free love exemplified its major defiance of authority.

Peter and I talked often on the phone. It was confusing—he signed off saying, "Hello."

Invariably I would say, "What?"

"We're finished with our conversation, aren't we?" Peter would respond.

"Yes, so why did you say 'hello'?"

"I don't like saying 'good-bye.'"

"Okay, Peter. Good-bye."

"Hello."

Not long after *The Wild Angels* went to the editing room, Peter became indirectly embroiled in a drug sting. Two of his buddies had rented a "hippie safe house" in Tarzana in the San Fernando Valley. After paying the first and last month's rent, the guys were broke and couldn't get a telephone. Peter put his name and credit on the line for them. He also stored some of his gear there, guitars and other paraphernalia.

Within a matter of weeks, a marijuana crop had been cultivated in the backyard of the house and the noise and odor of pot parties were becoming recurring nuisances to some of the neighbors. At two o'clock one morning, Peter got a call from Cass Elliot of the Mamas & the Papas fame. She was an overnight guest at the Tarzana safe house. Police had staged a drug raid and discovered Peter's gear. An investigation revealed the telephone was in Peter's name.

"You're in trouble," Cass told Peter. "Guilt by association."

Peter called his lawyer, Harry Weiss, who advised him to get out of town fast. Peter did, flying first to New York and then working his way back to Palm Springs. He did not call me immediately, which was a mistake. The next day his name was plastered on the front pages of four of the five Los Angeles dailies. The only paper that didn't try to exploit the Fonda name was the *Times*; it buried the story as a sop to father Henry.

All I could do at that stage was chastise the offending journalists and demand front-page coverage when Peter was exonerated of a crime he had not committed and had not even been charged with. But we knew it was coming. The year 1966 was one of transition, half modern and half medieval in its pretensions. Possession of marijuana was a serious crime, as were many other things we take for granted today. A Manhattan court had recently ruled *Fanny Hill* an obscene novel. Linda Lovelace, who would rocket to fame as the real Deep Throat, was a teenager in Texas; the only thing she could suck without going to jail was a lollipop. Peter was in trouble. Los Angeles law enforcement was hungry to prosecute a name figure for marijuana use, something not done since Robert Mitchum went to jail on the same charge back in 1949.

Weiss arranged for Peter to appear in a Van Nuys courtroom without fanfare. Peter and his friends were charged with possession of nine pounds of marijuana, a weight investigating officers calculated by adding several packets of birdseed they found on the premises to the actual stash. Peter was released on his own recognizance, pending a jury trial in six weeks.

Although Weiss was reasonably certain Peter would be acquitted, based on the flimsy evidence, I knew that Peter, and therefore his career, was in jeopardy because of the press. The papers were beginning to fall in love with the idea of knocking people off their pedestals. I kept hammering at my theme: acquittal deserved front-page coverage.

Peter was rightfully angry and defiant, but what he did next compounded his problem as well as my work on his behalf. It happened two weeks before the trial.

The Sunset Strip was undergoing one of its periodic cultural transitions. In the forties and fifties, the Strip had been old Hollywood's playground, a collection of glittering nightclubs, fine restaurants and popular lounges. More recently, members of the counterculture, youthful hippies, had gradually invaded it with no particular agenda aside from having a good time. The movement presaged a clash between establishment and anti-establishment, as owners and managers of old-line businesses complained that the hippies were ruining business.

On November 11, a group of three hundred young people congregated at one of their hangouts, Pandora's Box, at the corner of Sunset and Crescent Heights at the east end of the Strip. They rallied because businesses had pressured the city fathers to condemn the club and declare the property in the public domain, ostensibly to widen Crescent Heights Boulevard. The rally ended with the arrests of dozens of young people after two city buses were attacked; in one case, the passengers were forced off and the bus was burned. If there was anything good about the near riot, it was that Peter Fonda's marijuana story was lost in the shuffle of more recent news.

Incensed by what they considered police brutality, the leaders of the youth movement announced another rally the following week. Frankly, I did not pay much attention to what was happening. I was running a business and my offices were at the opposite end of the Strip. I knew, of course, that another confrontation between alienated youth and the police was at hand, but I didn't stick around at the end of the day to observe it. I went home.

Sometime during the night I received a telephone call from a photographer who was covering the riot. He was calling on behalf of Peter, who, with fellow actor Brandon De Wilde ("Shane! Come back, Shane!") and singer-musician David Crosby (Crosby, Stills & Nash), had been arrested while aiding his fellow hippies in the riot. Peter wanted me to get them out of jail and counter the potential bad publicity.

"Where are they?" I asked the photographer.

"They've been taken to the West Hollywood sheriff's station, but I think they're going to be shackled and transferred downtown."

The first image that flickered in my brain was a front-page photograph of Peter Fonda in shackles with a headline reading: Fonda Busted Second Time. Publicity of that kind was enough to negatively influence a jury in Peter's marijuana trial. I grabbed a 35 mm still-frame camera, hung it around my neck and took off.

The station house was a mob scene. Dozens of kids and young adults had been arrested and the booking process was underway. Peter, Brandon and David were in a holding cell. I began firing rounds from the Gatling gun of my imagination. Peter later wrote in his memoir: "From my cell I could hear my publicist, Jay Bernstein, raising holy hell in the booking room, demanding to see me."

I raised such a storm that a sheriff took me to Peter as if I were his privileged attorney. They neither searched me nor removed the camera that hung around my neck. The instant I entered the cell I told Peter to sit down and shut up. He did. I looped my camera over his head and dropped it to his chest. "Listen to me!" I said, leaning in close. "Here's your story. You were at the scene of the riot to shoot preliminary photographs for a documentary that you, Brandon and David are going to do about the changing culture of the Sunset Strip. This camera is your alibi!"

We looked at each other, our thoughts in sync. I went back to the booking room and started cornering journalists, hammering the fact that Peter had been caught up as an innocent filmmaker and if any of them wrote a big story about nothing, it could destroy his career. Later, Harry Weiss showed up and got all three of them released with no pending charges.

From the outset of Peter's indictment, both Harry and I had impressed upon him the necessity of his father testifying on his behalf at the trial, a ploy Peter was opposed to. Henry was on location in Arizona shooting a Western shoot-'em-up called *Welcome to Hard Times*. Two days before the trial I got a telephone call at home. My heart leaped; I recognized the voice.

"Mr. Bernstein, this is Henry Fonda. Peter says you need me in court this week."

"Yes, sir, Mr. Fonda. We do!"

"Well, tell me what my motivation is. Tell me what you want me to wear, what you want me to say and how you want me to act."

Peter was hardly more than a kid and I was only a couple of years older than him, yet I was being asked to coach a Hollywood legend. I offered Henry my advice as if I were directing a movie. Before his testimony, I loaned him a walking stick Sammy Davis had given me. "It's a prop that will lend you an air of dignity and wisdom," I explained. He followed my instructions to a T.

After the jury retired, Harry Weiss told me they were hung. It may have been a guess; he may have had inside information. Whatever, he was correct. The prosecutor chose not to retry the case, and Peter kept his freedom. The dailies ran front-page stories absolving him, and the Fonda name remained in good stead in the public eye.

Eventually Peter became a premier moviemaker. He understood the process as well as anyone, from preproduction to postproduction. His failure came about because of success. The mainstream industry hated *Easy Rider*. They didn't understand it; more important, they loathed the idea that a couple of young guys (Peter and Dennis Hopper) could go against the grain and produce a box-office blockbuster for less than a million dollars. It's hard to skim from a small budget, and there's no financial room to put your buddies on the payroll.

A few years later, when I lived in Elvis Presley's former mansion in Stone Canyon, Peter lived with me for a short time. He was in the doldrums. He had been relegated to working in independent pictures. After *Easy Rider*, Universal let him make one picture, and then they left him on the industry periphery. "They let me continue to work because of Dad," said Peter. "It was a game to them. They walked me on balls, but never let me get past third base."

In Hollywood, you never truly know who your friends and enemies are because many times they are one and the same. I was dining with a client at the Daisy, a popular Hollywood club on Rodeo Drive. A waiter came over and said, "Mr. O'Neal wants to speak with you." He pointed. Ryan O'Neal was standing at the cigarette machine near the door. His eyes were locked on me. A second man was standing on the threshold, guarding the door. I recognized him as Harvey Lee Yeary; he'd had a bit part in William Castle's ill-fated *Strait-Jacket*. He was doing better now, but not as well as Ryan. Ryan was starring in ABC's *Peyton Place*.

I sensed what Ryan wanted. I had been dating his estranged wife and Tatum's mother, actress Joanna Moore, while Ryan was engaged in a very public affair with Barbara Parkins, his co-star. Unfortunately no sparks ignited between Joanna and me—we were friends. A few nights before, we had gone by my place, where I needed to change clothes. We never left. Joanna, who had been drinking when I picked her up, got drunk and naked, and passed out on my bed. Nothing happened. At four, she woke up. "Where am I? Oh, my God! I have to go!"

I got up and put my clothes on.

"Did we do anything, Jay?"

"Yeah, you were great," I said.

"Oh, no! What did we do?"

"What did we do? You don't remember what we did?"

"Did we do . . . *it*?"

"How about five times?"

"Oh, my God!"

Now, at the Daisy, I excused myself from my client and went over to Ryan at the cigarette machine. When I offered my hand, he grabbed me, slammed me against a wall and put his nose in my face. Yeary stood guard at the gate.

"I'm gonna kill you, Bernstein!" said Ryan. His teeth were clenched. "You've been spreading stories that you fucked my wife five times in one night!"

I didn't say anything, but my eyes were darting about, looking for something I could use to crush his skull. His ears were smoking and his eyes were like red marbles.

"I'm gonna kill you," he repeated. "It may be tonight; it may be later. But I'm gonna kill you!" He released his grip on my shoulders, spun on his heels and left. Yeary followed him.

Ryan and I remained enemies, but ten years later Harvey Lee Yeary became one of my first official management clients. He had changed his name to Lee Majors.

One day I got a call from actor Gene Barry. He was peeved, and he wanted me to represent him. After a successful run as Bat Masterson, Gene was now starring in *Burke's Law*, another successful television series that had just completed its first season. He was angry with Aaron Spelling, the show's executive producer.

My ears perked. Aaron Spelling? It was he who tried to get me fired over the Sammy Davis, Jr., fight incident on *Dick Powell Theater*. Powell had subsequently died, and Aaron was now producing the first of his many successful series. Curious, I asked Barry what the problem was.

He said he felt ignored. He owned part of *Burke's Law* and was co-executive producer with Aaron. "But every time a press release goes out, there's only one name there," said Gene, "and it's Aaron Spelling!" He said Aaron's people ignored his complaints.

"I know how to handle Spelling," I told Gene.

A couple of days later I issued a press release that made trade-paper front pages. "Producer-star Gene Barry signs Gary Conway to be his co-star in ABC TV's *Burke's Law*." The body copy did not mention Spelling's name.

Fifteen minutes after the trades hit the newsstands, I got an irate call from Aaron. "Whoa, Jay! What am I? Chopped liver?"

"Aaron, I don't work for you. I work for Gene Barry."

Spelling took a diplomatic stance and invited me to come by his office at the old Four Star Studios, now CBS at Radford Row in the Valley. I had never met Aaron. He reminded me of a scarecrow in disrepair—thin as a fencepost, blond, with big, bulbous, expressive eyes and a scratchy voice that didn't seem to fit his frail frame. We sat down. He had Larry Gordon, his assistant, go fetch me a Coca-Cola. Today Gordon is my friend as well as one of the most successful motion-picture producers in Hollywood. In those days he was Aaron's legman.

Over Cokes, Aaron and I discussed the problem.

"It's like this, Jay. I busted my ass to get *Burke's Law* on the air, and here you come acting as though I don't have a place at the table. What goes here?"

What he was really saying was this: television is a producer's medium. He's the guy who makes the show happen. It's not like movies, where, after you sign a big name, everything falls into place around the star. In television, the producer is the star; he's the cohesive element that makes things happen.

We struck a deal: I wouldn't put out any news releases about Aaron's projects without mentioning his name, and Aaron's publicists wouldn't put out any stories concerning *Burke's Law* without mentioning Gene Barry's name.

I liked Aaron. He was fifteen years older than me, but he was youthful and hip. He had served a long apprenticeship in the industry, first as an actor, then as a writer and finally as a producer. He understood television as well as Sheldon Leonard did, which was a lot. Aaron was providing escapist entertainment for millions of people who did not have the time or the money to venture downtown to the local movie theater once or twice a week. He was giving them a temporary interlude in which their problems were forgotten. He was also making gobs of money.

Aaron was hardworking, determined to be the best producer in the business, quick of mind and terribly naïve. He was in the midst of getting a divorce from actress Carolyn Jones, and after our meeting at Radford Row I began to see him frequently on the social circuit. Aaron, Nick Adams, Bob Conrad and I, along with our girlfriends or wives, often went to parties or restaurants together. It was a long-ago time now lost, when business was business and fun was fun. You could argue all day with a competitor, but at night it was forgotten.

Aaron fell in love. He met a schoolteacher who lived in the San Fernando Valley; she consumed his conversations. "Why don't you bring her over here for dinner?" we asked. By "over here" we meant Hollywood or Beverly Hills. The Valley was erroneously stigmatized as the Ozarks of Los Angeles.

"She won't come," said Aaron. "She's not into the Hollywood scene. She thinks the glitz and glamour are phony."

Here was a guy on the verge of becoming one of the greatest television producers of all time, and he was nuts about a woman who hated Hollywood. All Aaron talked about was his "schoolteacher." He would go to her home in the Valley, and they'd light candles and be romantic.

At last, the schoolteacher agreed to go with Aaron to a Hollywood party. I don't remember whose house it was, but the guest list was laden with television stars. Aaron's girlfriend got drunk. Then she started making clandestine trips upstairs. Then she started making trips upstairs that weren't clandestine. Finally somebody caught her in bed with one of the male guests, a minor television star. He was maybe her tenth lover of the evening. She was a nymphomaniacal star-fucker! After the party, Aaron never mentioned his girlfriend again. He forgot her like a bad dream. I don't think he ever dated another Valley Girl.

Well, that was poor Aaron's dating prowess back in these early days. It's comical in retrospect. We were just kids back then, experimenting socially and professionally. I was always on the prowl, trying to date every beautiful girl I could. I was lonely because I was working around the clock.

And if my first mentor was Sheldon Leonard, my first role model was Guy McElwaine, my link to Frank Sinatra. He was a cucumber of the cool type, very smart, very debonair, and very much into his own world. He was the original Ring-a-Ding man, who knew how to thread his way through the Hollywood jungle. He was a second-generation movie man—his father had been a publicist at MGM. In his career, Guy was a publicist, an agent, a producer of some great movies and the head of a studio. He was Hollywood's everyman, with a touch of class.

Guy acted on both instinct and experience, going with the flow but always landing on his feet. When long hair was in, Guy grew long hair. When wide-collared open shirts were the fad, there was Guy with an open collar. These were temporary changes; in the end he always went back to French cuffs and diamond-studded links. At heart, Guy was a product of "old" Hollywood and all the glamour its antiquity implied. He was a vestige of a time past without ever realizing it. I admired him.

Barriers didn't bother Guy. He was elusive, involved in a lot of extracurricular activities. He was an Adonis, courting and seducing some of Hollywood's most glamorous stars and starlets. He ran neck and neck with Elizabeth Taylor in securing and disposing of spouses. He was married seven times.

We were in front of a restaurant when a young lady accosted him: "Hi, Guy, how are you?"

Guy's face drew a blank. The young lady was full of smiles and good humor, rattling reminiscences like a machine gun. Guy had not a clue as to who she was.

"How are Don and Ann?" she asked. "Do you still see Mary and Jim? I keep up with you in the gossip columns. I read that you're with Rogers & Cowan. How long will that last?"

Guy stared, trying to figure out who she was.

Finally the young lady realized she was forgotten history. "For God's sake, Guy!" she exclaimed. "I was *married* to you!"

Another star who desperately wanted to wring my neck occasionally was my client Michael Landon. Regardless of our personal and professional battles, Michael, in my honest opinion, was indeed a multitalented filmmaker. He was an actor, writer, director and producer. As an actor, he disdained personal publicity. He enjoyed the good life, and his power and prestige gave him opportunities most mortal men never have. Girls were always knocking on his dressing-room door and he didn't always send them away. It was an aspect of his private life he wanted newshounds to avoid.

In the late sixties, *Bonanza* was in the midst of its extraordinary fifteen-year run as one of television's most popular shows in history. Michael played Little Joe, the youngest brother in the Cartwright family. Little Joe was a beloved character, the one who drew women like a magnet, which happened to suit Michael perfectly.

Every hamlet, village and city in America clamored after Michael to appear at fairs, conventions and reunions. Of all the stars I knew, he was the most willing to participate. He felt the public had made him what he was and he wanted to give them something in return. When he wasn't working, he was often on the road promoting Main Street, U.S.A.

One such venture took him to a flower festival in Michigan. He was the grand marshal of the parade. I wasn't with him, but after the festivities he called me.

"How'd it go?" I asked.

Michael laughed. "Okay, until some kid threw a rock at me."

It was the kind of story I could make hay out of. The real story was as simple as Michael told it. A kid in a high-rise building had dropped a pebble from a window that landed on Michael's convertible. No injuries, no damage, no nothing—except I turned the pebble into a boulder. I took the story to Harrison Carroll at the *Herald-Examiner*.

"You don't expect me to believe this, do you, Jay?"

"Well, it happened."

"One little kid threw a boulder at Michael Landon?"

"Several kids," I exaggerated. "They rolled it out the window of a building. Had it hit Michael, it would have killed him."

Harrison loved offbeat stories, but you had to sell him. I put my name on the line. "It's true, Harrison. They probably weren't aiming the boulder at Michael, but it was his car they hit." I gave an inch of space between my thumb and my index finger. "He was that far from being killed. The officials wanted to stop the parade, but Michael wouldn't have it. He braved it out, even with the possibility of more boulders from more windows down the parade route."

The story ran the next day in Harrison's column. The wire services picked it up and headlines around the world proclaimed dramatically: "Little Joe Almost Stoned to Death," or "Michael Landon Escapes Rockslide in Flower Parade."

It was easy to get Michael's name in the newspapers and on television, but stories with a handle were hard to come by. This one worked, and I was proud of myself. When Michael returned to L.A., he gave me a call. I joined him for lunch at the Rangoon Racquet Club, a popular watering hole and eatery in Beverly Hills.

Michael wore a grim expression. He was cold, formal. We chatted; our meals were served and then Michael got to the point. "Jay, I've written two *Bonanza* scripts and directed one, but you keep publicizing Michael Landon, the person."

What he said was true, but there were mitigating circumstances. First, the public wanted information on Michael Landon, and his two scripts and one directorial performance didn't exactly overwhelm newspaper editors. Little Joe was a known commodity.

"Did you read the piece in *People*?" he asked.

He was going back a few weeks. Of course I had read the piece. I had arranged the interview. The reporter had promised he would stick to Michael's role in *Bonanza*. He hadn't. At the tale end of the brief item, he had delved into Michael's private life, which had been growing messy. "I didn't write the piece, Michael. I just set up the interview."

He cut me short. "Where in hell did you get the boulder story every newspaper is running? That's not what I told you."

"So? I exaggerated, Michael. That's what gave the story legs."

"But it's not true," he said with exasperation.

"Ninety percent of the stuff people read isn't true. But they want to believe it. Harrison Carroll wanted to believe it. The wire editors wanted to believe it. As a result, you've been in the news for days. Readers sympathize with you. They admire your courage under fire. You're a hero. Do you think George Washington really cut down a cherry tree?"

"I don't want to be a hero," he said. "I only want publicity for what I write and what I direct. You're fired."

My pasta was steaming on the plate before me. I picked it up, flipped it and dumped it on the table. "And fuck you, too," I said, exiting the premises. I felt humiliated.

By the time I got back to my office, I was really pissed. I had put a creative effort into Michael's public relations for a lousy thousand dollars a month, and now the ungrateful bastard had fired me. The next morning my attitude had not changed. Then my secretary buzzed.

"Michael Landon on line two."

I grabbed the phone. "Jay Bernstein," I answered gruffly.

"Hey, Jay! How's it going?"

"Just peaches and cream, Michael, as you can well fucking imagine."

"I've been thinking," he said with sheepish inflection. "Let's continue to work together."

During the next decade, through the rest of *Bonanza*, which still had five years to go, and through all of the *Little House on the Prairie* and *Highway to Heaven* series, Michael fired me another five times and hired me back four times. It was always touch and go, but after a while I got used to it. Landon was one of those stars, like Sinatra, I wasn't terribly fond of as a person. But he had a golden touch when it came to product. He did for human beings what Walt Disney did for animals—he made them poignant and likable. In most of *Bonanza*, he was just another actor in an ensemble cast, but *Little House* and *Highway* were his creations and he put his indelible stamp on them. I don't think anyone else in the industry could have made those series as successful as Michael did. Being a wonderful person wasn't his forte. He was driven by an urge to succeed, and if you got in his way, he'd run over you. To that extent, we were similar.

Welsh singer Tom Jones was already a bona fide hit when I became his publicist in 1968. In previous years he had been part of the swinging music scene, scoring hits with movie themes like "What's New, Pussycat?" and James Bond's "Thunderball." He was a powerful singer, masculine and roguish in appearance, with an onstage bare-chested presence that at least one nameless woman found extraordinarily sexy.

Gordon Mills, Tom's manager, hired me to launch the singer's first American performance, at the famous Copacabana in New York City. The Copa was a supper club with an intimate atmosphere that allowed an entertainer to move about in the room as he performed. I had a front-and-center table with half a dozen guests in case Tom's debut needed extra bodies. It didn't. The place was packed on opening night.

During his performance a strange incident occurred. Tom was moving from table to table, stopping here and there, singing directly, as if personally, to some of his female fans. Suddenly a woman stood up, slipped off her panties and handed them to him. Gordon Mills told me later that Tom was startled; women had slipped him dinner napkins with their telephone numbers written on them, but never their underwear.

Later that year, Tom opened at the Flamingo Hotel in Las Vegas. After a few days Gordon called me. The crowds were small and lukewarm. Tom wanted to be more than a saloon singer who had to compete with the clink of cocktail glasses. "Think you can do something for us?" Gordon wanted to know.

I flew to Vegas and took in the Tom Jones show. It was sexy and dynamic, but I didn't think it had the oomph to put him over the top as a long-term Vegas hit. It needed a push, a headline-making push.

I talked to Tom and Gordon. They had old-fashioned concepts and came up with the same type of stuff rockers had been doing for years.

I went to my suite to think about it. In the process I remembered the knickers incident at the Copa. I had an idea that might work.

By this time, through Sammy and other clients, I was well-known in Vegas by management. It wasn't difficult to persuade the hotel to give me a couple dozen bogus keys with the Flamingo logo on them. I then went to a lingerie shop and bought several pairs of ladies' lacy silk underwear.

That night I stood at the entrance of the Flamingo showroom. When I saw a good-looking young woman without a date, I approached her. She was usually with another girl or one of a trio. I chose the ones who seemed extroverted and hungry for a laugh. I offered one of two deals. I would give twenty-five dollars if she would throw a room key on the stage while Tom was performing or fifty dollars if she would throw a pair of panties.

I had no trouble getting girls; they were like actors at central casting. Now I had to choreograph the show. I wanted one girl here, one there; I needed them spread throughout the room, planted in strategic spots. Furthermore, timing was everything. They needed to wait until Tom had supposedly worked them into a frenzy with his sex appeal.

Tom was in the dark; he knew nothing about my gambit. The show began, and in his usual way Tom began working up to his most popular songs—"It's Not Unusual," "Delilah" and "Help Yourself." He had great presence, his own style (helped by his friend Elvis) and a sort of water-front masculine appeal. He wore tight pants and his shirt open to his navel. He was belting away when the first girl threw a room key. Tom paused ever so briefly, swept up the key and looked at it in one quick gesture, and then continued singing. A couple of minutes later another girl tossed a pair of panties. Tom picked up his pace. Another girl tossed a room key.

It was like shots of electricity suddenly bolting through the room. Tom really began to sing and move, convinced that he was motivating the women by virtue of his sexuality. The women responded in kind, and the more they did, the more magnetic Tom became. The room keys, the panties, Tom's gyrations and his sensuous songs—they added up to an explosive performance, both onstage and off.

I stayed in Vegas a week, repeating the same routine every night. Gordon and I purposely left Tom out of the loop. By the time I went back to L.A., Tom thought he was the most magnetic man on the planet. During the second week, however, without panties and room keys, the show lost its magic. It was good, but it lacked that indefinable dynamic called sex appeal. Gordon gave me a call; I returned to Vegas.

I got more keys and another bunch of panties. This time, however, I invited members of the press to attend and gave them the Bernstein royal treatment before the show. The same thing happened: Tom began to jive and the women went nuts. Each night was wilder than the one before. The press coverage gave the campaign its needed kick. By week's end, the hotel had enlarged the letters of Tom's name on the marquee and women were lining up at the ticket window. I went back to Los Angeles and kept up with the coverage in the papers. There were no more bogus keys and panties bought at wholesale. The real things were now landing on the stage. Tom was transformed into an authentic Vegas star. What began as a gimmick had become a phenomenon.

Tom eventually moved to ever-larger showrooms—the Hilton International, Caesar's Palace, and the last I heard he was packing the room at the MGM Grand. I've always felt a sense of pride in that particular campaign. I was a ghost, an invisible man who motivated the audience in obscurity.

In addition to individual performers, corporations came my way because they sponsored television shows. I was hired to publicize and promote them. I represented AT&T, U.S. Steel, General Mills and Procter & Gamble, among many others. Inherent in the job was taking care of corporate executives and their advertising reps when they came out from New York or Dallas or Chicago. They thought Hollywood was la-la land. They had two goals: breaking par and bedding a starlet.

In the beginning, I was naïve. I actually fixed these guys up with girls who were my friends. "Margo, would you like to go out with the head of a major corporation?" "I'd love to!" The day after the date, however, she'd call me: "God, Jay, the guy tried to tear my clothes off!" I got identical reports from four out of seven girls. It was disgusting, but I needed those big accounts to pay my office nut; they kept me in business.

Before Heidi Fleiss, the hot madam in town was a woman named Alex. I went to see her. She had a big, elegant house in the Hollywood Hills. I told her my predicament and the type of playboy men I represented who visited Los Angeles. "I need dates for these guys—dates who look like college girls, who dress like college girls and flirt like college girls. They need to be sunny and fresh and fun and sexy, while dining on lobster and champagne. At the end of the night, however, they need to let their dates get lucky."

Madam Alex was delighted to help me. We agreed to a fee, which under the circumstances seemed reasonable. The main criterion was the maintenance of secrecy. I didn't want the girls ever to reveal their true occupation. The chicanery worked better than I anticipated; some of the corporate geeks actually fell in love, or thought they did, never realizing their new all-American girlfriends were hookers. Like most plans requiring subterfuge, however, the scheme had one major flaw: it seemed too easy.

One afternoon, my secretary said there was a beautiful young woman in the outer office who wanted to talk with me. I took a peek; my secretary's judgment was on target. The girl was stunning, about twenty years old. I invited her into my office. She quickly turned the conversation to the purpose of her visit. "A friend of mine told me she was doing some work for you."

"Oh, what kind of work?"

"She's on a list you use to set up dates with clients of yours. I'd like to be on that list."

I shrugged. "Did your friend explain everything to you?"

"Yes."

"And you're okay with what you have to do?"

"Oh, sure."

She was wearing a wire. It was a Jaik Rosenstein sting. Three days after I rejected buying an ad from him, Jaik ran a banner headline in *Hollywood Close-Up*: Publicist Runs Call Girl Ring. The sheet sold out at Schwab's. I thought I was finished.

The following week Jaik ran a scandalous story on Robert Evans, head of production at Paramount. The story about me rang of truth; if I sued, the facts would ruin me. The Evans story, however, had not a thread of truth. I don't know who, but someone acted: *Hollywood Close-Up* abruptly stopped publication when its office was blown up. Strangely, it was rumored that Rogers & Cowan were the culprits. Jaik Rosenstein faded into oblivion, and nobody ever mentioned my "call girl ring" again.

George Hamilton understood publicity as well as the best press agents— he could have made a fortune in public relations. I worked with George on and off for years. He shared Nick Adams' attitude about Hollywood money, although it was the only trait they had in common. "I came out here with $75," he said proudly. "Now I owe $750,000!"

In 1970 he gave me an anxious call. "Jay, I need your help. If you want a big account, I'll give you the Evel Knievel production I'm going to do."

Evel Knievel was the daredevil motorcyclist who got his rocks off by trying to jump over rows of buses and trucks and natural wonders like the Snake River Canyon. He often missed his landing mark and ended up in the critical ward of a hospital with a bunch of broken bones. When George called me, Evel had just crashed while trying to jump over something like a thousand buses at Caesar's Palace in Las Vegas. He had been transported to an outlying hospital in Los Angeles.

"I don't have the story rights yet," said George, "but I just talked to Evel, and he said if I can set up a big press conference for him today, here at the hospital, he'll give me the rights."

As a favor, as well as a challenge, I told George I would do it. Unfortunately, Evel's daredevil jumps and subsequent injuries had become so commonplace that most editors relegated his press releases to page forty, and that was often for thirty-eight-page newspapers. Furthermore, the hospital was in the desert somewhere on the fringe of "the valley"; that is, in the middle of nowhere.

Nevertheless I called my guys together—I had about fourteen really good publicists then—and we went to work, burning up telephone lines to every journalist, columnist and wire reporter we could contact. We called television and radio stations and rag writers; we called everybody and begged them to attend Evel's press conference at four p.m. at the desert hospital.

By the time we exhausted our sources, I had a sinking feeling. I asked my Green Berets what they thought. The consensus was that maybe four people would show up, six at most. George had emphasized that Evel wanted a "big" press conference. I took my guys with me to the hospital.

George had set up a terrace area as though preparing for a presidential news conference. By four thirty p.m., it was evident that no member of the press was remotely interested in quizzing Evel about his latest escape from death. Not one reporter showed up. My guys were standing around like so many cacti in the hot sun, and George was wringing his hands. "Go get Evel," I said. "We'll be the press."

He took off. We formed a semicircle of chairs on the terrace concrete and sat down with pencils and notebooks in hand. A few minutes later Evel was trundled out of the hospital in a wheelchair, his arms and head bound in bandages and his legs in casts. He wore a serious expression, as if he were about to announce the cessation of the war in Vietnam. He stopped and motioned for us to draw closer, which we did, scraping our chairs on the concrete.

Here we were, fifteen publicists in chairs surrounding Evel Knievel in a wheelchair looking like a mummy, two nurses sweating in the sun in their white uniforms, and George Hamilton standing at Evel's shoulder like a nervous aide beside his commanding officer. I was sitting closest to Evel's left hand. He looked at me and said, "Hi, I'm Evel Knievel. Who are you, and who do you represent?"

I stared at him, thinking fast, wondering if he was smarter than we were. "I'm Jay Bernstein, Mr. Knievel, George's publicist"—I turned quickly to the person on my left—"and this is Stan Rosenfield . . . of the *Los Angeles Times*." Evel smiled. Stan, catching my lead, turned to the person to his left and said, "And this is Stan Moress . . . of the *Herald Examiner*."

Around the semicircle it went, with each of my troupe introducing the one next to him and coming up with the name of the place of his employment: *The Daily News*, the *Hollywood Reporter*, *Variety*, Associated

Press, United Press International, until at last, with all legitimate sources used, they were actually making up names of papers and magazines. I was proud of them; each was smart enough not to use the name of a television station, suspecting Evel might ask where his camera crew was.

After the introductions the news conference proceeded. We asked the same insipid questions Evel had dealt with a thousand times. But it worked, and after we wrapped I told the guys they had to expend a real effort to get something in the papers, especially in the ones we said we represented. The next day we landed stories in about half of them. Evel was apparently pleased; George got his rights, and Jay Bernstein Public Relations went on to represent the movie.

I went to Acapulco with a girlfriend and another couple to relax a few days, staying at a downtown hotel. But just a few minutes after we arrived, I stepped on a sea urchin. As I quickly and painfully discovered, it affects one in the same way a twelve-gauge shotgun shell would if it went off inside your foot. It was the most excruciating pain I have ever felt. I needed badly to get to a hospital, but we were told there wasn't one, so I ended up in a doctor's office: Taco Cedars-Sinai.

"Your foot is full of spines," the doctor told me.

I didn't need an explanation. I needed a painkiller.

"They are alive," continued the doctor. "If we don't get them out, they'll begin to flow into your body like sperm flows from a woman's vagina into her ovaries."

"Shit!" I screamed. "Do what you need to do! I don't want to get pregnant from these things!"

I was lying on a surgical table and didn't think I could take the pain much longer. Through clenched teeth, I said, "Doc, give me something to kill the pain."

He shrugged. "I have no anesthesia, señor. *Lo siento*."

"Low what? No anes-fucking-thesia?"

Two male nurses entered; they looked like the zombified prizefighter in *The Harder They Fall*. They pinned me to the table while Jekyll extracted the needles, one by one, digging into my flesh with a syringe. I passed out.

When I came to, I had a cast on my lower leg and foot and a pair of crutches. Back at the hotel, I collapsed on my bed and slept restlessly for several hours. I woke to a ringing telephone. Taco Bell was back in business.

"Jay, it's George."

"George who?"

"George Peppard! I'm in a heap of trouble, and I need you!"

He was in Boston, shooting the pilot for *Banacek*. The day before, George had picked up one of the extras on his set, a young woman who had initiated a flirtation. He had invited her to his hotel suite for dinner. Later, while they were making love, she bit him on the neck like a lioness.

"So you hit her, I suppose."

"No," he said, which surprised me because George had an explosive temper. "I was shocked; it was so unexpected. It wasn't rough sex at all. I mean, shit, her bite brought blood. Then I saw that she was expecting me to hit her. She *wanted* me to. So I shoved her out of bed."

"What happened next?" I asked.

"She grabbed her clothes and ran through the lobby in the buff."

"Where are you staying?"

"The Ritz-Carlton."

"The Ritz-Carlton has the most conservative clientele in Boston!"

"It's worse than that," said George. "She was screaming, 'George Peppard raped me! George Peppard raped me!'"

It smelled like a setup, but I let George continue.

"So the cops come and arrest me. When I posted bail, I called the studio, but nobody would talk to me. The same thing at NBC."

"Did it make the papers?"

"Page two everywhere, including the *L.A. Times*. 'George Peppard Accused of Rape.'"

"That's why those bastards at the studio and the network wouldn't take your calls," I told him. "All of a sudden, they don't want anything to do with you. You're anathema to them."

"You've got to come and get me out of this shit."

"What's the weather like?"

"It's snowing."

There were no flights from Acapulco to Boston. The fastest route was via L.A. When I arrived at LAX wearing tropical threads, Marsha, my secretary, was waiting at the gate with a change of clothes, an overcoat and a packed suitcase. I hobbled to the men's room, my foot beating a tattoo of pain. I couldn't get my pants over the cast. Marsha had to help me change.

By the time I got to the Boston Ritz-Carlton, George had received a telephone call from an anonymous person who said the rape charges would be dropped if he forked over $20,000. "It's extortion," he said bitterly.

I was not surprised by the call, but I *was* surprised by the amount of money being demanded. While airborne, I had considered George's predicament from every conceivable angle. I thought he would be hit up for something like a quarter of a million dollars.

"Pay it," I said.

George being George said, "The hell I will!"

"It will cost you a hell of a lot more if you fight it, George."

"I don't care," he said. "Nobody's gonna extort money from me!"

We hired a private detective and a fleet of lawyers. I got in touch with some underworld characters through Las Vegas connections; two weeks later it unfolded that the scheme was an inside deal, a police setup. Two cops had come up with the scam. After busting George's "victim" on drug and prostitution charges, they blackmailed her, telling her she was going to prison unless she cooperated with their plan. The cops managed to get her on the set as an extra.

Meanwhile George had spent in excess of $20,000. Vindicated, I thought he should quit. "No fucking way," he said.

He went to court, and I went with him. I remember the judge telling the girl how horrible she was, as if the cops had been persuaded by her to join the scam rather than she by them. They got light sentences, which pissed George off. I called a press conference and told the reporters turnabout was fair play. George had been accused of rape on page two; I demanded his vindication be on the same page using the same size type and the same space, à la Peter Fonda seven years earlier. The result was better than I'd requested. The story got front page across the nation. L.A.

Associated Press reporter James Bacon said it was the first time in his memory that a person was accused on page two and acquitted with a front-page headline.

George and I went back to the Ritz-Carlton. NBC and Universal were burning up the phone lines with congratulations. Hollywood was alive and well.

Susan Hayward was an idol of my youth who became my client, and later a close friend and confidante. At times we were more than friends as we occasionally became romantic when she was extremely depressed and lonely. She was getting ready to fly to Africa, where I had arranged a safari trip for her with accommodations at William Holden's Mount Kenya Safari Club. A couple of nights before she was scheduled to leave, I took her to see Aretha Franklin perform. After the show, we went to Aretha's dressing room. Aretha was nervous, upset. As Susan and I left, Aretha asked me to call her the next morning.

I called. Aretha's problems were compounding by the moment; pre-performance "nerves" were becoming a minor part of her psychology. I hung up. Susan was packing.

"Why don't you go with me to Africa?" she said.

"I can't. I've got too many problems to tend to."

"Like what?"

"For one, I've got to babysit Aretha. She's a mess."

"What's wrong with her?"

I explained, to the best of my knowledge. Among other things, Aretha was having marital problems. She was tied up in knots. "She needs a crutch, and I'm it," I said.

Susan's eyes lighted up. "Why don't you have her come with me?" she said enthusiastically. "She can be my maid. No one will know who she is, and she can have a good rest."

I looked at Susan; she was serious and expectant.

"Well?" she said.

I cleared my throat. "Susan, that's sweet of you, but I don't think I can ask Aretha Franklin to pose as your maid."

"Why?" asked Susan.

I didn't answer. Susan belonged to another generation. She was incapable of switching gears in the face of old age. She was too set in her ways. Her solution to Aretha's problem was the problem in black versus white relationships, innocent as it appeared. The only real solution was time . . . a long, long time.

I stayed and helped nurse Aretha out of her depression. But she was just one of dozens of clients, all with problems of one sort or another. I was becoming more disenchanted by the moment. I was managing careers and mindsets under the guise of a publicist when I was really a psychologist. I needed a change—a career change.

Chapter 10

FARRAH-MANIA
AND *CHARLIE'S ANGELS*

I was a Rams football fan with season tickets. I invited Sonny Bono to go with me to a game. The idea was to drink a few beers and have a good time. When I picked him up in my limousine, he asked, "Do you mind if Lee Majors comes along?"

I didn't mind at all. Sonny recently had done a cameo on Lee's successful television series, *The Six Million Dollar Man*. I didn't know Lee, but he had been on the periphery of my life twice. His first movie role had been in *Strait-Jacket*, the mask movie that sent my old girlfriend Leslie Parrish into hysterics, and he had been Ryan O'Neal's backup when Ryan threatened me at the Daisy because I was seeing his estranged wife. In those days Lee had been Harvey Lee Yeary. He had come a long way. He was his own man now, a veteran television superstar.

I was living in a void — plagued by boredom and acute depression. I was managing Glenn Ford and Charlotte Rampling, but my public-relations business was falling behind. I'd lost much of my interest in it. Actors, because they were so insecure when unemployed, were unreliable, and corporate accounts bored me. I thought Lee might be a potential management client.

Sonny and I picked up Lee and went to the game. Lee was a handsome man, athletic and masculine, but also shy and taciturn. After several beers, he began to loosen up. Sonny, who felt he owed me something for helping resurrect his career, encouraged Lee to hire me as his publicist. I didn't mention that I would prefer to manage him. After the game, Lee pulled me aside. "I'll hire you for a thousand bucks a month, Jay," he said, "but you have to represent my wife for free."

"Who's your wife?"

"Farrah Fawcett-Majors."

He explained that she'd had a few modeling jobs and a couple of minor television roles. She'd recently done a pilot for Spelling-Goldberg called *Charlie's Angels*. ABC had it on their March schedule. Farrah and Jaclyn Smith, another model turned actress, were playing second-fiddle to Kate Jackson, the show's star. It was about three women detectives. I yawned. Lee was my priority; Farrah would be just another name on my list of clients.

The timing was good. I was in need of a movie hero. Bill Holden was making his last major movie, *Network*, but he was no longer capable of carrying a film on his own merit. George Peppard was floundering, lost in the sea of Machiavellian Hollywood waves. John Wayne, suffering lung cancer, was making his last movie. The new stars were Dustin Hoffman, Al Pacino and Robert De Niro, fine actors but not replacements for the brilliant heroes of the past. Jack Nicholson and Warren Beatty were nearest to the stars of old, but they were into antihero roles, a shift in storytelling I thought detrimental to the cultural influence of movies in times past. I saw Lee as a potential international hero in the mold of Clint Eastwood or Charles Bronson.

Lee invited me to his home to meet Farrah. It was a very unusual meeting. As I looked at her, she smiled. I smiled back—time stopped. The moment lasted an eternity. I felt spellbound. I saw a magical, golden glow around her; it was an extraordinary feeling. Farrah was *literally* breathtaking. I knew at that very moment that a superstar was born and I was her launching pad.

But Hollywood was replete with beautiful women, as I was firmly reminded by Lee, who did most of the talking, making it clear he was head of the household. Farrah's role as an actress was subsidiary to their domestic life. It was something to keep her busy. Farrah laughed in genial agreement. She was quiet, but not shy. She knew when to speak, when not to speak. It wasn't that Lee had trained her, but rather that she was perceptibly and innately bright.

I kept my thoughts to myself about making Farrah into a Superstar. Lee was the star in the Majors household. Farrah was an adjunct, an appendage, as far as he was concerned. Lee was like Bill Holden and George Peppard—conservative, old fashioned and narrow minded. A wife's place was in the home, not in front of a camera. Lee was the breadwinner and the decision maker. Even with all my deep, intuitive and surreal feelings about Farrah and her star potential, none of us that night had a real inkling of what lay in the bright future; it was too fantastic to contemplate.

In the beginning of my relationship with Lee and Farrah, I felt like a babysitter. In his absence, Lee wanted me to escort his wife to various functions. It wasn't easy to satisfy his demands; taking Farrah about town was time-consuming. I enjoyed being with her, but it was disappointing to see her plodding through the routine of trying to stay on the periphery of the Hollywood game. She had enjoyed success as a model, but now, after a so-so career as an actress, she had assumed the role of a thousand other Hollywood actresses, that of a has-been, no longer a wannabe.

I repeatedly told Farrah not to worry about anything. As long as she followed my rules and took my advice, things would dramatically turn around for her and her career. I plotted all day and I schemed by night, and in my sleep, I dreamed about it.

One afternoon I took her to *The Merv Griffin Show* at a studio in Hollywood. Farrah was one among many star wives participating in a fashion show. For me, it was another humdrum episode; I had more important things to do. I sat through the taping, talking with various people between shots. When it was finished, I got Farrah and we left through the stage door with several other couples. Then another extraordinary thing happened.

Three dozen fans were waiting outside, which wasn't unusual. What *was* unusual is they only wanted to see Farrah. They collapsed on us, ignoring the other wives who had modeled. It wasn't just a crowd; it was a swarm of fanatics, all wanting to be near Farrah. It was a new experience for me. Farrah radiated something extra, a quality esoteric and ethereal. Hair rose on the back of my neck. It was uncanny, but the instant I saw the reaction of her fans it reaffirmed to me that Farrah was going to be a Superstar. I resurrected a word from the Kennedy years: *charisma*. She had it, a magnetic quality that defied description. When we got into our limousine, I said, "Farrah, I'm going to make you a Superstar."

"Oh, Jay! Don't be silly." She saw nothing of the sort. She had been going with the flow since her arrival in California in 1969. Her career had not been a struggle as it was for most actresses, although nothing of importance had come her way. She'd had minor parts in *Myra Breckinridge* and *Logan's Run*, and a few forgettable television roles. I think she had given up on being a star, if she had ever wanted to be one. She was wholesome, not desperate, a beautiful woman dedicated to her husband and her domestic responsibilities. She had more interest in sports than in movies or television. She spent her time playing tennis, swimming and being Mrs. Lee Majors.

Suddenly my mind-set changed. I had been dwelling on heroes—more precisely on the lack of them. Watergate and Vietnam had changed everything. After Nixon's fall, political heroes were absent from the American landscape. Vietnam had made military heroes a thing of the past. Sports figures were no longer loyal to their fans or team, except for one season; Joe Namath was advertising pantyhose. Forget heroes; maybe America was waiting for a heroine, someone who was not only gorgeous but who espoused values. I saw that heroine in Farrah. She didn't smoke, she didn't drink, she was into fitness and exercise (I thought she perspired Perrier water) and she was beyond beautiful.

She was heavenly. I saw her as America's new role model.

Nobody seemed interested in *Charlie's Angels* except Aaron Spelling, Leonard Goldberg and Fred Silverman, president of ABC Television Entertainment. Lee certainly wasn't, and I don't think Farrah gave it much thought. The buzz was that Spelling-Goldberg had produced a dud.

That was not unusual; most television projects failed. The bottom line, as always, would be the Nielsen ratings.

The week the pilot aired, Patty Hearst was kidnapped in one of the more lurid and perplexing cases since Leopold and Loeb. The news dominated the airwaves. I felt *Charlie's Angels* would be overshadowed by Hearst. After all, it was an escapist fantasy about three women detectives. Patty Hearst was real.

The two hour TV movie debuted on March 21, 1976. The critics lambasted it, but the show received a phenomenal 54 share, which meant over half of America was tuned to it. It was a gargantuan rating. No one could doubt that ABC would give Spelling-Goldberg a green light to develop the show into a dramatic-action series for the fall season.

My emphasis had already shifted from Lee to Farrah. She couldn't act, but she had spunk and a natural ease in front of the camera. I thought acting classes would help, but she vetoed my suggestion: "I'll never take acting classes, Jay. Don't bring it up again!" She wasn't against tutelage, but it was too time-consuming. She was an outdoor girl, an athlete.

I needed a game plan, a way to exploit her assets. As if by accident, Farrah solved my problem.

In June, just before *Charlie's Angels* went into series production, she showed me a new pinup poster of herself. I was bowled over. It was tasteful, yet the sexiest picture I had seen since I was a kid. It reminded me of the World War II pinup poster of Betty Grable. Grable, however, had been a star that made a poster. As I looked at Farrah's photograph, I realized the reverse could be true also—a poster could make a star.

The brainchild of the poster was an executive at the Pro Arts poster company. When Farrah was asked to pose in a bikini, she dismissed the idea—not the poster but the bikini. She also rejected their photographer, choosing fellow Texan Bruce McBroom, whom she'd met while doing *Myra Breckenridge* in 1969. She had chosen a one-piece red bathing suit, and McBroom shot a series of photographs alongside the Majors' pool.

The photograph was not nearly as revealing as other cheesecake pictures of the day. Farrah appeared in profile, her head tilted back, her hair as dry as the Sahara, with a wide, radiant smile. The swimsuit was wet, and it clung tightly to her lithe body, exposing her full breasts, something Betty Grable had been prevented from doing. When I saw the poster shot I instantly perceived an angle for a campaign—nipples. No mainstream celebrity had ever been so exposed. "I can promote this," I told her. "I can merchandise this."

She shrugged, expressing no excitement.

"This can be something big," I continued, "just like you're going to be big."

She laughed. The poster was no big deal. She had done it, that's all, and whimsically.

One salient idea I learned in college was that history repeats itself. It was time for a new pinup poster. I wouldn't draw commission from it because I was on a flat retainer with no perks. It was a challenge, that's all; I thought I could change history while simultaneously repeating it.

Farrah was almost thirty. Traditionally, the perfect celluloid woman was under twenty-five. When Betty Grable did *her* famous poster, she was twenty-four. Elizabeth Taylor was twenty when she made *A Place in the Sun*; Lana Turner was twenty-one in *Honky Tonk*; Jane Russell twenty-two when she did *The Outlaw*; Jean Harlow was dead at twenty-six. If there were women who had become star sex symbols at an older age, they lied about it.

The age attitude was not a Hollywood creation. It was a cultural holdover of a Victorian concept regarding marriage, and it was still in play in the mid-seventies. Essentially, if a young woman was not married by her twenty-fifth birthday, she was a spinster. We were in the midst of the women's liberation movement, but for all their good intentions, women progressives had failed to resolve the stigma of age, married or not. I remember when Raquel Welch, today still one of the most beautiful women in the world, turned thirty but claimed to be twenty-five.

I asked Farrah if she would mind if I revealed her age in a publicity campaign. To my surprise, she didn't give it a second thought. She shrugged and said, "No. Why should I?" On September 14, ABC aired the *Charlie's Angels* pilot again. It took fourth place in overall ratings. Eight days later the first episode of the series aired. Suddenly we didn't have enough pinup posters to meet the demands of retailers, and the printing presses starting rolling twenty-four hours a day. Farrah's poster was a star before she was. It became the biggest seller in pinup-poster history—12 million copies. Millions of teenage boys and young men had their first sexual experience with Farrah Fawcett. She just wasn't there in person.

When Farrah celebrated her birthday, she was the most famous thirty-year-old in the nation. She received a half-million letters from young women, saying in effect, "I'm twenty-six, and I thought I was over the hill. Thanks to you, I realize I've got a few more years to get my life together."

Poor Lee. When I first met him at that Rams game, he had seemed ebullient, confident and supremely mature. It was the beer; it fogged my observation. Lee was as insecure as any actor I ever knew. He was unprepared for fame. He could be rude to his fans and uncommunicative to his colleagues. He was a television heartthrob who lived in fear of losing his wife.

We shared one common interest—sports. If I had business to discuss, I warmed him up by talking sports. And we were both gamblers. He was good; I was not. I was a risk-taker. Lee said, "I'll be your bookie. Why give your commissions to someone you hardly know? Let me have them." I did, and he had no qualms about taking them.

His vocabulary seemed limited to a few sports words, like *hike*. His sign language was prehistoric. A high five was his most expressive gesture. "Gimme five!" he would cry when excited, and then slap the shit out of my hand.

He was making tons of money and his innate conservatism demanded that nothing change the status quo. He transmitted his philosophy to Farrah. My problem was selling them new ideas, turning no into yes. Lee wanted to be blameless. He argued with me vociferously before acquiescing, because if an idea failed he would then have a scapegoat. That was Lee's mentality: wary, self-serving and self-protective. He once advised a friend: "When you go to Hollywood, hire yourself a smart Jew." I was his Jew.

Lee had a cabin on a lake in some mountains north of Las Vegas. It was his retreat from a world he didn't feel comfortable in. When Farrah was working and he was not, he would often go alone to the cabin and stay two weeks at a time. He had a boat and he would fish by himself, just Lee and the fish. It reminded me of Leslie Parrish and her cats.

His wilderness experiences sounded like he was reliving the life of Henry David Thoreau on Walden Pond. I went to the cabin with him once, thinking it might give me a chance to establish a better rapport with him. His father and another friend from Kentucky joined us. We were supposed to be gone a week. It was one of the worst experiences of my life.

The cabin was smaller than my kitchen and the refrigerator hadn't been cleaned out in two years. The four of us were cramped in the hut of a cabin like cellmates in jail, yet no one ever said anything of importance. The boat was hardly big enough for one person. We were four men leading lives of quiet desperation. There were no elephants or lions or Cape buffalo to stimulate the flow of adrenaline. The great wide world beyond that little cabin and that little boat and that little lake no longer existed.

After twenty-four hours of communing with nature I began to go stir-crazy. We fished hour after hour, catching nothing and seldom speaking. I roughed it two days, and then I bade the trio farewell and hightailed it back to Los Angeles. I needed some polluted air in my lungs.

If Farrah was hesitant about becoming a star, she wasn't uncooperative. On a personal level, Farrah and I developed a very special friendship that would last the rest of our lives. Shoot, we were having the time of our lives! We teased each other and tried to have fun when we could; however, there just wasn't enough time in the day. I was extremely driven and focused. She went along with everything I asked, which was a lot.

All summer long, while *Charlie's Angels* was being filmed, she gave lunchtime interviews. On a staggered schedule, I brought in forty top national and syndicated journalists, people I had dealt with over the years. I briefed each of them for a solid hour before I took them to Farrah's trailer. I preached to them about symbols and mythical goddesses; I gave each a poster. By the time they met Farrah, they were preconditioned, totally in sync with my agenda without realizing it. I stayed for the interviews.

When questions about foreign affairs and abortion and a hundred other controversial topics were asked, I interrupted and steered the reporters in other directions. I declined interviews with writers who might be hostile, and I turned down requests for Farrah to appear on talk shows. I wanted to build an image; I had to control the questions and the environment.

"If somebody wants to meet the girl next door, they should go next door," I told Farrah. "We need to create a mystique. You represent apple pie, baseball and the American flag, but your wholesomeness must be imitated, not shared. A national treasure. An icon. You are part of the American dream. Remember that—a dream. You are unattainable."

Charlie's Angels had been intended as a vehicle for Kate Jackson. By the time the series aired, however, Farrah was bigger than the show.

In pop culture people are interested in stars, not artists. Meryl Streep is a great artist, but most movie fans don't know much about her private life. While Farrah was reaching her peak, her fans' need for information about her could not be sated. She was known globally as simply "Farrah." When a celebrity is recognized by just one name, it is sometimes referred to in our business as achieving "iconic" status. It's the pinnacle of the business for an actor. Always to be remembered, and never to be forgotten. With Farrah, it came amazingly quick. The Farrah phenomenon was something the world had never before experienced with a Hollywood starlet, or any mortal woman in the history of mankind, for that matter.

An overnight female goddess on earth. The phenomenon was so intense, it became known as a *thing* within itself. Farrah-mania some even called it. She became everything to everybody. Men, women and children all adored her for many different reasons. Farrah the sex symbol, role model and all-American superstar.

In the beginning, Aaron Spelling was smart enough to use Farrah's newfound status. He probably pushed the poster as hard as I did. To his credit, he certainly shared my foresight, as he had his writers reevaluate the role of Farrah's character, Jill Munroe, and give her equal time with Kate's character. For the rest of the year, the show was trying to catch up with Farrah. I was receiving over two hundred calls a day from journalists around the world. I began to cut back. I had gone for quantity in the beginning; now I wanted quality.

When UPI's Vernon Scott said Farrah was the next Marilyn Monroe, I knew we had reached a new plateau. Farrah wasn't remotely like Marilyn, but I capitalized on the comparison. It was the hair. Marilyn had been the last blonde to achieve stardom. Before Marilyn, with few exceptions, female stars had been brunettes; since Marilyn, until Farrah, most were brunettes again. Where Farrah differed from Marilyn was in her intelligence. The "dumb blonde" was out.

I didn't ignore Lee and my other clients, but it was Farrah who consumed my thoughts. I wanted to make her the most famous woman in the world. Yet to become her de facto manager, I had to overcome a stubborn barrier—Lee's ego. "The term 'personal manager' sounds like we don't know how to take care of ourselves," he said. Then, almost inadvertently, he gave me the green light.

We were poolside at their Bel Air home. Lee was exasperated, tired of phone calls, press pressure and contract negotiations. He and Farrah were working Monday through Friday on their series. Farrah was doing magazine photo shoots nearly every weekend at my place in Stone Canyon. "We're overwhelmed," said Lee. "It's hard to keep up with everything. The business deals are too many to think about. You've got to handle some of this stuff, Jay."

"A lot of this is not the job of your public-relations man, Lee," I said. "If you want me to take over, I'll be glad to do it. But we'll have to strike a personal-management agreement."

Lee looked at Farrah. "Looks like we've got a manager, darling." Then he looked at me. "How will it work?"

I told him I needed authority to make career decisions, after consultations with him and Farrah. "I know where the quicksand is, and where the crocodiles and cannibals are," I explained. "I can help you avoid them. I'll serve as a buffer between you and potential problems."

"You'll be the villain instead of me, right?" said Lee with a laugh. "When something gets screwed up, it's your fault. Right?"

I received $1,000 monthly from each and 5 percent of their incomes from acting, excluding *Charlie's Angels* and *The Six Million Dollar Man*, which preceded me. I got nothing from ancillary activities, like product endorsements and commercial revenues. It wasn't a good deal for me, but that's how badly I wanted to get into personal management full time.

I began the slow phase-out of my public-relations business. It was transitional and could not be done overnight. I had many employees to take care of, and I wanted to keep a few choice clients as backups to Lee and Farrah. I wanted to be the first multiple-client manager in the business. It was a new concept.

Farrah, Lee and a few others became my whole life. I did it all day long, two shifts a day, and when I went to sleep at night, I dreamed about them—mainly Farrah.

My goal was to make Farrah a star in every possible medium. When I was growing up, movies had been the medium of mass entertainment. By 1976 the medium was the media. Everything was interrelated: movies, television, radio and publishing. There was no single venue of importance; they all overlapped. It was complicated, because the free-enterprise system demanded a vast array of ownership. I had to deal with dozens of executives every week.

Fabergé, the cosmetics and hair-products company, had a subsidiary motion-picture division, Brut Productions, which I had represented a couple of times, launching movies such as *A Touch of Class*. George Barrie, the founding father, was an unusual executive. He was a businessman with acumen, but also a talented songwriter, sometimes teaming with Sammy Cahn. He was a two-time Oscar nominee. Combining show business with the cosmetics business, George was responsible for creating the celebrity-endorsement method of selling products.

I arranged a meeting with George and his son Richard, who was succeeding his father as president of Fabergé. I low-keyed it, not knowing exactly what I could pull off. I had nothing to sell except a name and an image—Farrah's. I was looking for a product Farrah might endorse. What I found was a gold mine. When we finished, I had a three-year deal for

Farrah at $1.5 million per year, a total of $4.5 million. She would serve as a consultant and spokesperson for one of their new products, Farrah Fawcett Shampoo. Before we signed, Farrah was the second-billed actress in *Charlie's Angels* at $5,000 per episode; after we signed, she was rich.

Farrah owed Fabergé sixty days a year, to be used shooting commercials, promoting products and consulting. I was not opposed to their use of her time except when she was on her set. I remembered when Sammy Davis, Jr., almost killed himself doing a Broadway show, a television show and a movie all at one time. I knew the toll it had taken on him, and I didn't want that to happen to Farrah.

At the zenith of Farrah-mania, I fielded literally thousands of bizarro offers from all over the world. It was utterly insane, but it was one of the many hats I wore as her personal manager. Everything from Farrah toys to Farrah toothbrushes, to Farrah dolls, candy, clothing, lunchboxes and absolutely everything in between. I had never seen or heard anything like it before. The manic frenzy of offers our way never stopped—all my phone lines were constantly lit up and completely on fire.

I did my very best and was successful in shielding her from the steadily building intensity and pressure from all the offers, demands and pandemonium that was crashing in all around us.

I was so dedicated to my clients in those days that my behavior verged on abnormality. With rare exception, I was willing to take a bullet for them. My attitude had begun at Rogers & Cowan. Philosophically, I had been opposed to company policy, which essentially was to side with the media during a dispute between a client and a member of the press. Warren Cowan once told me, "Stars come and go, but the people that do you favors in the press are always there." I disagreed with him. I believed my allegiance belonged to my client.

My rationale was simple: if I went to my doctor and he said, "Get out of here; you have a fever," he wouldn't be doing his job. Robert Shapiro didn't defend O.J. Simpson because he thought he was innocent. He did it because it was his professional duty. I felt the same way; I was there to protect my clients and I didn't shirk my duty. My clients were my family.

We were having dinner at the Rangoon Racquet Club—Farrah, Lee, Charlotte Rampling and I. Farrah needed to go to the ladies' room. To get to the restrooms one had to go through the bar, a long narrow room that ran parallel to the dining room, separated by a short wall and lattice framework. I told Farrah I would escort her.

The cocktail lounge was full of people, mostly men, and it was late enough that more than a few of them had reached their limit. We walked through the bar without event, and I waited for Farrah in the hallway outside the ladies' room. As we came back, one of the guys sitting at the bar recognized her. "Farrah, I hear you're a lousy lay!"

Farrah was not yet accustomed to celebrity, neither its upside nor its downside. She was still very much a little girl from Texas with limited experience in the tough world of Hollywood.

"Farrah, did you hear me? They say you're a lousy fucking lay!"

Shocked at the man's audacity, Farrah whispered, "I'm getting Lee." Big trouble was on the horizon if Farrah told Lee what had happened. Lee was a macho man of the old school, one who had no reservations about backing up his machismo with action. He was tough, and he did not treat fools lightly.

All of this happened in seconds—the man's remark, Farrah's shocked reaction and the image I conjured of Lee's wrath and his potential violence. I imagined Lee ending up in jail. There was no upside if Lee became entangled with the guy, so I acted.

I turned and slugged him with a full-fisted roundhouse that sent him tumbling to the floor. Before the guy could get up and react, the bartenders and waiters hauled him outside.

Lee never knew the cause of the incident. Farrah was smart enough to keep her mouth shut. When we returned to our table, we passed off the action as typical barroom mayhem. Lee shrugged, and we continued dinner. It would be years before I realized that taking a bullet for a client was foolish.

Chapter 11

SUPER SUZANNE SOMERS AND *THREE'S COMPANY*

I wanted a backup to Farrah, not a replacement—another actress I could cultivate, nurture and develop into a different high-octane star. I had dozens of offers for Farrah, but she couldn't work another project until *Charlie's Angels* went into hiatus at the end of its production season. We were offered two choice big-screen movies, *Coma* at MGM and *Foul Play* at Paramount; I had persuaded Colin Higgins to write the latter for her. But if I had a backup, I could capitalize on some other offers.

I locked my eyes on Lynda Carter, a PR client who met the criteria I felt necessary for success. She had talent, her self-presentation was superb and furthermore she possessed a quality that appealed to me. But most important, she had a platform from which I could launch her into the celestial heavens of superstardom: she was Wonder Woman on television.

Lynda was almost perfect management material. She had one minor flaw—a tendency to get extremely nervous when small talk was required. I once took her to a party at the home of Jon Epstein, who produced the *Columbo* series. My beeper went off. It was an important call and I excused myself to go to a telephone. To leave Lynda among admirers hardly seemed rude. I didn't give it a second thought, although as I was leaving she gave me a pointed glance, as if to say, "Please hurry back!"

I was gone four minutes, no more, but time enough for Lynda to grow frantic. More than frantic, she was an absolute wreck. The people she was talking with or, more accurately, listening to, seemed as harmless as garden flowers. Nevertheless I extracted her from the circle and once we were alone she told me her problem. Small talk frightened her; she couldn't do it—it drove her nuts.

It wasn't Lynda's inability to make small talk that kept me from making her a superstar. Rather, it was the nemesis I'd met before, one that would confound virtually every management client I would have in the future. This time it was in the person of Ron Samuels, the son of Maury, who'd owned the Jerry Lewis Restaurant back in the days when Leslie Parrish and I were together. Ron and I were friends, and when he called me wanting to know if I would introduce him to Lynda Carter, I didn't give it a second thought. Ron had become a successful commercial agent and I didn't question his intentions. Had I known he and Lynda were going to fall in love, I might have refrained. They not only fell in love and got married, but Ron, rather than me, became her manager until the gilt of love melted and they got divorced some years later. My educated guess is that just like most Hollywood marriages that fail, theirs was lacking something fresh, someone or something new. There is always the lure of the tempting Hollywood social life. They likely just weren't having any fun anymore.

I was never one of those Hollywood socialites who accepted an invitation to the "opening of an envelope," but I did maintain a full social life. Farrah and Lee often joined my date and me, usually for dinner, and in their absence another client replaced them. After I moved into the Elvis Presley mansion in Bel Air, I had parties every other weekend. I received hundreds of invitations but attended only those I deemed important.

When Kurt Frings invited me to a party honoring Elizabeth Taylor, I accepted immediately. Kurt was agent for some of Hollywood's most glamorous women—Elizabeth, Carroll Baker, Tuesday Weld, Angie Dickinson and Audrey Hepburn, to name a few. He was a native of Germany, an ex-boxer and a youthful man even in his sixties.

The occasion was a lobster luncheon. Thirty-nine people were present—everyone except Elizabeth. She arrived two hours late, then struck up a standing conversation with Eddie Dmytryk, who had directed her in *Raintree County*. The rest of us were seated, and most were getting antsy. I was not. I watched Elizabeth. She was shy—uncomfortable at being guest of honor. She was using Dmytryk as her crutch. By the time she sat down the lobsters had become shrimp.

Kurt loved to throw parties, and it was an honor to be invited. When I first met him, his guest list was always star-studded. Time took its toll, however, and Kurt suffered a debilitating stroke. His stable of actresses left him, and his birthday parties became the extent of his social life. He was in a wheelchair; he could hardly speak. I remember his first party following his stroke. His girlfriend put it together. Every star in town was present to pay respects to the famous old agent. A year later, I received another invitation. This time there were six stars, and the next year the only guest I knew was me.

I felt badly for Kurt, but I understood the fleeting nature of Hollywood loyalty. Since he could no longer help anyone, he was being quickly forgotten. Before I left the party, I was in one of his bathrooms. A lipstick lay on the counter. I picked it up and wrote in huge letters on the mirror: "Kurt, I love you, and I'll always be your friend. Jay Bernstein."

Next year I received another invitation. A handful of people were there, and again I was the only guest I knew. When I went to the bathroom, I was taken aback. My note of the year before was still on the mirror. The mirror had been cleaned around it, but the letters remained in bold red. It was a nice compliment to me, but a sad reminder of the evanescence of fame.

The evanescence of fame is usually accompanied by its many warnings. Which reminds me of a famous actress named Suzanne Somers. I did not discover Suzanne Somers; she discovered me. She was a publicity client of Jay Bernstein Public Relations, assigned to account executive Stu Erlich. The first day she walked into my office, I didn't realize she was already a client. She asked me to manage her career, which was something of a joke. She was thirty-one, barren of style, terribly naïve, with a resumé that was almost blank. She had recently made a picture called *Ants* in which she played a corpse. She had mouthed three words in *American Graffiti*. What she had, though, were guts and a sense of humor. When I turned her down, she laughed it off with a ditzy giggle. A couple of weeks later she was back in my office. "I want you to manage my career," she repeated, as if we'd never discussed it before.

I was usually brutally honest, but I liked Suzanne and abstained from telling her that she didn't have a career for me to manage. It wouldn't have made a difference. Suzanne was one of those ambitious wannabes who took the word no as a temporary barrier. We were similar. It was the fence syndrome—if you can't go around it, over it or under it, then blow it up. Suzanne was a dynamite expert chock-full of dreams and ambition.

She bugged me a half-dozen times over a period of several weeks. She managed to get on the *Tonight Show*, independent of an agent, and read a poem she had written. She had chutzpah. Then she showed up at my office with a real proposition. She was excited and full of confidence, intent on her goal, which was to demolish the fence that stood between us.

"I want to be as big as Farrah," she said. For the first time she was speaking from strength, although it was exaggerated. She had just been cast as the third lead in a new series, *Three's Company*, a midseason sitcom replacement calling for six episodes. "I'll be making $2,200 per episode," she said. "I'll give you every dime of it if you'll manage me."

I saw Suzanne as a contemporary Judy Holliday, an analogy I couldn't use because most people didn't remember Holliday. By now, Farrah had established her own identity as Farrah, so I told the press Suzanne was the next Marilyn Monroe, which she wasn't. I used the comparison to get attention. It was strictly a publicity gesture, a gimmick to get her some recognition before she blossomed into the sexy comedic genius she is.

Together, we screened all of Marilyn's movies. Suzanne picked up Marilyn's movements, the swing of her hips and the way she cooed and blew kisses. She and her soon-to-be-husband, Alan Hamel, tried to dominate my nightlife, which to a degree they did, but I felt it was important for her to get all the exposure she could. As we left restaurants, I would whisper to Suzanne, "Do Marilyn," and she would, perfectly, for the paparazzi and legmen.

It worked; the press picked up on it and Suzanne received gobs of print coverage other actresses would die for. The cocoon phase lasted six months; then we dropped the Marilyn shtick. To me she was always a takeoff of Judy Holliday; to America she was Suzanne Somers.

An old showbiz adage is "Timing is everything." With Suzanne it was. I sensed that people, and therefore the press, were getting tired of seeing and reading Farrah, Farrah, Farrah. I never remotely felt Farrah had run her course, but after seventy-five magazine covers in hardly a year's time we had begun to saturate the market.

Farrah didn't laugh much; she was the cool blonde. Suzanne was a comic relief. She laughed all the time. There was another factor. Suzanne was as unique as Farrah, except she didn't come from another planet. She had a touch of "everywoman" in her—people could identify with her down-to-earth attitude and appearance; it was easier for women to look like her than like Farrah, whose beauty was too remote for the average woman to strive for. Of course, when I first met her, Suzanne didn't look like Suzanne. The Suzanne that people came to know and love, we created.

I don't remember how subtle I was (Suzanne says I was never subtle about anything), but in my effort to make Suzanne over, to make her as beautiful as she could be, I tried to duplicate some of Farrah's look. I got Suzanne to use the same makeup, the same hairdresser. I tried to distance her from San Bruno, California, where she had grown up. San Bruno was her bane, her failure, a place where she couldn't make it as the weather girl on local television. She was my first student in Princess Training.

And Suzanne had that certain "it," which needed to be exploited. My initial plan, which worked, was to get her on every magazine cover I didn't want Farrah on. I knew the big ones, like *People* and *TV Guide* and *Newsweek*, would follow in time, but the important thing at the outset was to splash her photograph on the myriad lesser but still prominent periodicals. Magazine saturation was paramount because television entertainment news followed their lead. Robin Leach said when Farrah was on the cover of a supermarket throwaway, sales jumped a million copies. By the end of the first year, Suzanne had graced the covers of fifty magazines.

Once Farrah had catapulted into icon status, my telephone never stopped ringing. One persistent caller was Carollyne McNichol, a former actress turned stage mother. Her message was always the same: "My daughter is going to be a star, but she needs you."

I didn't call her back. She never came to my office, but she telephoned constantly, three, four times a day. "My daughter—"

Finally I answered. "Who's your daughter?"

"Kristy McNichol. She's starring in ABC's *Family*."

"Send me her resumé."

I'd never heard of Kristy McNichol, but *Family* was a successful series, an unlikely Aaron Spelling project. Unlikely because it didn't fit his normal model. It was not camp fantasy, but a serious drama about American values. Kristy had fifth billing, four big marks shy of being the star. She was fourteen years old. When Carollyne called back, I told her, "I don't represent kids."

"She's more than a kid," said Carollyne. "She's going to be a big star. If you'll manage her, it will speed her success."

I gave in, thinking that the only way to get rid of this woman was to represent her daughter.

Kristy was an archetype of thousands of young actors past, present and future. She had a look and a quality and a modicum of talent. Most important, she had a vehicle, *Family*. Without proper management and guidance, she probably would have remained undiscovered when her series ran its course. What she needed was someone who could put a spotlight on her. Aside from a few commercials and bit parts, *Family* was it; she'd never been in a movie for television, much less for the big screen. I went to ABC and screened three episodes of *Family*. Kristy had something. It was always inexplicable, like pornography. I couldn't define it, but I knew it when I saw it. Kristy had potential, but before I finalized the deal with her mom I wanted to meet her.

She was a kid, but she was enthusiastic and confident. Carollyne did most of the talking for her, but that was okay. Kristy never would have become an actress had it not been for her mother. When I left the meeting my horizon had broadened. I saw in Kristy a star, but not as a backup to

Farrah or Suzanne. Kristy, because of her age, had to stand on her own. We had to capitalize on her role in *Family* before the series ran its course. I saw her as a new Margaret O'Brien.

By now my dance card was full. I was working two-and-a-half shifts a day, on Farrah, Suzanne and Kristy, in that order, followed by another half-dozen clients, and dreaming nightmares about them when I slept, which was not often. I lost weight, but I never lost focus. At last, however, I needed help to get me through the day. I went to a doctor.

"You've got to slow down, Jay."

"I can't."

He gave me a prescription for some uppers. They worked, adding two or three hours more to my workday. A month later I was back in the doctor's office.

"You've got to slow down, Jay. You've got to get more sleep."

He gave me a prescription for Valium, to counter the uppers when I went to bed. It was the Judy Garland cure. I didn't have a studio doctor like she'd had at MGM, but it was the same thing. I had a Hollywood doctor who understood the pressure of the industry.

I had never taken recreational drugs, although they were always there. Even after I experienced smoking pot with sportscasters Curt Gowdy and Don Meredith (one funny and very smoky weekend spent on an epic fishing adventure), I used it only occasionally to soothe my nerves. Most people in Hollywood used drugs to gain confidence and overcome inhibitions; I had confidence aplenty and inhibitions were generally absent from my psyche. What I needed was sound sleep, if only a few hours a night.

Valium became my friend and nemesis simultaneously—this was before medical science realized it was addictive. I went from five milligrams a night to ten; then I jumped to twenty. By the time *All That Jazz* came out a couple of years later, I was up to forty milligrams. One morning I looked in the mirror and said, "Jay, you've become Bob Fosse's clone!"

Trying to keep pace was next to impossible. But I couldn't slow down no matter what drug I was on. And Lee Majors was driving me crazy. He wanted to produce and star in movies under his and Farrah's banner, a newly incorporated company called Fawcett-Majors Productions. Since becoming Colonel Steve Austin, Lee had done eight movies of the week, six of which were Austin spin-offs of *The Six Million Dollar Man*. His only TV movie with an adult theme was *Francis Gary Powers: The True Story of the U-2 Spy Incident*, based on the Soviet shoot-down of America's most sophisticated spy plane during the Eisenhower years. But none of the movies helped elevate Lee's career.

Then I came across a teleplay about ski-injury rehabilitation, which I thought fit Lee's capabilities as an actor. He read it, liked it and gave me the green light to package it for Fawcett-Majors Productions at Universal, where Lee could get it financed.

The story was about a double-amputee Vietnam War veteran living in self-pity, until a friend jolts him back to life by teaching him to ski. It was called *Just a Little Inconvenience*, which was the attitude the veteran assumed about his physical challenge at the film's conclusion.

I had once represented James Stacy. After he co-starred with Susan Hayward in *Fitzgerald and Pride*, Jim was riding his motorcycle with his girlfriend when a drunk driver struck them. The girlfriend was killed and Jim lost his left arm and left leg. He continued to act, although roles were sparse due to his handicap. I cast him as the double-amputee in *Just a Little Inconvenience*. Barbara Hershey was cast as the love interest.

The movie was filmed in Canada's Banff National Park. I stayed in Los Angeles. Principal photography had hardly begun when I received a panicked call from Lee. His story was almost too wild for my imagination. Jim Stacy had tried to rape Barbara Hershey. Apparently intoxicated, he had knocked the door to her suite out of its frame and attacked her.

Incensed and frightened, Barbara wanted to quit the show and go home; Stacy was still out of control, and Lee was concerned about adverse publicity hurting the movie as well as his career. "What can I do?" he wanted to know. "When Universal finds out what happened, the shit is gonna hit the fan!"

"Get your people together and tell them not to call the studio," I told him. "Then confront Stacy, put him flat on his back like a turtle, pin your foot to his throat and tell him he can fuck up his own career all he wants to, but he's not going to fuck up your career!"

Evidently Lee followed my advice. He called me back and said, "Okay, I've got Stacy straightened out, but just in case he wants to try something else, I'm putting two security guards with him at all times."

The production continued without further problems. After all was said, done and in the can, *Just a Little Inconvenience* was a good movie, and when it was televised in the fall of 1977, it was well received by the critics. Since I had found the property, packaged the movie, sold it to the network and done sundry other things to make it happen, I thought I should be credited as executive producer. But Lee refused to put my name in the credits, which initiated the first small breach in our relationship.

Charlie's Angels sparked what became known as TV's "jiggle" revolution. The focus shifted to Farrah because she made a sexy poster and didn't wear a bra. It wasn't planned; it was just Farrah. She didn't like bras. Kate Jackson was not pleased; had she gone braless no one would have noticed. It was a quirk of nature. I didn't have to exploit Farrah's braless look; the media did it for me—they couldn't help it. Farrah was a phenomenon. Kate blamed it on me. Tough. Farrah was my client and Kate was not. Her hostility toward me would simmer and finally boil over in the years to come. By the end of the first season, *People* featured Farrah as one of its Personalities of the Year and *Scholastic* magazine ranked her number one personal hero of high school students. (President Carter was number sixteen.)

Success, however, was not without its internal problems. Lee in particular was grumbling behind the scenes. While Farrah's career had taken off like a rocket, Lee's was becoming a spent bullet. *The Six Million Dollar Man* was on its last legs, and Lee resented that his wife was suddenly bigger than he was. When the final episode of *Charlie's Angels* aired May 22, 1977, everyone seemed to sigh with relief. Hiatus, that period of time between seasons, was welcomed by all. Lee and Farrah were going abroad. The Shah of Iran, whose son was a big fan of *The Six Million Dollar Man*, had extended a personal invitation.

Before they left, we attended the People's Choice Awards at the

Ambassador Hotel. Farrah had been chosen Best Female Newcomer and *Charlie's Angels* was selected as Favorite Television Drama. My date and I sat with Lee and Farrah and Aaron and Candy Spelling. At some point Aaron began table-hopping and Farrah went to the ladies' room. Candy was talking about all the fun things Aaron had in mind for the next season of *Charlie's Angels*. Lee interrupted her: "There's not going to be a next season, at least not for Farrah. She's not going back to the series." With that, he stood up and excused himself from the table.

"Candy, don't pay any attention to Lee," I said. "He's had too much to drink. He had eight beers. I counted them."

The next morning I went to Lee's office at Universal Studios. His mood had not changed. "The Fawcett-Majors family makes $55,000 a week, Jay, and $50,000 of it comes from me," he said. "When I get up in the morning, my wife is gone; when I come home at night, she's still on the set. That's not my idea of a marriage, and it's going to change."

Trying to dissuade him would have been a waste of time, but I needed a logical reason for Farrah's quitting the show. What was I going to tell the press? Lee had the answer.

Farrah had been working on a handshake agreement, which was common in Hollywood. Spelling-Goldberg was selling tons of commercial products based on the *Charlie's Angels* characters: mugs, dolls, T-shirts, lunch pails and a host of other items. They were paying the actresses 2.5 percent, a standard fee. Farrah had wanted a bigger cut, based upon her poster deal, from which she received 10 percent. That was our angle—Farrah did not have a signed contract with Spelling-Goldberg. Most important, it was legitimate. Farrah had approached Aaron many times, requesting a renegotiation, but he had always ignored her.

Lee had thought things out carefully. "When I hired you, Jay, it was with the understanding that the star is never the villain," he said. "The manager takes the blame, and that's what I want you to do now. I want you to take the heat. That's what I'm paying you for."

I left his office in a fog. Lee was pulling the plug on Farrah and *Charlie's Angels*, and Good Soldier Jay was going to be blamed for it. It was a stupid move on Lee's part, but he was hell-bent. He wanted Farrah home, not on a studio set nine months out of the year. What he didn't realize was how stubbornly the Farrah Fawcett myth had taken hold, not only with the public but also with Farrah. After tasting celebrity, it would not be easy for her to give it up. It was human nature.

At the moment, I had to figure out a way to reduce the impact Lee's decision would make on the industry. This wouldn't be easy. You didn't just walk off a major television show. *Charlie's Angels* would no doubt continue without Farrah, but Spelling and Goldberg would not sit back and let an actor walk away from a series with impunity. They had to protect their turf, and I knew they would.

I called Aaron. He offered to renegotiate her salary.

"That's not the problem, Aaron. Farrah doesn't want to be in *Charlie's Angels* anymore. She's quitting."

"She can't quit," he responded. "She has an agreement with us."

"That's the problem. It's not in writing."

"Bullshit. A handshake agreement is valid."

"Aaron, you know that Lee and Farrah are not satisfied with the commission you're paying for merchandising products using her name and image. They don't agree with you, never did. There's no contract there."

"We have a verbal agreement."

"Farrah doesn't think so. Lee doesn't think so. And their lawyer doesn't think so."

A pause, and then Aaron said, "You know the park across from the Beverly Hills Hotel? Meet me there in thirty minutes."

We hung up. I went into my James Bond mode and had Jack, my chauffeur, drive me to the park. Aaron was waiting. His limousine was at the curb and he was sitting on a bench, his chauffeur standing alongside him like a bodyguard. Aaron and I shook hands.

"You won't mind if Roger frisks you for a wire, will you?"

I laughed. "Are you serious?"

He was. I let Roger frisk me, and then, like an undercover cop in a Spelling-Goldberg TV production, I turned to Jack and said, "Frisk Aaron, will you, Jack?"

Aaron raised his arms; Jack ran his hands up and down his body.

Acknowledging to each other that we were free of wires, Aaron and I sat down. Jack and Roger went back to their respective limousines and stood at attention.

"Have you thought about this seriously?" Aaron asked rhetorically. "If Farrah walks, you're going to lose your place at the table. You and Farrah will never work in this town again."

"She's walking, Aaron. There's nothing either of us can do about it."

"If it's money, we can negotiate."

"It's not money."

"Then what the hell is it?"

"She doesn't want to be an Angel anymore."

The conversation was over. Aaron stood. "Actors don't break contracts with Spelling-Goldberg with impunity, Jay."

"Farrah doesn't have a contract to break."

We left. I felt empty. It was a shame, because I sensed that Aaron had been willing to give Farrah the moon and all its cheese. How far he would go with his threats, I didn't know. But I knew Aaron, and he would not lie dormant. Not only was Farrah's career at risk, but mine, too. Aaron and I were playing hardball again.

The first episode of the second season of *Charlie's Angels* was scheduled to go into production June 1. Everyone was on pins and needles, except Farrah. Spelling and Goldberg thought she would show up after all. Maybe I did too. Farrah had always seemed remote from business, as opposed to work, as if it were something that flew over her head. "Are you sure this is what you want to do?" I asked.

She answered sharply. "I don't have a contract with them, Jay. I never had a contract with them. Every time I told them what I wanted, they ignored me. No contract, no Farrah."

This was a side of her I'd never seen. She was more in tune with the business end of show business than I had realized. She didn't show up. What many people thought was a bluff turned out to be real.

"It's not about money anymore, Jay," she said. "If it was about money, I'd let you make a deal with them. It's about time now. Get me a movie role that only takes eight weeks."

It was really about Lee. Farrah wasn't unhappy with the show; she was unhappy because Lee was unhappy. She didn't want to argue with him anymore.

Production halted on *Charlie's Angels*. Spelling-Goldberg filed a $7 million breach-of-contract suit against Farrah. Through their lawyers we were further notified that Spelling-Goldberg would seek a court injunction to prevent Farrah from taking other acting jobs until the suit was resolved.

"Jay," said Lee, "we're leaving this in your and our attorney's hands," and he and Farrah took off for Iran.

Suddenly I was alone, really alone. I was persona non grata at Twentieth Century-Fox and ABC; no one would return my calls. The word was out that anyone, producer or studio executive, who appeared to be cooperating with Farrah might become entangled in a legal suit for abetting her leaving *Charlie's Angels*. Aaron was using the tried-and-true means of the Hollywood blacklist, a tool that had served to destroy many careers in the past. Hardball. I exercised my throwing arm. I was one lone man against a powerful production entity and the number one network in the nation. I began to plot ways to outwit them.

Quitting the show didn't remotely dampen my ability to keep Farrah's name and image in the news; rather, it enhanced it. The June issue of *New Times* magazine ran a cover headline that read: "Absolutely Nothing in This Issue about Farrah Fawcett-Majors."

Within days of Farrah and Lee leaving, however, I felt the jaws of the pincer pressing harder. When ABC threatened to pull all its productions from the Paramount lot, the studio was suddenly no longer interested in Farrah starring in *Foul Play*. Goldie Hawn was cast. MGM rejected her for *Coma*, replacing Farrah with Geneviève Bujold. Hollywood had seven major studios, but not one was willing to talk with me about casting Farrah in a movie, even though she was the hottest item in America. I began to look for independent financiers.

Farrah and Lee had been abroad ten days when I received a telephone call from a friend who wrote for the *Star*—Robin Leach, later of television fame. When Robin called, it usually meant trouble. "Jay, you should know this," he said confidentially. "The *New York Post* is coming out with a cover story next week that identifies Farrah as having been arrested and convicted of shoplifting."

I thought I knew everything about Farrah, but this was something new. As the alleged facts unfolded, it wasn't a pretty story. A few years before, Farrah had been accused of stealing a dress from an upscale boutique in Century City. She had gone to court and been found guilty, although her penalty was essentially a reprimand. Two days after her court appearance, she had been caught stealing another dress at the same store. This time the judge gave her a choice of sentence: jail or psychiatric treatment.

Farrah and Lee were unreachable. I tried to get through to them at the Shah's palace in Tehran, to no avail. I had to act. I had no knowledge of what had really happened, but I knew Farrah was not a thief. So I did what I had done on other occasions: I made up a story. The important element of damage control, which all good politicians realize, is to counter bad publicity with a plausible rebuttal.

Here was my refutation: Farrah was a young model starting her career. She managed to obtain a photo shoot but didn't have an appropriate dress to wear. She went to a store in Century City, bought a dress on sale and took it home, only to find that it was ripped. When she took it back, the store clerk would not let her exchange it because it was a sale item. Farrah argued, but the clerk was adamant: "No exchanges or refunds for sale items." Angry and desperate to make the photo shoot, Farrah went to a rack, took a new dress without a rip in it and left the store. As a result, she was arrested, charged and found guilty in criminal court.

This was during the time of massive protests and confrontations with authorities across the country, particularly at Berkeley, where Jane Fonda was making headlines in her fight against the "establishment." Farrah, incensed over being convicted for something she did not think she was guilty of doing, went back to the store after her trial and took another dress in plain view of the clerk in a defiant demonstration of her outrage. As a consequence, she was arrested again.

When she appeared before the same judge, she challenged the authority of the store—after all, she had paid for the original dress, only to find it ripped—but the judge didn't buy her youthful if misguided defense. "You're not Jane Fonda," he told her, "and if you were, you'd get the same sentence."

I gave my version of Farrah's story to the Associated Press. By the time the *Post* came out Monday, it was an old story with a plausible explanation. It was one of the few times a tabloid cover featuring Farrah's photograph did not increase sales. People looked at it and said, "I already know that story," and passed.

I never did ask Farrah the true story, which was probably more plausible than the one I had invented. After her second court appearance, incidentally, she chose psychiatric treatment.

Chapter 12

BLACKBALLED

Being blacklisted hurt me more emotionally than it did professionally. I had no doubt that I, and therefore Farrah and my other clients, would continue to function as viable and profitable entities. I had overcome barriers all my life. It was a matter of out-thinking my opposition, of being more creative. But for a man who had come to Hollywood wanting to be accepted, it was a low blow. It buckled me.

My girlfriend and I were having dinner at the Bistro; the chatter and noise were incessant. Usually, you could hardly hear the conversation at your own table, much less that of others. Yet I kept hearing the word *Bernstein* lift out of the cacophony like a four-letter refrain. At first I thought it was my imagination. As I listened more closely, however, I realized it was real.

At last, at a table from which my name was obviously emanating, I saw a man stand and wobble toward me like a big, fat goose. I did not know him personally, but I knew him by sight and reputation. He was a line producer at ABC and he was obnoxiously drunk. He approached, red-faced and glassy-eyed, his arms swinging apelike. Behind him, I saw two other men push back from his table and stand, as if to serve as stunt doubles if required.

"You're shit in this town, Bernstein," said the man as he wobbled to a stop.

"Perhaps," I said, "but you're shit-faced."

"You're just another Sammy Glick Jew," he slurred, referring to the unsavory antihero of Budd Schulberg's famous Hollywood novel, *What Makes Sammy Run?*

I stood. He took a couple of steps back. "If you want to go outside, let's go," I said. "But remember this: you're going to have to kill me, because if you don't, I'm certainly going to kill you."

He didn't want to go outside. "You fuckin' Glick-assed Jew," he said, and then he wheeled and went back to his table.

The incident was my first but not my last confrontation. It really had nothing to do with Aaron Spelling; it had everything to do, however, with my tactics, or what was presumed to be my tactics. Hollywood had more braves than chiefs, but every brave wanted to ascend to chiefdom. Most were a feather short.

If intimidation was the new modus operandi, then it was best for me to be seen as the intimidator rather than the intimidated. Since Hollywood wasn't the popularity contest I once thought it was, I decided to make a personal transformation. The next time someone threatened me in public, I wanted him to be aware of the possible consequence.

I was prone to accidents, probably because I was a daredevil. I had three walking sticks given to me in succession by Sammy Davis, Jr., George Peppard and Lee Majors after I suffered injuries skiing, mountain climbing and hunting. I began to carry one (eventually I collected four hundred of them) wherever I went. I told friends my stick was an affectation, but in reality it was a weapon. I grew a beard—not a Papa Hemingway bush, but a neatly trimmed hirsute cover that lent my face a hint of danger. I started dressing in black: black coat, black shirt, black pants. I didn't wear a hat, but I was copying the look of the bad guys in the old Saturday-afternoon matinees. Sometimes, depending on where I was going, I carried my .38 in a shoulder holster, often pulling my coat back so the weapon could be seen. I wanted my enemies, and the enemies of my clients, real, imagined or potential, to think twice before they tangled with me. I wanted them to fear me, and they did.

I pursued Kristy McNichol's career with the same diligence and vigor I gave to Farrah's and Suzanne's. With Kristy, however, it was easier. She was a natural actor, and her contract with ABC allowed her to work during hiatus with no restrictions. Diane Berkeley was in charge of NBC's movies for television. I went to see her. "Kristy McNichol is happening," I told her. "Why don't we find a TV movie for her?"

We did. It was *Summer of My German Soldier*, a love story between a Jewish American teenager and a Nazi soldier incarcerated in the South during World War II. It was a perfect vehicle for Kristy. I put together a tentative package and took it back to NBC. They bought it.

The movie was a successful showcase that received a high rating. With the Emmys coming up, I initiated a campaign for Kristy. She won not one but two Emmy statuettes. She won for *Summer of My German Soldier* and for her ongoing role in *Family*. We were on a roll.

Carollyne McNichol wanted more. She drove me nuts. She was as relentless as Suzanne Somers, although I don't ever remember her coming to the office. It was always telephone calls, a dozen a day. I didn't have time to answer them. One time she tracked me down at the Polo Lounge. "You've got to do something for Kristy," she said gravely.

Kristy's career was in excellent shape, but Carollyne was a stage mom, afraid it would suddenly be over.

Things in Hollywood often connect when you aren't expecting it. I was having lunch with Larry Gordon, the same Larry Gordon who fetched me a Coca-Cola the first time I met Aaron Spelling. Now he was a motion-picture producer of note, who later became bigger than a note. He was prepping a Burt Reynolds vehicle called *The End*, a black comedy about a dying man who wants to commit suicide.

"How's your movie coming along?" I asked.

Larry was a Mississippian with a heavy southern accent. "Purty well," he answered, "except I cain't find the gull to play But's dawter."

"How old is the daughter?"

"She's uh teenager."

"I've got her," I said. "Kristy McNichol, one of the kids in *Family*."

By the time I left, Kristy had the part. I don't think she even had to read for it.

Next, trying to capitalize on Brooke Shields' *Blue Lagoon* success, I put Kristy in a similar project with Chris Atkin. It was a so-so script, but Kristy and her mother wanted to make some money. She was doing movies, and she was hot.

When Farrah and Lee returned from abroad, Lee wanted me to go on a jaguar safari in Nicaragua. It didn't make sense because the country was on the brink of revolution; also, I didn't have time. Lee was threateningly persuasive, however, and I was forced to buy the plan. Farrah was smart; she stayed in Bel Air.

Four men were in our party. We flew to Managua, and then drove into the hinterlands of a third-world country marked by its rough and angry terrain. Fortunately, all of our party had been inoculated, because deep in the jungle everyone we came across suffered from malaria.

We traveled by Land Rover, a cumbersome vehicle not adept at crossing swollen rivers. Our first barrier was a wide, rampaging waterway that appeared too deep and swift to cross, but we commandeered a raft large enough to ferry our vehicle. Following his instincts, Lee Majors became the stud of the group—the Six Million Dollar Man transformed into Jungle Jim.

We crossed the river and entered a torrential rainstorm. I crawled under a tarpaulin in the back of the vehicle until we made camp. I had been on a lot of hunting expeditions and enjoyed camping out, but we were ill-prepared for this excursion. We had hammocks that we tied between trees; they filled with water as the rain poured. A slight body movement would tilt the hammock and suddenly you were dumped into the swelling water and mud, wallowing and thrashing like a drowning man. It was miserable.

The second night I grew fed up with the rain. "Somebody owns this property," I said. We had a team of pack bearers, all of Spanish descent, none of whom could speak English. I asked in my broken Spanish if they knew of any houses in the area, and one of them volunteered to take me on a scouting trip. Four miles up the road, we came to a house in the middle of the jungle. It was the headquarters of a cattle ranch. The owner invited us to take shelter in his home.

We went back and got the rest of our group, but Lee wouldn't go in the house to meet the owner and his family. He was afraid they would recognize him from television. "I want to remain incognito," he said. We were in the middle of nowhere! He stayed in the truck, but the rest of us accepted the cattleman's generosity. About four in the morning, someone knocked on the door. It was Lee, with a sheepish expression. The patron invited him in and gave him a bed. He and his family didn't know Lee from Simón Bolívar. The next morning we were served pancakes as if we were at IHOP in West Hollywood.

Meanwhile, all the locals were talking about impending revolution, which made us uneasy. One night, the eleven natives who made up our pack bearers and kitchen crew disappeared. It was approaching dinnertime before we realized there was no activity at the camp kitchen. We called after them and scouted the property, but not one of the hired help was to be found.

We went into a defensive mode without even discussing the issue. Everyone just assumed we were in trouble, including me. It was as if we were in a Western movie, waiting to be attacked and killed by the Indians. We talked little, but the general feeling was the crew would come back with reinforcements to get our weapons. What would happen to us, we didn't know. It was dark and eerie, and we were hungry.

We still had a campfire. In the flickering light I saw a big black insect crawling on the ground. I said to one of the guys, "I'll bet a hundred bucks you won't cook that bug and eat it."

"Yes, I will," he answered.

"I'll take half of that bet," said Lee.

We grilled the bug in a frying pan. I lost the bet. Lee and the guy split it, as if they were eating a baby crab.

Their dinner added a moment of humor, but it did not dispel our fear of being attacked by rebels. The night grew deeper and darker. We didn't say much to each other, but we automatically assumed positions on the periphery of our camp, one man facing east, one west and so forth. No one took charge and hardly ten words were spoken after the bug was devoured, but we were ready to defend ourselves. We were four Texans at the Alamo.

The night was quiet, the only sound the occasional clicking of a rifle bolt. Then, after two or three hours, we heard noises approaching, as if Indians were preparing to attack. We waited in position, ready to fire at the first sign of assault.

Finally one of our lost crew came into the flickering light of the camp-fire, then another one. They were drunk, the whole lot. Much earlier, unbeknownst to us, one of them had taken the truck down the road and gotten a flat tire. When he didn't return, his fellow crewmen had gone looking for him. They found him at a Nicaraguan cantina in the boondocks.

The next morning I asked one of our guides how we were going to find jaguar in the middle of the jungle. He rubbed two sticks together and started some kind of voodoo talk. That was it for me. I didn't give a shit if I ever saw a jaguar. The others agreed.

When we returned to Managua, a local advertising company offered Lee $35,000 cash to do a beer commercial. Lee tried to up the price to $50,000; they passed. Later, we were sitting at the hotel pool. The same reps sent us a big tub of beer, which we took as a gesture of conciliation after Lee's business negotiation had collapsed.

After we returned to the States, someone called Lee and told him he was on Nicaraguan television every five minutes in a beer commercial. While we were sitting at the pool swigging beer, the advertising agency had filmed us with a telescopic lens. Lee wanted me to sue them. It was the one time I didn't take the heat; I had no idea how to sue a company in Central America.

The revolution started two weeks after we returned to California.

People thought I was sleeping with every woman I represented. I wasn't—with one exception. I slept with the beautiful British model-actress Charlotte Rampling when she was my houseguest for six months. To my chagrin, we never had sex, even though we shared the same bed.

It wasn't Charlotte's doing; it was mine. After she finished *Farewell,*

My Lovely with Robert Mitchum and John Ireland, she wanted to remain in California. She and Bryan Southcombe, her husband, had a big argument. She was staying; he was going back to England.

It was Bryan who made arrangements for her to stay with me. Before leaving, he said, "I trust you, Jay. You're a southern gentleman, and I expect you to honor your upbringing."

I did, although I let Charlotte move from a guest bedroom to mine. She didn't want to sleep alone. It went no further than that. I had given my word to Bryan.

"Oh, come on, Jay," Charlotte would say. "Surely you've been to bed with Farrah."

"No, I haven't," I told her. "I have a sense of honor with certain moral rules attached. I represent Farrah's husband as well as her. It would be wrong of me even to think about having sex with her."

"Oh, come on, Jay! There's got to be more to it than that!"

There was. Farrah was an athlete, and sex was not a spectator sport to her. I didn't want to be compared with Lee Majors or later Ryan O'Neal. Sex to Farrah was like gymnastics or tennis or jogging; she did it, and then it was done. "Jocks should be with jocks," I told Charlotte.

"What about Suzanne?"

"Sex is part of her spirituality. It's not a sport. I doubt if she's ever cheated on Alan. It's not her nature. Achievement, money and companionship—those are the driving forces behind Suzanne's psyche. She grew up differently from Farrah. Suzanne had nothing when she was growing up. Now that she has something, she wants to keep it."

Charlotte laughed. It seemed silly to her because she was a free spirit, a flower child of the sixties. I managed her career by day and slept with her by night. Not once did we have sex. When she returned to Europe, she divorced Bryan and married Jean Michel Jarre. That marriage didn't last either.

Farrah seemed unconcerned that we were blacklisted. When the Spelling-Goldberg suit was filed, she asked Charles Silverberg, her lawyer, "Can they take my home away from me?"

"No," said Silverberg.

"Then let Jay handle things," she said. "I have an appointment with my hairdresser."

We couldn't sit around and wait for a court to decide her future. If she wanted a career, she needed to stay in the game. I was counting on her competitive nature, the part of her that hated to lose. ABC didn't control the industry—they just thought they did. Spelling-Goldberg wasn't the only production company in the business; Aaron just thought it was. I burned up the phone lines looking for a movie for Farrah, but to no avail.

Then I got a call from Rudy Durand, an independent producer. It wasn't about Farrah. He'd just produced and directed *Tilt*, with Brooke Shields; he wanted me to launch the movie's release. "Mel Simon financed it," Rudy said. "He lives in Indianapolis and owns about a million shopping centers. Give me fifteen percent, and I'll help you get his account. I want you to work hard on *Tilt*, because Mel has lots of money and he's going to be making dozens of movies."

I checked out Mel Simon. He didn't own a million shopping centers, but he owned ninety, which was good enough for me. More important, he had opened an office in Los Angeles. He was in town.

I made an appointment with him. A New Yorker, he had found a home in Indianapolis via the army. Like me, he had been stationed at Fort Benjamin Harrison; but after his discharge, he remained. He got into the real estate business, and by 1977, his company owned over 12 million square feet of retail property in enclosed shopping malls.

We got on famously. When I pitched Farrah as a lead motion-picture actress he advanced me the money to find a script for her. Putting a deal together with Mel was crucial. His company was making motion pictures in volume, which would assure major distribution.

I also made a deal to publicize all of Mel's movies. It amounted to $115,000 per year, which was a good account. I called Rudy and gave him the news. His kickback would amount to $17,000 a year; not a bad profit for a single telephone call.

"But you've really got to publicize *Tilt*," he said.

"Don't worry, Rudy. That's my business."

Famous last words. When I screened *Tilt*, I couldn't figure it out. Brooke played a teenage pinball wizard traveling cross-country with a musician, challenging other pinball champions. It was weird. Rudy had crazy point-of-view camera angles from inside a pinball machine. It didn't make sense to me. I didn't think it was releasable.

Meanwhile I found a screenplay for Farrah, which was good news and bad news. The script originally was a vehicle for Woody Allen and Diane Keaton, written by Woody and Reginald Rose. That was good. It was in turnaround, and I bought it without reading it. That was bad. I thought, "If it's good enough for Allen and Keaton, it's good enough for us." It was one of many mistakes I made in launching Farrah's first picture.

Somebody Killed Her Husband was the story of a young woman whose husband is murdered. If she and her lover don't find the real killer, they'll be blamed. Its inherent problem was that Farrah would have to play against her image as a glamour girl.

If the story presented problems, the package didn't. Martin Poll, who had made the award-winning *A Lion in Winter* with Katharine Hepburn and Peter O'Toole, was brought in as producer, as well as a secondary financier to Mel and a third party. Lamont Johnson was hired as director. I negotiated $500,000 for Farrah, an unheard of sum for an actress who had never made a theatrical picture. The money was critical; it would motivate Lee to approve the deal, which he did. *Somebody Killed Her Husband* was set to begin production in December 1977.

Farrah was a dynamic commodity, regardless of being blacklisted. Harry Weiss said he had a deal for her. He was the lawyer who defended Peter Fonda during his marijuana trial. Harry was representing two entrepreneurs with an idea that would require Farrah's name. It sounded preposterous, but I'd just had a dream in which I became a billionaire from the proceeds of a crazy gimmick like the Pet Rock. Thus I met with Harry and his clients. One was a jeweler, Edwar Kalpakian; the other was Keith Gaede, of the wealthy Irvine family of Orange County.

Their idea was a gold pendulum the size of a pecan sculpted like an old-fashioned water faucet with a drop of gold water clinging to its spout.

Naturally, they wanted to call it the Farrah Fawcett Faucet. Absurd as it sounded, I did not dismiss the idea. I had another dream. It was about a huge tanker truck dispensing Farrah Fawcett Water through Farrah Fawcett Faucets.

When I told Farrah about the idea, she laughed nervously. "Jay, I can't do that!" Money was of less consequence to Farrah than her pride; she had done the poster, elevated to Fabergé, and now she wanted to be engaged in projects that commanded a modicum of respect.

Meanwhile, Weiss got in touch with Farrah's attorney. Harry's clients were willing to pay $200,000 cash for Farrah's endorsement and a piece of the action if she would promote the faucets on the independent television channels. Farrah asked me to deliver her answer: No.

I did, and I didn't. I told Weiss the deal wasn't big enough for Farrah to give it consideration. A couple of days later, Harry called me back. His clients would raise the advance to $500,000. A half-million dollars was nothing to sneeze at. I told Farrah; again she said no.

I still did not kill the deal. I told Harry his clients would have to start with a $750,000 figure before Farrah would consider it. He said he would get back to me. When he did, his clients had approved the new offer. Now I thought Farrah should give it consideration. Not too long before, she had been making $5,000 per episode on *Charlie's Angels*.

Farrah, too, found the idea less disrespectful than she had in the beginning. Personal integrity has a limit. We talked it over, and she decided to do it.

I went forward with a publicity campaign built around a contract ceremony for the Farrah Fawcett Faucet. Weiss and his clients wanted the signing to be held in Orange County. Farrah agreed to everything; all she had to do to pick up a quick $750,000 was show up, sign the contract and make a few television appearances. It seemed like manna from heaven.

The signing ceremony was scheduled for three p.m. on a given day. I was there; Harry and his clients were there; Peter Fonda was there with Miss Orange County; everybody of importance was there, except Farrah. At three twenty she paged me. "Jay, I'm sorry," she said nervously.

"Apologize to them. Tell them I just flew in. I'll be there as soon as possible."

On my way back to the delayed signing ceremony I had an idea. I tried my best to make my face grow ashen white. I drew Harry and his two principals into a corner. Each of them had a terribly anxious expression. "Listen, guys," I began with the saddest voice I could muster, "Farrah simply can't go through with this. She hates the idea of promoting a faucet on television, regardless of her being its namesake. She just won't do it."

The men looked at each other, desperate. "Is there anything we can do?"

I sighed. "If she doesn't have to personally promote the faucet, and if you'll raise her fee to a million dollars, I think I can talk her into it. But you'll have to trust me to persuade her. I can assure you that you can't."

They went to another corner, huddled in a brief powwow and came back. Harry spoke for them. "They feel they have no other choice," he said. "They'll do it."

"Trust me," I said. "If I don't persuade her, I'll resign as her manager."

"How are we going to promote it without Farrah?" they wanted to know.

"When she first came to Hollywood, she didn't have a job," I said. "Edwar was the only person who would help her. He gave her a job when she needed it. Now he comes to her with the faucet idea, and Farrah, being a Good Samaritan, wants to help him. That's your story. I'll even get her to give a Farrah Fawcett Faucet to Lee Majors. Maybe he'll wear it dangling from his six million dollar neck."

Farrah arrived; I drew her aside and explained the new deal, emphasizing that she would no longer have to promote the faucets. It went in one ear and out the other. I don't think she ever realized I had taken a $200,000 offer and jacked it up to $1 million solely for the use of her name.

I wasn't finished. I had no idea if the faucets would sell or not, but I was reasonably certain the investors, for all of their enthusiasm, would never profit enough to pay Farrah. I went back to them. "Farrah will sign the contract, but she wants you to place a letter of credit in a bank trust department from which she will draw $333,000 for the next three years." They agreed, hyped as they were on selling zillions of Farrah Fawcett Faucets.

The idea was good enough to get a *Cosmopolitan* cover. Then it started going south, although not so far and fast that Farrah didn't get one more perk. The guys made the faucets, at least a few thousand of them, and planned a big opening promotion party at the Bistro, one of Beverly Hills' upscale restaurants. When I told Farrah, she said, "I'm not going."

I called the guys back. They were flabbergasted that Farrah would not attend their kickoff party. "Look," I said, "Farrah's a businesswoman. Her time is valuable."

"Is there anything we can do?" they wanted to know.

"Well, she's been wanting a racquetball court at her house—"

"If you can get her to come to the party, we'll pay for it."

Farrah agreed. She came to the party and stayed fifteen minutes.

The bottom line: Farrah made a million dollars and got a new racquetball court for signing the contract and going to a party. The entrepreneurs sold maybe seventy Farrah Fawcett Faucets for a hundred dollars each. I got zero, since my contract excluded commission on merchandising deals.

A year or so later, Keith Gaede approached Farrah saying, "Please, you've got to let us out of this deal." Farrah's answer was decidedly no. Keith offered her jewels—diamonds, emeralds, sapphires, anything—if she would release him from the line of credit payments. "No way," said Farrah. People always underestimated her.

Chapter 13

DEMONS
AND ANGELS
ON TRIAL

Farrah did not see herself as an actress. From the outset, her acting career had been a lark, a reason to be in Hollywood. She had become a successful model, but her real forte was sports; she enjoyed nothing better than athletic competition. She couldn't stand to lose, at anything. I once saw her break a tennis racket against an iron railing because she lost a match. In lieu of acting classes, I thought, her competitiveness might serve as a surrogate.

When Martin Poll cast Jeff Bridges as Farrah's co-star in *Somebody Killed Her Husband*, I was pleased. Jeff was young, experienced, athletic and vigorous. He was also a good actor with two Oscar nominations behind him. I thought his professionalism might motivate Farrah to excel, just as sports did. Jeff would bring her acting up to par because Farrah would work hard to compete with him.

In December, Farrah and I went to New York to begin filming. Lee remained in Hollywood, finishing his last season of *The Six Million Dollar Man*. He would wrap in March, a few days after we finished production.

So far, we had defied Spelling-Goldberg and ABC. We were doing precisely what they had tried to keep us from doing: making a movie. It was apparent the minute we landed at Kennedy International that Farrah's reputation with the public could not be reversed by a lawsuit in California. She was a national celebrity. Farrah-mania had taken even stronger root and amazingly was still growing. No matter where we went, crowds clamored to be near her. We had to hire an army of bodyguards. She was iconic—the stylish hair, the natural smile, the beautiful eyes. If she could only act . . .

We'd hardly begun production when Fabergé executives came calling. They wanted Farrah for a promotion in Chicago. They didn't give a damn about the movie—Farrah Fawcett Fabergé Shampoo was more important. She went to Chicago on a weekend; when she returned, she was dead tired.

Then Fabergé executives came again. They were like a smug army in Givenchy suits, all but Richard Barrie. It was apparent, at least to me, that Richard was enamored of Farrah. That was okay, but there weren't going to be any more weekends in Chicago, or anyplace else. Farrah had a movie to make, and, with the exception of Richard, I barred Fabergé reps from the set. It wasn't good public relations, but I felt it had to be done.

Fabergé was only one problem. Lamont Johnson, Farrah's director, was one of those millions of men who became infatuated with her. I don't know exactly what happened because I wasn't there, but Farrah told me he cornered her and tried to stick his tongue down her throat. Being rejected by his star hurt the director's feelings, which meant he would probably try to get revenge. He did, near the end of the shoot. I was in my hotel suite when Farrah called me. She was in tears. "Jay, I need you!" she cried. "This man is trying to humiliate me!"

In the midst of a scene that required Farrah to climb up a wall, Johnson started screaming directions at her as if she were a moron. Finally he yanked her down a ladder, dragged her to a room just off the set and chastised her so-called incompetence for the benefit of the cast and crew who were waiting outside the door. Macho man!

Five minutes later, I walked on the set. I think it was at Macy's Department Store. Farrah was two floorless floors above, climbing a lattice wall, and Johnson was screaming at her again.

"Cut!" I yelled. Everybody looked at me, including Johnson. Suddenly our roles were reversed. Now I was the one who was intimidating. I waved my walking stick and got in the director's face. "Listen, you sonuvabitch! Don't you ever fucking yell at her again!"

Lamont was speechless. He had to eat crow because he was afraid I'd cane him if he didn't. I finished my tirade, asked Farrah if she was okay and then left the set as abruptly as I had arrived. She had no more problems with her director.

There were other problems, however, that were in my exclusive domain. When I made the deal for *Somebody Killed Her Husband*, I was naïve. I had put together many television projects, but movie contracts were different. I was no longer dealing with a barrage of network legal technicians who did virtually the same deal day after day. I was negotiating now with two or three individuals and their lawyers who were intent on making a bundle of money in one fell swoop. On the surface everything seemed okay. I asked for $500,000 for Farrah, and got it. I wanted a summer release for the movie, and that was fine with them too, or so I thought.

Halfway through the production schedule, Columbia, with whom Simon's company had negotiated a distribution deal, said, "We have good news. We have a release date in October."

October? I had been promised the summer. Teenagers, the core of our principal market, didn't go to the movies in October. They went in June, July and August; the demographics showed it. When I complained, I received a breath of foul air: "A summer release is not in the contract; if it's not in the contract, it doesn't exist. Read your contract."

I read the contract; it was all about money. I read it again. I reread it for days. Three key words were missing: *to be released*. While their absence echoed in my brain, I picked up on another phrase, this one in black and white: "*Somebody Killed Her Husband* shall be Farrah Fawcett-Majors' first filmed motion picture." Farrah had guaranteed that *Husband* would be her first *produced* movie, but the contract said nothing about it being her first *released* movie. I wondered if I could squeeze another production into Farrah's schedule and get it cut, edited and scored before October.

I called Elliott Kastner, a friend who had produced *Where Eagles Dare*, *Harper*, and *Farewell, My Lovely*. Elliott had a mixed bag of successes and failures, but he always had a project in the hopper. "Elliott," I asked, "how would you like to make Farrah Fawcett's first released movie?"

"Come on, Jay." He laughed. "She's filming right down the street as we speak."

I explained my dilemma and the facts of the contract, which said nothing about Farrah's second production being released before her first production. "How would you like to have her first released movie?" I asked again. "The Cannes Film Festival is three months away. You can sell it sight unseen if you can guarantee me a late-summer release date."

He had a shooting script with Richard Harris attached to it, a detective story. If Farrah liked it, she could have the female lead, which would require three weeks' work. We negotiated a tentative deal giving Farrah $200,000 per week, a total of $600,000—$100,000 more than she was making from *Husband*. I told Elliott I needed seventy-two hours to think about it.

The potential deal with Elliott was strong enough for me to call a meeting with the principal moneymen of *Husband*. It took place in an eighth-floor suite at the Manhattan hotel where Mel Simon was staying. With Mel were Martin Poll and Skip Brittenham. After the usual amenities, I told my story, namely that I was going to make another picture with Farrah and release it in advance of *Somebody Killed Her Husband*.

"You can't do that!" one of them said.

"Read the contract," I responded. "It specifies that *Husband* is Farrah's first produced picture. It doesn't say it will be her first released picture."

When it dawned on them that I was not only serious but firmly intent on getting Farrah's second produced picture in release before her first produced picture, one of them climbed into an open window and threatened to leap eight stories to his death. "I'll be ruined," he screamed.

"Tough shit," I said. "Read the contract."

Anger became frustration. If I beat them to the punch, they might be in deep trouble. Everything hinged on Farrah's first released movie. If it failed, what could one expect from a second movie in October? I was Jesse James holding a loaded gun to their temples.

"Jay, you can't do this to us," was their constant refrain.

Finally I reneged on the Kastner deal. First, he wasn't sure he could get a picture in the can for a late-summer release, and I wasn't certain he could either. Second, my overriding concern was for the men I was fighting with. When I had first sought a movie deal for Farrah, I found no takers. Then Mel Simon came along, and he, with his partners, put up the money. I didn't feel comfortable stabbing them in the back, although I was still unhappy about the October release. "If I forget the Kastner deal," I told them, "it will cost Farrah $600,000."

They offered to raise her pay from $500,000 to $750,000, plus a "best effort" promise to try to get a summer release rather than October. Farrah's new salary was retroactive, which meant her pay was increased 50 percent. It gave me leverage in negotiating her next movie. I ended up doing three movies with Farrah, and she received $750,000 for each.

When I told Farrah I had negotiated a quarter-of-a-million-dollar increase in her pay, she was lackluster. "Oh, how nice," she said. I was not surprised. I had learned to accept praise from only myself when I did something important—"Attaboy, Jay!" I would tell myself. "You did a good job!"—because praise seldom, if ever, came from the client who benefited from my skills.

Husband wrapped. On the plane home I told Farrah I would have another picture for her before year's end.

"I can't do another one, Jay. I'm having too much trouble with Lee."

"What do you mean?"

"Lee says *he* should be doing movies, and I should be home playing the wife."

Life was in the midst of one of its reversals. When I got involved with the Majors, Farrah was a housewife who dabbled in acting. Her first episodic television role as the second-billed Charlie's Angel brought her a drop in the bucket compared to Lee's salary. Now he was bombarding her with an old but true story: "I never see you anymore. I want a wife, not a star." They were involved in a Hollywood conundrum that was usually insoluble.

I stared at Farrah. We were midstream, and it was a little late to change horses.

"He's jealous of my success," she continued. "I went through this with him on *Charlie's Angels*, and I don't want to do it again. I don't want to fight with Lee."

"So what's the bottom line, Farrah?"

"Unless you can get Lee some movies, too, I can't do any more. I don't want to continue."

I whistled under my breath. It wasn't a sigh; it was a reaction to being hit by a bolt of lightning. But that was Farrah. She wasn't naïve; she knew how to use leverage to get what she wanted. What she wanted was to rid herself of Lee's professional jealousy.

"Lee hasn't done a theatrical movie in years!" I countered.

"I don't care," she said. "Either get him a movie, or don't expect me to work anymore."

Enter Charles B. Pierce, an independent producer, director and writer with the credentials of a sleight-of-hand artist. Pierce was one of those rare creatures in Hollywood—a dreamer with a track record. He wasn't an amateur, but he was close to it. An Arkansan, Charlie had made what amounted to a home docudrama about sightings of a swamp monster back home in Wal-Mart country. It was a modest effort that catapulted box-office returns into the sky above drive-in theaters. *The Legend of Boggy Creek* had given Charlie the financial wherewithal to pursue other film projects, most dealing with history. By the time I ran into him, his next rendezvous was with the first Vikings in America.

"Why don't you cast Lee Majors as your lead?" I suggested.

Charlie thought Lee would be perfect, which didn't surprise me. What did surprise me was the $400,000 plus 10 percent of the gross that Charlie was willing to give up to get him. What surprised me further was that Lee was willing to take the deal and wear a Viking costume. I whistled under my breath again.

The Norseman was a piece of shit, and I knew it. But Farrah had laid down the terms—if I didn't get Lee a picture, she wouldn't work anymore. It wasn't that I didn't want to get Lee a good picture, it was that I couldn't. Until the lawsuit with Spelling-Goldberg was settled, Lee's name in the mainstream industry was as anathema as Farrah's. Of course, I didn't tell Lee what I thought of the script; I would let him figure it out for himself.

If he ever realized it was a clinker, he didn't show it. The $400,000 was more important to him.

As usual, I saw an opportunity to put some of my other clients to work. With Pierce's approval, I did most of the casting. I didn't know if Susie Coelho could act, but the story had an Indian girl who could neither speak nor hear. I put Susie in the role. One day I ran into Cornel Wilde, who had just written his autobiography. He said he would sell a copy to me for one dollar if I would put out a news release saying I'd read it. I gave him a buck and signed him up to do the movie. Then I got Mel Ferrer, Audrey Hepburn's husband, who I hadn't seen since back in my Las Vegas days in the early sixties. It was a good cast. The only problem was the script.

I threw a dinner party. Among my guests were a dangerous cast of characters, prominent among them Lee Majors and Robert Lecky. Lecky was in charge of development for Simon Productions. I don't remember all the guests, but I know Brenda and Mel Simon were there, and of course Farrah, so on the surface it was a friendly gathering. The crux of what was to come was over a Mel Simon movie that Lee had wanted to star in. Lecky had turned him down because he didn't think Lee's acting style projected enough emotion for the lead character.

Cut to after dinner. We'd drunk a lot of wine; the dinner plates had been removed. We were ready for brandy and coffee. Voices were low, conversations having come down to one-on-one between persons sitting beside each other. Suddenly the mood was broken: "You sonuvabitch!"

It was Lee, who had been talking to Lecky. Now he wasn't talking. He was raving, cursing, bemoaning what he thought of Lecky for having rejected him for the past movie role. Everyone looked, all equally stunned, but it was Bob Lecky who was frightened, his eyes wide, frozen in their sockets, his body stiff as the chair he sat on.

Lee leaped up, his face red with anger. He began to flail his arms and swing his fists as if he were going to roundhouse Lecky. He ranted; he raved; he grabbed the window curtains, and, like the Burt Young character in *Chinatown* who began to thrash in the Venetian blinds when

Jack Nicholson showed him compromising pictures of his wife with another man, Lee looked like he was going to eat them. The rest of us were speechless.

"You turned me down, you sonuvabitch!" Lee shouted, and suddenly I realized what his rage was about. I poised to interject myself between Lee and Bob before Lee swung a blow. I wasn't going to let a guest get injured, which all of us were certain would happen. Then Lee let out a wild, maniacal yell, chicken-flopped his arms a couple of times, spun around to face Bob, smiled like a hyena and said calmly, "Is that enough emotion for you, Lecky?"

The Spelling-Goldberg-ABC civil suit lingered in the background during the filming of *Husband*. A trial had been scheduled, postponed and rescheduled. Farrah's lawyer was always skirmishing, trying to outflank the corporate crowd. To me, it was like a stay of execution. I saw it in Biblical terms. When the final scene was finished in New York, it was a slingshot victory, but only a thump on Goliath's nose. We had done what Aaron didn't want us to do: make a motion picture independent of his company. We had won a battle, but the war continued. The trial was reset for April in Los Angeles Superior Court.

Farrah was briefed and prepped. Her legion of fans held vigil outside the courthouse; dozens more were in the courtroom. The press made up two phalanxes of combatants: one for Farrah, one for corporate America. I was surprised by some of their stances. Wrote journalist Vernon Scott: "Pity the poor television producers who build hit shows with non-stars only to discover they have created monsters who not only bite the hand that feeds them but devour everything in sight."

Every action stems from a point of view. That's why education is important. If you understand the other person's perspective, you can develop tactics and strategize accordingly. I couldn't figure Scott. Reporters usually sided with the underdog, knowing their own shoe leather was expended primarily for the benefit of their publisher. Scott's attitude made me nervous; I respected him as a journalist.

Farrah played cute and coy on the stand. I watched the jurors. They were faceless, wearing masks that hid their emotions. Aaron could win; we could win. I had no idea; Silverstein had no idea. I cringed every time my name was mentioned. Courtroom dialogue never expresses the truth on either side—it is manipulative, designed to distort. I decided to take a shot at winning without conferring with anybody, including Farrah's lawyer.

The trial was in its fourth day. It was going nowhere and getting nastier as it advanced into the void. By law the two sides were obligated to hold a settlement conference. I sent word secretly to Aaron's lawyers that I wanted to talk. Whether I had that authority made no difference to me. Something had to be done. The courtroom dramatics had become a pissing contest, the lawyers urinating on each other.

Later, I was in the men's room taking a leak. I looked over my shoulder and saw Aaron's lawyers surrounding me in a semicircle, like three linebackers waiting for the ball to be snapped. I didn't have anything against these guys, but I thought this was a little much, circling the wagons in the men's room. But this was life and death, David versus Goliath. I zipped up, turned to them and swung my walking stick as a gesture of contempt.

"Here's what I want you to tell Aaron," I said. "It's no longer about Farrah. It's about me. You want a settlement, but you haven't offered me anything. You can't stop me from making a living; I'm too smart for you. You can't threaten me, because I don't give a shit. You can't keep my kids from going to Buckley School, because I don't have any kids. You can't keep my wife from joining share, because I don't have a wife. To stop me, you have to kill me. It's that simple, because if you don't kill me, you won't stop me."

They looked at each other, confused, because they had no one else to go to. If a deal were to be struck, it had to be struck with me. I left them standing in my wake.

The next day, I got a call. "What kind of settlement is Farrah willing to negotiate?"

"She's not negotiating anything," I said. "Farrah's not going back to *Charlie's Angels* as a regular, ever. But she's willing to do three episodes per year for two years at $100,000 an episode. Six cameos, $600,000.

Aaron wins; we win. The amount of Farrah's compensation will be kept under lock and key. That's it. You can take it or you leave it."

That afternoon the settlement came to fruition. The trial was dismissed. Farrah was an Angel again. Who won? Obviously, Farrah did, although Aaron gloated that he did. That was okay with me.

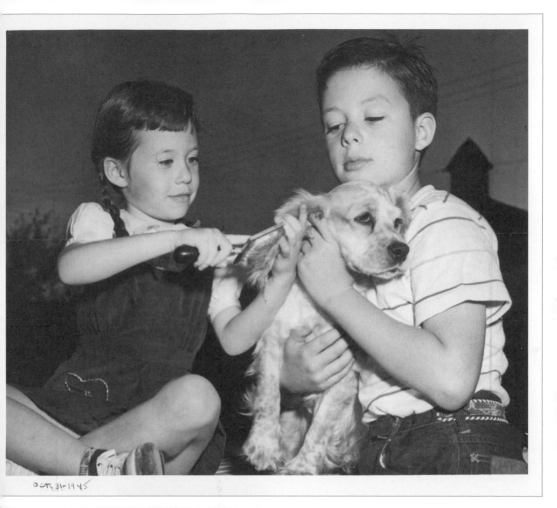

^ Jay and his sister Jan prettying up their dog for the camera. (COURTESY BERNSTEIN FAMILY)

< In uniform in the early 1960s. (COURTESY BERNSTEIN FAMILY)

^ (clockwise from top) Sammy Davis Jr., Peter Lawford, Dean Martin, and Frank Sinatra in *Sergeants 3*. (© UNITED ARTISTS/PHOTOFEST)

< Jay in his teen years. (COURTESY BERNSTEIN FAMILY)

Jay Bernstein
PRODUCER / DIRECTOR

^ Jay, with his signature cane in hand, and Mickey Spillane at the wrap party for *Murder Me, Murder You* in Beverly Hills. (RON GALELLA/WIREIMAGE)

^ Stacy Keach as Mike Hammer. (CBS PHOTO ARCHIVE/GETTY IMAGES)

< Jay Bernstein, with Mary Frann in 1987, behind the scenes of *The New Mike Hammer*. (© CBS/PHOTOFEST)

^ Jay and Farrah. (PETER BORSARI)
<

^ The best Christmas present a boy could receive in 1976. (CURTIS D. TUCKER/ANN TUCKER)

^ Jay with Linda Evans.
(PETER BORSARI)

< Suzanne Somers in 1977.
(HARRY LANGDON)

Chapter 14

SUPER STARLETS:
FARRAH AND SUZANNE

With the trial behind us, and Lee on location in Florida filming *The Norseman*, Farrah and I went to Cannes. Mel Simon's people had arranged for *Husband* to be screened in France, although it wasn't in the competition. The idea was to sell the movie to distributors and expose Farrah to the world as a big-screen actress. I had never been to the festival. I haven't been back since; a return would have been anticlimactic.

Farrah was a model turned television actress turned celebrity star turned phenomenon. She was the festival's biggest attraction since Brigitte Bardot in 1956. It took us three hours to get through the crowd at Nice. Then we motored to Cannes, where we drove through backstreets and alleys until we arrived at a small villa in a clump of villas in the hills above the town. Mel had taken care of everything, which included five security guards for Farrah.

I don't remember the exact schedule—it was five days of hectic activity—but before we arrived in Cannes proper, we went to a party on Stavros Niarchos's yacht. I had met Niarchos in Africa with Bill Holden and I would meet him a third time with Suzanne Somers. His yacht was spectacular, so big that a helicopter sitting on its pad looked like a speck. It was a floating hotel laden with art, including the famous Andy Warhol painting of Elvis Presley hanging over Stavros's screening-room door. Unfortunately, Farrah became seasick.

With rare exception, I did not get involved romantically with clients. I had not lied to Charlotte Rampling, but Cannes was different. It was so romantic in the hills overlooking the city that I considered making a play for Farrah. We had our own little villa with a fireplace and candles flickering like fireflies in the night. As I watched her glide about, I could hardly keep myself at bay. At last, however, my head won out over my heart. I refrained from making a move because I wanted Farrah to continue thinking I was the smartest person alive. If I made a move and failed (and I'm sure I would have), I would be reduced in her eyes to a stupid dreamer.

Being at Cannes meant you had to attend a screening at the Palais des Festivals. We were told explicitly, "If Farrah doesn't go to the Palais, we will never show a film of hers, ever."

It was not an idle threat. An official said, "Raquel Welch didn't go, and her films were thereafter barred." It was tacit, but a law nevertheless. When you accept the invitation, you are expected to participate. We went to the Palais.

I don't remember what was being screened; it made no difference. I should have realized something eventful was on the horizon from the elaborate planning that went into our traffic route. We changed cars four times, so we wouldn't be followed.

We drove first to the Carlton Hotel, where Mel's people had reserved a suite of rooms. While Farrah was getting ready, I went to the casino to rid myself of some money. As I was returning to Farrah's suite, I ran into Robin Leach and invited him to join us.

The invitation was a mistake. When Farrah saw Robin, she picked up the only handy item (a banana, fortunately) and threw it. Bingo! She hit him in the forehead. Then she began to curse him for a story he had written in the *Star*. The incident presaged a night of horrors.

Finally we went to the theater. Thousands were waiting on the sidewalk and street in front of the Palais. José Eber, Farrah's hairdresser, was with us. He was so intimidated that he wouldn't get out of the limousine: "It's too dangerous!"

I looked at Farrah. Fear was written on her face too. But we had to make an appearance, so I edged the door open. The crowd fell back, and I helped Farrah out. We took only two steps before the crowd swarmed us like bees at a hive. Frantic, Farrah turned back to the limousine. "Oh, my God!" she cried. "It's gone!"

It wasn't. The throng that encircled us camouflaged it. We had been promised police protection, but the cops seemed scant. In fact, the entire Cannes force was on duty, all seventy-eight of them! The horde was simply too great for the meager force to contain, although they tried gallantly.

We edged toward the theater like snails. Somehow the police formed a cordon around us. Behind them were the paparazzi, and behind the photographers were the fans, thousands from around the globe, pressing toward us. When we reached the steps leading up to the theater, I thought we were home free. Then it happened. The crowd surged, the paparazzi fell forward, and the police line broke. Tiers of people began to fall upon each other, pushed by the weight of the crowd behind them. A vise was closing. I tried to shield Farrah with my body, and was hit in the head by a camera. It was scary, like a scene from *The Day of the Locust*.

At last the cops managed to form a line in front of us and a line behind us, moving us inch by inch until we reached an elevator. The door opened and they shoved us in. We stayed caged until they cleared the gallery of spectators from the actual theater entrance; then they came for us and escorted us into the lobby of the Palais.

During the screening I made arrangements for us to exit the theater through a back door. For once the festival officials didn't stick to protocol. They agreed, and we had a heavy police escort back to the Carlton.

The next day a police captain came to see me. "Please, we hope you won't say anything about the incident last night," he said.

I had no intention of saying anything, but I was surprised to be sought out, considering that hundreds of journalists and photographers had been present. It turned out that several people had been crushed and killed. "If it gets out," said the policeman, "no one will want to come to Cannes."

Lee finished *The Norseman* and went straight to Brazil to make *Killer Fish*, an exploitation movie I put together with Carlo Ponti, who was supposed to produce it. Again, I got Lee $400,000 and a piece of the action. It was filmed in a terrible place named Angra dos Reis. The whole episode was tragic, but Lee wanted to be in movies. Without Lee and the supporting cast—Margaux Hemingway, Marisa Berenson and Karen Black—the movie would never have gotten off the ground.

The minute I returned from France, Lee was on the phone. "Carlo Ponti didn't show up," he said. "He sent his son, who doesn't even go to the set. The director can't speak a word of English, only Italian. The cast speaks English, but the fucking crew only speaks Portuguese. This is one fucking mess. Get your ass down here!"

Reluctantly, I went. It was mid-May. I hopped a plane with a bag of California spring-summer clothes, not considering that Brazil was on the other side of the equator, where winter had firmly set in. It was the beginning of the worst movie experience of my life. When I arrived, the wind-chill factor pushed the thermometer to near zero. My first thought as I walked across the tarmac was, "I've got to get out of here, fast!" But Lee wouldn't let me leave. I had to do everything, ranging the gamut from production designer to production manager.

Angra dos Reis was a hellhole. En route to the set one day, we passed a downed horse in the patchwork road. It had broken legs. When I went back to the hotel in the afternoon, the horse was still there, suffering from its wound. A week later, it was still there.

I couldn't handle it. After three weeks, I said, "That's it. I'm out of here." I had a good excuse. Back in Los Angeles, some friends were throwing a birthday bash for me. I packed my bags, offered everybody my condolences and farewells, and started for the airport with a driver. For some reason I felt uneasy—something was amiss. Then I discovered I didn't have my passport. We turned around and drove back to the hotel. I told Lee about my passport.

"I know," he said. Obviously, he had it.

"Where is it? I've got to get the hell out of here," I said.

He wouldn't tell me. "If I have to stay here, then you have to stay here." It was a sick joke, but I stayed until the movie wrapped.

Farrah and Lee weren't the only thoroughbreds in my stable. I had Suzanne and Kristy, Robert Conrad, Jennifer O'Neill and Susan Saint James, among others. In total I had eleven management clients. Victor French was another one, but he was going through a divorce, which was all he could talk about. He was constantly depressed, which depressed me. I got tired of being depressed, so I persuaded him to get another manager.

I had high hopes for Jennifer O'Neill, though. She was the first "10." I had first represented her as a publicist, thinking she could become the next superstar. *Summer of '42* was her vehicle, the story of a young woman falling in love with a kid. It made Jennifer a star, a sex symbol, but then she fell in love for real and disappeared in Europe. She was gone too long to capitalize on her stardom. Timing is everything.

Bo Derek, a beautiful woman whom I did not represent, was the second "10," but the nomenclature stuck with her. She got it from the movie of the same name, the idea of which was taken from *Summer of '42*. It was a switch on the ages—an older guy and a young girl instead of an older woman and a young guy.

A few years after the success of *Summer*, Jennifer returned to her ranch in the South. I helped her get a Disney picture called *The Black Hole*. She rented out her ranch and her horses and all the things she loved because the movie was going to take a long time to shoot. She came to California and leased a house. Then the geniuses at Disney decided she should have her beautiful long hair cut off, although anyone with even a pretension to recognize beauty knew it was a mistake. She cried as they cut her hair.

She had a meeting with her agent and business manager at the old Gaiety on Sunset. It was a long meeting. Driving home, she ran into a parked car and was injured. An ambulance took her to Cedars-Sinai Hospital, where she was put in intensive care. I wanted to be the first to send her flowers and a card, but Disney beat me to it; they managed to check her blood count for alcohol. The home of Mickey Mouse and Goofy and Bambi sent her a pink slip. Walt was dead, and the management of the studio was now under Michael Eisner, the guy who later gave Michael Ovitz $100 million for working one year.

When she got out of the hospital, Jennifer sued Disney, which was like suing the U.S. Treasury Department because you don't like the look of a penny. Disney doesn't have a whole floor of lawyers for nothing. She never got a dime. Eisner replaced her in *The Black Hole* with Yvette Mimieux, who should have been a professor at Harvard.

Disney, the house that Walt built, had become a corporation interested solely in the bottom line.

By summer 1978, Suzanne Somers was a bona fide star. *Three's Company* was the hottest sitcom on the air and she had evolved into a comedic phenomenon. She made the covers of *TV Guide* and *People*, benchmarks for Hollywood celebrities. Now she wanted to be a movie star, but without the preamble most actresses experience in their climb up the ladder of success. I received no movie offers for her, and the projects Farrah didn't want were not suitable for Suzanne's talent. Finally I found a little "beach" picture that was already packaged with the exception of the star. It was a TV movie called *Zuma Beach*. One of the producers was Brian Grazer; the co-writer was John Carpenter, and the supporting cast included Rosanna Arquette, Tanya Roberts, Timothy Hutton, Delta Burke, Perry Lang and Parker Stevenson, young unknowns with talent. Suzanne complained there were no stars in the cast. "That's because you are the star," I told her.

The movie was a piece of television fluff, but it would be her first starring role, something she'd dreamed about all her life. Yet she was hesitant, primarily because Alan Hamel (whom she had now married) thought she should be in a major motion picture with a top-of-the-line director, seasoned stars and a cast of thousands. Alan equated television stardom with movie stardom, a mistake I had already experienced with *Somebody Killed Her Husband*. And Suzanne, for all her popularity, was not on the iconic level of Farrah.

"There weren't any stars in *American Graffiti* either," I reminded her. "But now almost everyone associated with the film are stars: George Lucas, Francis Coppola, Ron Howard, Richard Dreyfuss, Harrison Ford and you."

Ultimately Suzanne was persuaded, not by me but by the money. The fee I negotiated was more than all of her previous paychecks combined. After *Zuma Beach*, I got her another TV movie, *Happily Ever After*, co-starring Bruce Boxleitner, another unknown. It was filmed in Palm Springs.

Suzanne was inexperienced, but she was intuitive. Her hairdresser, who'd been at the studio for thirty years, put her hair up in a beehive. Suzanne didn't feel right about it, but she was afraid to tell the hairdresser she didn't think it worked for her character. It gnawed at her; on the third day of shooting she went to the producer and told him she was uncomfortable with the coif. She was too inexperienced to realize it was too late, that her character had already been established on film, and the cost of changing the hairstyle and reshooting her scenes was prohibitive. The producer shunted her complaint aside. "Oh, it looks great!" he told her.

Disappointed, Suzanne lowered her head. The man was wearing unmatched colored socks. She thought, "How would this guy know about hairstyles? Look how he dresses!"

Suzanne was learning. When she told me about the experience, I gave her some advice. "Use your gut instinct," I said. "Don't depend on others, especially someone who started in the system with Thomas Edison. When you think something is awry, speak your mind immediately but diplomatically."

Before *Happily Ever After* was completed, I closed a deal at CBS for Suzanne to cohost a TV extravaganza in Guadalajara, Mexico, with John Ritter. I don't remember the bottom line, but Suzanne received something like $50,000, a low-end fee because of the company's "favored nations" relationship with John. In other words, they couldn't pay Suzanne more than they paid John, and John's deal was set in concrete.

In lieu of money, I asked for perks for Suzanne. The network execs looked at me as if I were crazy. Movie stars like Elizabeth Taylor got perks. But television stars? No way! Just for the hell of it, I stuck to my guns. They agreed to fly Suzanne from Palm Springs to Guadalajara in a private jet. Anything else? "Yeah, I want the plane to be green, Suzanne's favorite color."

Farrah flew in the Fabergé jet, the most glamorous private plane in the world. Suzanne was afraid of flying, but a plane like the Fabergé jet was enticing. When her transport arrived at Palm Springs, however, it was a small (although beautiful forest green) Learjet. Suzanne developed a case of the nerves. She got on the plane and off the plane. She wanted a jumbo. Alan didn't help. He kept saying, "Suzanne, if you're scared, you don't have to go." Of course she *did* have to go; we had a contract to fulfill. I urged her to get back on the plane, but every time she seemed willing, Alan threw a wrench: "Honey, if you're upset, you don't have to board." It was the first but not the last time he worked to turn Suzanne against me.

Finally I persuaded her to get on the plane, and we flew off to Guadalajara.

I was still anathema at ABC, which was stupid on their part. I was managing stars, not wannabes, and stars were known commodities. Greed is ever present in Hollywood, and I've known few executives who wouldn't pursue a star if given the opportunity. I saw the guys at ABC as flapjacks, one pancake short of a stack. Farrah wasn't the only star I managed, and two of them had series at ABC—Kristy and Suzanne. The network should have been answering my phone calls. I didn't take being rebuffed by fat-cat executives lightly. I thought it over and came up with an idea unique in the annals of television. I called it the "network crossover."

I discussed it with Suzanne and Kristy's mother. After they agreed with my plan, I met with Bud Grant, president of CBS Entertainment. I had to act fast and secretly. I did, making exclusive deals for Suzanne and Kristy, both still under series contract with ABC, for CBS projects during hiatus. The cruncher, though, was CBS's promise of a series for each actress after their ABC shows—*Three's Company* and *Family*—ran their courses. As I recall, Kristy got a million-dollar contract, more money than her mother had ever dreamed of. Suzanne got $3 million.

When the deal became news, the ABC hierarchy had near coronaries. Never before had anyone taken two hot network properties to another network. It was a first, but I was playing a dangerous game. ABC network executives were power players, although most suffered tunnel vision. They were tied into now, not into tomorrow. It was during this period that Aaron Spelling, often my enemy, paid me a supreme compliment: "Jay has chutzpah, but he also has a first-rate mind."

Years later, after Alan Hamel effectively brought Suzanne's television career to an end by making outrageous demands, Suzanne wrote a book in which she criticized my CBS deal. She said I did it for money. I laughed. Of course I did it for money! And I remember how happy she was to get it.

I'm often asked what happened to Kristy McNichol. After I propelled her into the limelight, a man named Jerry Zeitman went to Carollyne McNichol with a proposal. Up to that time, I had been everything for Kristy—manager, agent and publicist. Zeitman said he would manage Kristy for free if Carollyne would enter into a production partnership with him, explaining that they would henceforth control Kristy's productions and share equally in the huge but unforeseen profits. The main thrust of his argument was to get rid of me: "Why pay Bernstein 15 percent, when I will do the same thing for free?"

It was probably not a difficult decision for Carollyne. People often think they can duplicate the efforts of professionals without realizing what is involved. Furthermore, I had a problem with Kristy's brother, an actor who wanted me to represent him. When I wouldn't, he became a Gatling gun of negative verbiage aimed at me. At any rate, I was fired, Zeitman took over, and now, when people ask me what happened to Kristy, I answer them honestly: "I don't know."

Chapter 15

MICKEY SPILLANE AND MIKE HAMMER

I was flying to New York to meet with Dino De Laurentiis, the Italian financier and producer. On the plane I recognized the short, stocky, tough-looking man sitting next to me. He'd been starring in Miller Lite commercials for ten years, but I would have known him anyway. He wasn't an actor; he was a writer. When I was a teenager, his racy pulp gumshoe novels had thrilled me endlessly. Three of them had become detective classics—*I, the Jury*; *My Gun Is Quick*; and *Kiss Me, Deadly*—and his fictional detective, Mike Hammer, was one of my heroes. The man was Mickey Spillane.

Once airborne, I said, "'She walked toward me, her hips waving a happy hello.'"

Mickey looked at me, not quite knowing what to say.

I threw out some more quotes: "'Women stuck to him like lint on a blue serge suit.' . . . 'You know how to punch a woman? You hit her in the mouth with your lips.'"

He laughed, probably thinking, "This guy's a nut, but at least he's read my books."

I had, all of them, and so had millions of other people. At that time, Mickey was the fifth-most-translated author in the world, behind Lenin, Tolstoy, Gorky and Jules Verne. Some publishers called Ian Fleming the English Mickey Spillane, but Spillane was compared to no one.

I introduced myself. The instant I mentioned Hollywood, Mickey said, "I don't like Hollywood, and I've never met anybody from Hollywood that didn't try to put the screws to me."

Mickey was not the personification of Mike Hammer, his fictional hero. Where Mike was hard-boiled, Mickey was a pussycat. Mickey thought things out, but Mike worked on instinct. What Mickey had were preconceived ideas drawn from his essential conservatism. He was blunt and to the point. When *Cagney & Lacey* became a hit on CBS Television, Mickey told *TV Guide*, "It's a good show, but it's not realistic. You're looking at fantasy. I'm not macho, but I just take exception to watching women cops. That's a job for guys."

I agreed with Mickey. You could exaggerate reality on television, but there was a limit. *Charlie's Angels* had been escapist entertainment, but *Cagney & Lacey* was trying to make people believe its stories.

"In the old days," said Mickey, "I always tried to keep Hammer my current age. That way I could relate to his experiences. But look at me now! I'm sixty-five. Who in hell wants a sixty-five-year-old detective running around solving crimes. That ain't very sexy!"

He reminded me of an aging actor, like William Holden, who was always looking for that last great script with a role that would close out his career on a high note. Mickey hadn't written a Mike Hammer novel in years, but he still thought about it. "I'm going to do one more," he said, "the big one. It'll be my swan song."

To Mickey, Mike Hammer was a state of mind, an ideal. "Ya see, we don't have heroes anymore," he explained. "Look at the drug users among ballplayers today. What kind of role models are they? There are no political models. Every time I take a look at a guy like Tip O'Neill, well, I wouldn't buy a used car from him. He's a backroom dealmaker, not a leader." It was as though I was talking to myself.

Mickey had no pretensions. He was born in Brooklyn and reared in New Jersey, the only child in a family of modest means. When it came time for him to go to college, he knew he would have to pay for it himself. He enrolled in Rutgers, but "they wanted me to be a jock, playing ball and swimming and stuff. I didn't have time for scholarship duties, so I switched to Kansas State because it was cheaper. I was already writing because I had to support myself."

His greatest disappointment was the movie and television industry. "It's all garbage. Think of what kids have to look at, and if you're an adult and watch it, then you've got a loose screw. Who wants to waste the time? People watch it because it's free. There ain't no responsibility in Hollywood. It lures young people because it offers a dream. Their eyes get big and wide at the prospects, and when it's too late they suddenly discover they're one of a million out-of-work actors. It's a shame. What most actors make wouldn't pay my beer bill." He was even harsher on producers and directors: "The guys who tried to translate my work to the screen were idiots and incompetent slobs."

By the time we were halfway through the flight, we were friends. When the plane landed, we were partners. We made a one-dollar deal that gave me the right to develop and produce Mike Hammer movies for screen or television. The deal had three caveats: Hammer had "to wear a snap brim hat, have short hair and carry a .45, not a sissy .38."

I didn't have a dollar bill. I tried to give him a five. "No, just send it to me," he said. As with Bogart and Rains in *Casablanca*, it was the beginning of a beautiful friendship.

Back in Hollywood, I pitched *Mickey Spillane's Mike Hammer* to the networks. No one was interested. Motion pictures and television shows reflect the mood of the times; politicians—usually the president—make the mood. CBS and NBC turned me down (this was before cable), saying the Hammer character was too rough and tough for contemporary audiences. Jimmy Carter was president and the national mood was soft on violence. Current detective shows portrayed cream puffs as private eyes, like Barnaby Jones and Cannon. The network hotshots thought gumshoes should be like Buddy Ebsen, avuncular if not downright grandfatherly. I pitched Mike Hammer as Dirty Harry with a sense of humor, an old-fashioned detective who solved cases the cops didn't, couldn't or wouldn't, and then laughed about it. The problem was, I didn't have Clint Eastwood. I put Hammer on the shelf and decided to wait for a better day.

I eventually did find my Mike Hammer. It was in the form of one of

America's *purest* actors—Stacy Keach. I can easily summarize in a few sentences my adventures with Stacy Keach. And I love to tell the story. It's a happy story. It's a story about the star of one of the hottest television series in America. About an actor who became a star, who learned his lesson, who then helped America broaden what we will accept to give people another chance, who then goes on to have a wonderful family, a wonderful life and a wonderful career. Like me, Stacy was a fighter. He had heart and the man never gave up. He never quit. But I am getting a little ahead of myself.

Chapter 16

ANGELS CAN'T
BE CENTERFOLDS

In Hollywood, you usually know who you're dealing with. That's not necessarily the case with international producers. When I put *Killer Fish* together for Lee Majors with Carlo Ponti, I had never met Ponti. He had "people," a horde of lieutenants and aides to deal with, mostly by telephone. Ponti was married to Sophia Loren, so he had more pleasurable things to do.

Dino De Laurentiis had people, too, but he wanted Farrah so badly for a movie that he felt it necessary to meet with me in person. I met him in his office in New York City. Dino was sitting behind his desk getting his hair cut.

"Ah, Jay, ah, Jay, ah, Jay! I have this picture perfect for the Farrah. Wind and rain and love in the storm. It's perfect for the Farrah!" He acted as if we were blood kin, and I'd never seen him before in my life.

The barber didn't miss a clip as Dino made his pitch. The movie was *Hurricane*, a multi-million-dollar remake of a 1937 classic. "Roman will turn her into an even bigger star!" he exclaimed. Clip! Clip!

Roman was Roman Polanski, the Polish director recently self-exiled back to Europe to escape a statutory rape charge in Hollywood. He was a great director, but his off-camera behavior was not fiction. I found Dino's proposition distasteful; I thought Farrah might also, and I was certain Lee would. The movie was going to be filmed on a remote island in the

Pacific; telephone communication would be minimal. I wouldn't be there; Lee wouldn't be there; and if Farrah became unhappy with Roman's intentions, well . . .

Dino offered $2 million. I turned it down. I foresaw nothing in *Hurricane* but trouble. As it turned out, the picture was miscast with Mia Farrow, and Swedish director Jan Troell replaced Polanski. It was a bomb, even though it had a stellar cast in support of Mia, including Jason Robards, Max von Sydow and Trevor Howard. The storm Dino's special-effects crew reproduced on a remote island cost him 30 million bucks.

Later I turned down a second De Laurentiis offer. He wanted Farrah to star in *The Fan*, the story of a Broadway actress who is stalked by a psychotic admirer. I thought it was too dangerous, and might put Farrah at risk of copycat syndrome.

Meanwhile, Suzanne had a guest role on a Paul Anka television special produced in Monte Carlo. It was Anka, Suzanne and Donna Summers. Alan went with Suzanne, and I took Marna Winter, a wisp of a girl Lee and I had met in Atlanta a couple of years before.

I recognized Stavros Niarchos's yacht anchored in the harbor. We had hardly dropped our own sails before an invitation arrived at the hotel. Niarchos was having a big dinner party and he wanted Suzanne as his special guest.

My memory of the yacht during the Cannes Film Festival failed me. If anything, it was bigger than I remembered, as big as Spelling's *Love Boat*, except it wasn't a set. It was real.

The dining room was set up with two major guest tables, one for Niarchos, who placed Suzanne beside him, with Alan on Suzanne's other side, and Niarchos's current inamorata, Princess Somebody, at the other table, seated beside me. It was an honor to be assigned a seat beside the princess, but when Marna and I went to the table there was only one empty chair with a guest card—mine. I was taken aback, but before I could signal what I perceived to be a mistake, little Marna was escorted away by one of myriad major domos. I watched her for a moment and then the crowd swallowed her.

I sat down, but I couldn't get Marna off my mind. She was hardly more than a teen, and I was worried about her. I kept looking from table to table, but I never spied her among the two hundred or so guests. I felt badly because I pictured her sitting in the kitchen with the hired hands. I tried to make the best of the dinner, chatting amiably with the princess, who spoke English as if she'd just finished a weekend crash course at a school in Tijuana.

Before and after dinner, we suffered through numerous toasts and flirtations and broken conversations. When it was finally over, I excused myself from the princess and went in search of Marna. The guests seemed to have grown in number and I suspected Niarchos had a secondary list of invitees for the after-dinner cocktail party. Then I saw her, looking a little elfin standing among the crowd of spectators. I rushed to her. "Marna, I'm so sorry you didn't get to sit with me."

Her eyes sparkled. "Oh, I had a great time!" She had been seated at a peripheral table with Ringo Starr. "And he's so funny and just wonderful and—there he is! Ringo! Ringo!"

Ringo came over with his longtime girlfriend, Nancy. We went through the introductions, which seemed ridiculous, since every time Ringo and I came across each other it was the same song and dance. Over time, we must have been introduced to each other a dozen times.

When I returned to Los Angeles, the first telephone call I received was from Nancy. Ringo was still in Monte Carlo, she said. "I'm lonely." I was never a saint, but this time I went over the cliff. I had an affair with Nancy, short-lived as it was, but an affair nevertheless.

She had an apartment in a clump of buildings on Sunset Boulevard that included Schwab's, the famous drugstore where so many starlets were supposedly discovered. Nancy and I would often tryst there, even after Ringo returned home. Finally we broke it off. The relationship had reached the point where she would be with me one night and Ringo the next, without Ringo knowing that she was cheating on him. My guilt overwhelmed me. I told her I couldn't continue. "It's best," she said, "because I really love Ringo."

Dissolve to a year and a half later. I read in a scandal sheet that Nancy had sued Ringo for breach of promise. She claimed he had promised to marry her; when he backed out—wham! She wanted her share of his fortune. Ringo had found a new girlfriend and Nancy felt cheated. I later heard that Ringo settled with her for a couple of million dollars.

I felt doubly bad because I didn't have the guts to enter the fray and tell Ringo how she had cheated on him, with no less than me.

By 1978 Farrah had been on the cover of almost every major magazine in the world. The exception was *Playboy*, which usually featured a cover shot of its Playmate of the Month with a nude spread inside.

I was often invited to parties at the Playboy Mansion, although I was never more than an acquaintance of Hugh Hefner. I liked Hef, but his personality required a coterie of yes-men as friends, much like Sammy Davis, Jr.'s had, and mindless loyalty was not compatible with my personality. Hef and I were social friends, nothing more, and through him I met many of his editors and members of his magazine staff. It was September when I called the *Playboy* office.

"How would you like to have Farrah Fawcett on the cover of your magazine?"

Playboy acted fast, and Claude Mougin photographed the cover shot. Farrah's body was in profile, leaning back, her head facing the camera at an angle. She wore spiked heels with inlaid diamonds and her right leg was raised in an inverted V. She held a glass of champagne, pricked her beautiful white teeth with a diamond-studded olive toothpick and wore a long silk shirt with the top buttons open, the left sleeve falling loosely from her shoulder. It was tasteful, sexy and far removed from pornography. The photo *Playboy* chose didn't even reveal cleavage. It was scheduled for the December 1978 issue with the caption Farrah Comes Back ... Big.

The shoot went fast, as if *Playboy* was afraid we might change our minds before Mougin clicked the first shot. Then they called Lee. "What date can we set for Farrah's nude layout?" Lee went into paroxysms— nude shots had never been part of the package. They called me. "What about the nude layout, Jay?"

"What nude layout?" I asked. "Farrah isn't doing a nude layout, and she never was. Nude shots were never in the mix. The idea never came up."

"Well, we've got to do something. What about an interview?" said an editor.

Playboy interviews were in-depth, running ten to fifteen pages. Farrah was neither willing nor experienced enough to talk about world affairs and answer the sophisticated questions *Playboy*'s interviews entailed. I said an interview wouldn't work, which threw *Playboy* into a panic.

"Come on, Jay. We've got to do something!"

I was nervous. I didn't want to blow the deal. We needed it. *Somebody Killed Her Husband* was ready to open and I foresaw a box-office dud. I needed to keep Farrah's name and image out there, in front of the American public. Suddenly I got an idea. "Remember when we were kids and played Twenty Questions?"

"Yes."

"Send me twenty questions. I'll give them to Farrah and get her answers to them."

He did. I gave them to Farrah; she shrugged, gave them back to me and dashed off to play tennis. I answered the questions and sent them back to *Playboy*. This was 1978 and they're still using the Twenty Questions format today.

Chapter 17

GETTING SUNBURN

The release date for *Somebody Killed Her Husband* was sped up to September 28. I was nervous. Not only were we going to lose Farrah's audience of high school and college kids, but I had a sinking feeling the movie had been the wrong vehicle for her. It was not a bad movie, but it had no dazzle. It obviated what Farrah was about—glitz, glamour and apple pie. The story required her to play against type, portraying a young housewife who always had a kid in her arms. I needed another deal before *Somebody* came out.

I had dinner with a producer who was doing a project with Robert Mitchum and Raquel Welch. He'd had a fight with Raquel, and now he wasn't sure he wanted her. Would Farrah be interested? After *Somebody Killed Her Husband*, which had begun as a project for Woody Allen and Diane Keaton, I was gun-shy about projects developed for other people. I demurred.

Then I read that producer John Daly (later of *Platoon* fame) had picked up the screenplay in a turnaround deal. Mitchum and Welch were no longer attached to it. I got a copy of the script, read it and liked it. It was a drama about an insurance investigator who gets a model to pose as his wife in an effort to crack a murder-suicide case in Acapulco.

I went to Daly. The word was out that Farrah's price was $750,000. Daly did not balk. He was having problems, but money was not one of them. He couldn't keep a cast together. I told him I would take over the executive producer's role, and he was amenable. The only barrier was Lee, who was still opposed to me receiving screen credits. With Daly, I again demanded that Farrah's name be above that of her co-stars, plus approval of cast, director and crew. He agreed.

The Bind was a semi-serious drama that needed a strong male lead to play against Farrah. Daly had secured Harrison Ford, which was good—he had just finished *Star Wars*. Lined up as director was Bryan Forbes, who had done *King Rat* and *The Stepford Wives*, among others. On paper the names looked great, but resumés don't take into account personalities.

Forbes and Ford had a difference of opinion. I wasn't present for the misunderstanding (I did not meet either of them), but it was severe enough that Harrison decided not to do the picture. While we scrambled to find another star, Forbes walked. We were scheduled to begin production in weeks, and suddenly we had neither a male lead nor a director.

Richard Sarafian's name came up—he was a drama director. We got in touch with him, discussed the project, and he committed. All we had to do now was replace Harrison Ford.

Through the years I had kept in touch with Guy McElwaine, who was now a major talent agent. I told him our casting problems.

"Can you change it to a comedy?" he asked. "Peter Sellers is looking for a project."

I knew Peter. I called him; he was interested. I talked to John Daly. We were excited about the possibility of securing Sellers, so we agreed to have the movie rewritten.

The whole episode was fool's play. Three weeks from shooting, we were translating a drama into a comedy. We didn't have Sellers on contract, only a semi-commitment; yet we had a contract with a drama director.

Before we sent the new script to Peter, McElwaine called. Peter had taken another movie. We were in a quandary. We had a new script, now a comedy, but with no leading actor. We needed to act fast, but nobody seemed able to shift into high speed. A thousand names came up, but none seemed suitable or quickly negotiable. Then Charles Grodin's name was mentioned.

I was not a Grodin fan, but he had a flare for low-key, deadpan comedy. Desperate, I thought that if Charlie could play the part like Sellers, it might work. I got in touch with his agent. He expressed interest, but said he would have to talk to Charlie.

It was agent-babble. I had no doubt Charlie would want to do the movie, which concerned me. Our preproduction publicity had emphasized the drama of the story. All actors aspired to serious drama; I wanted to make sure Grodin understood we were now going to make a comedy. I called his agent again. He said Charles not only wanted to do the movie, but that he understood exactly what we expected of him.

When Charlie arrived in Acapulco, my greatest fear came to a head. He had with him his physical trainer, a box of toupees and a sophisticated swagger. I was scared. Grodin saw himself playing Cary Grant.

On top of all that, we needed a new title. *The Bind* no longer fit. I was thinking about it one afternoon while sunbathing poolside at the Villa Vera. I fell asleep on a chaise longue, roasted for a couple of hours and woke up with a title: *Sunburn*.

Lee was prepping for *Steel*, his third Bernstein-packaged picture. It was clickety-click-click-click! Three pictures back to back to back, each at $400,000 for Lee, plus a piece of the back-end profits, if any. Lee and Farrah were getting rich. I was working my ass off and getting little.

Steel was to be filmed in Kentucky, Lee's home state. Lee was one of those people whose life was always stuck in the past, in Kentucky where neighbors seemed to be a mirror image of himself. They had little of importance to say to each other. Lee grew up a loner just like his neighbors.

Before the production began, Lee persuaded me to go to Kentucky with him—he wanted me to see his hometown. His stepparents were nice folks, seemingly as shy and insecure as Lee. They took us to dinner at the Holiday Inn, which they said was the best restaurant in town. Another couple, contemporaries of Lee's folks, joined. During dinner the second woman kept staring at me. At last she said, "Are you a Jew?"

"Yes," I said, caught off guard, "I suppose I am."

"Then where are your horns?" she asked, as if she were a doctor inquiring how long you've been experiencing chest pains.

"When I was a boy, my parents had them manicured off," I said.

She dropped the subject.

After dinner I was given the grand tour of the town, around the court-house square, through various neighborhoods. "See that house?" said the woman, pointing at an upscale house with a tailored lawn. "That's where Middlesboro's Jew lives."

On *Steel* we had a problem far more serious than Lee's theft of my passport in Brazil. The movie required a stunt that had never before been performed. Previously a stuntman had jumped out of an airplane in a Burt Reynolds movie, but the scene was shot in such a way that it appeared the plane was much higher than it really was. Our picture required a stuntman to fall from a building that was much higher than the plane had been in the Reynolds picture. Lee and I met with A.J. Bakunis, our stuntman, before the company went to Kentucky to begin principal photography.

"Can this be done without your getting killed?" I asked Bakunis.

"Hey, that's what I do," he said confidently. "I'm a stuntman."

Weeks later, I was in Acapulco on *Sunburn*. I got a call from Lee in Kentucky. "You're an asshole," he said.

"Tell me something new."

"Bakunis got killed doing that stunt jump."

It wasn't my fault any more than it was Lee's, but he was angry because I wasn't there to hold his hand. It was a tragedy, plain and simple.

A few days later, I told Lee I was taking the executive producer's credit for *Sunburn*. He had a conniption fit. "If you put your name in the credits, I'll fire you," he told me. "And I'll have Farrah fire you."

I was angered by his intransigence. He was jealous of Farrah, and he was jealous of me because I was with her more than he was. "You can fire me, Lee, but I'm going to have my attorney write a letter to Farrah's attorney with a list of all the women you've fucked during your marriage. It will be accompanied by instructions for the letter not to be opened until I'm fired."

A silence lingered at the end of the line. Then Lee said, "You wouldn't do that."

"Try me," I said.

We hung up. I put my name on the credits of *Sunburn* as executive producer, then instructed my lawyer to send the letter to Farrah's lawyer. Neither Farrah nor Lee fired me, at least at that time. Later, when I *was* fired, Farrah's lawyer called me regarding the letter.

"What about it?" I asked.

"Well, I opened it today."

"And what was in it?"

"Eight blank pages."

Somebody Killed Her Husband did not set box-office records, but neither was it a bomb. The reaction of the critics was strange—they generally panned the picture but lauded Farrah's performance. (She had, indeed, tried to compete with Jeff Bridges, and honed her skills in the process.) We were disappointed, of course, but it didn't seem to be a bad start considering we had made the movie without industry sanction or aid. I had higher hopes for *Sunburn*. We wrapped in December, and I headed for Tucson, Arizona.

Robert Conrad and I had remained friends through the years, and I had continued to represent him as a publicist and sometimes as his manager, off and on. The year before, I had come up with an idea. No one had ever done a TV movie based on a defunct series. The more I thought about it, the more I realized *The Wild Wild West* was not necessarily dead. The next time I saw Conrad I broached the idea of resurrecting the series as a two-hour TV movie.

"Let's do it," said Conrad enthusiastically.

I called Ross Martin, who had co-starred with Bob in the original series. Because of a heart attack, Ross hadn't worked since *The Wild Wild West* had been canceled in 1969. He was feeling good, though, and excited about the prospect of resuscitating his role.

CBS owned the old show and therefore the title and characters. I thought it would be easy to get the rights for a new television movie, but when I told the honchos at the network what I wanted to do they balked. "You can produce it," they told me, "but it has to be a CBS project." I wasn't averse to their counter, except for the producer's fee: $35,000. It wasn't much in the scheme of things, far less than most producers received for a year's work in a project. But I had no alternative.

Once the project was packaged and ready to go, I announced publicly what we were doing, proudly emphasizing my genius at coming up with the idea of producing the first television motion picture based on a defunct series. Then Bob called me with bad news. He had an opportunity to take another job that was extremely lucrative. I couldn't argue with him; without him, I wouldn't have put the project together to begin with. We delayed production for a year.

Meanwhile a lot of producers jumped on the bandwagon with similar projects. Anytime you come up with an original idea in Hollywood, you can rest assured it will be repeated in the next cycle of production. The protection of intellectual rights is nil; only when threats come from outside, such as piracy by Chinese entrepreneurs, does the industry unite in self-preservation. In the maelstrom of Hollywood, new ideas have fifteen minutes of originality and are rarely attributed to the real creator. I was the first to announce the idea, but by the time we actually filmed *The Wild Wild West Revisited*, several other defunct television series had risen from the dead. Nevertheless, we went forward with our production in Arizona. Burt Kennedy was the director and Paul Williams played the villain against Robert Conrad and Ross Martin.

The movie did well enough that CBS gave me a sequel, *More Wild Wild West*. When we did that one the following year, I got Jonathan Winters as the guest star. Again we ended up with a good movie, one I was sure would get high ratings. Then some network genius threw a wrench into the mix. The programmers decided to split the movie into two one-hour shows for eight o'clock Monday and Tuesday airings, times in which women were the primary viewers. It was a ridiculous idea. It did poorly both nights and that was the end of *The Wild Wild West*.

Chapter 18

CREATIVE CON-ARTISTS

Ron Meyer, one of the founders of Creative Artists Agency, invited me to lunch at Harry's Bar & American Grill in Century City. I accepted his invitation, primarily because I was curious. My relationship with CAA had been less than optimal. In fact, it didn't exist. To explain requires a brief journey in history to a time before CAA existed.

Around 1968, I had gone to the William Morris Agency with a proposal. I had friendships with most of its principal executives, especially Sam Weisbord and Norman Brokaw, and I persuaded them to let me represent the agency in public relations. I already had two other talent agencies, but Morris was the big client.

An inter-office memo made the rounds suggesting that when an agent had a client in need of public relations, he should be sent to Bernstein. I got about twenty important clients through Morris channels; in turn, I sent people to the Morris office, like Ricardo Montalban and Susan Hayward. It went back and forth like that for several years. Michael Ovitz, for example, gave me the *Barney Miller* TV show.

Rowland Perkins probably helped me more than anyone at Morris. After he gave me a big account, I wanted to do something nice for him. I thought about it. Rowland's head was as hairless as a cue ball. I decided a toupee would be an excellent gift. I went to Jay Sebring, the hair stylist who was later murdered along with Sharon Tate and others by the Manson psychopaths. I got Jay to make Rowland a hairpiece, but when I got the bill, I almost flipped. It was $800. As it turned out, for sheer joy and pleasure, it was the best $800 I ever spent. The toupee changed Rowland's life—overnight he went from nerd to Superman.

About the time I signed Lee Majors, Ovitz, Perkins and three other packaging agents jumped the William Morris ship and started their own midnight firm, Creative Artists Agency. There was nothing wrong with them going into business for themselves, but when the sun came up they had taken a slew of Morris clients with them. I knew all five of the CAA rebels and liked four of them. The only one I didn't get along with was Bill Haber, who had once been secretary for Sy Marsh, CAA. "Guys, I'm not political," I said. "I don't even vote, so I don't want to get involved in agency politics. But I'll be happy to do your PR until you're able to afford to pay me. You won't owe me any back money. When you get off the ground, we'll start from scratch."

It was a good deal for CAA, with the possibility of a good deal for me if CAA became successful. Haber, however, who accused me of being a double agent for William Morris, blackballed me. It didn't help my case that I was close to Weisbord, then president of Morris, who said upon learning of the rebel defection that he hoped the children of the CAA executives would "breathe poison air." So Haber had some ammunition to fire at me, and he did. I didn't get the account.

During the next two or three years it got worse. CAA became a power-house agency. One of my friends said Haber's criticism of me was relentless, a daily carpet bombing. I not only didn't get CAA as a client, but the agency blacklisted me. Word came back to me that if a CAA client signed a management contract with Bernstein, he would be released from the agency.

I was the first person blacklisted by CAA, and years later, when Ovitz was blacklisted himself, I had a good laugh. Never before had the old adage "what comes around, goes around" sounded so visionary.

Then, out of the blue, Ron Meyer called me. I liked Ron. Of the top CAA echelon, I thought he was the sanest and most reasonable. When he invited me to lunch, my clients included Lee, Farrah, Suzanne, Kristy,

Susan Saint James, Jennifer O'Neill and several other top actors and celebrities. Only two of them had agency representation, and none at CAA.

"Jay, we've been wrong about you. I apologize," said Ron as we took our seats.

"Thank God," I told him. "It's been difficult not having a relationship with CAA."

"It's not going to be like that anymore. We'd really like to work with you."

We chatted like old friends and ordered lunch. Finally Ron got back to business. "We need to wipe the slate clean," he began. "We've talked about it at the agency. The consensus is that we'd appreciate you giving us your clients for agency representation."

He looked at me as if he'd just come up with a way to harness thermo-nuclear energy. Because I was the first multiple-client manager, I usually served multiple functions: manager, public-relations rep and sometimes producer. I was essentially performing as my clients' agent also, barely within the framework of the law.

"What?" I said. "Are you nuts?"

Ron was proposing that my clients give another 10 percent of their income to CAA. Most of them were already giving me 15 percent. If I went along with his proposal, they would now be giving a total of 25 percent, 15 to me and 10 to CAA, which meant I would eventually get fired by all of them, a result Ron no doubt understood. CAA was so used to railroading people that Ron Meyer apparently thought I would jump at the chance to be railroaded myself. I was insulted, so I did what I usually did in similar circumstances. I picked up my plate of pasta, turned it upside down and dumped it on the table. Then I walked out.

A few months later, I was in the parking lot of Ma Maison. A guy walked up to the car next to mine. It was Bill Haber. "This town isn't big enough for the two of us," he said, as if he were auditioning for a Saturday-afternoon Western.

I looked down at him and said, "Well, when are you leaving, Bill?"

He got in his car and drove away. I had just renewed my imprint on his enemies list.

At that time I was blacklisted at ABC, NBC and CAA, and also by Army Archerd, noted columnist for *Daily Variety*. I didn't like Army, but I didn't dislike him, either. I just thought he went too far with his machismo.

At a party at Red Buttons' house, Army and I had got into a shouting match. I don't remember why, but it's a pretty good bet that it was about his wife, of whom Army was more protective than a mother hen over her flock of chicks. When the argument appeared to be advancing toward fisticuffs, Vince Edwards came up behind me and pinned my arms. That's when Army swung a roundhouse to my jaw. It almost knocked me out.

At another party (I think it was the opening of Gucci's in Beverly Hills), a man lit a cigarette. It was before smoking became politically incorrect, but Selma Archerd told him to put it out anyway. The guy told her to go fuck herself. Army slugged him. Rather than firing Army, *Daily Variety* moved his column from page two to page nine. He was buried for about two months. I remember thinking, "When that's the punishment, you don't learn to correct your mistakes."

Eventually Army became the most important columnist in the trades, so when he blacklisted me, it hurt. It was over the birth of Sy and Molly Marsh's child.

Sy and I were long-time friends, dating back to the days when he represented Sammy Davis, Jr., at William Morris. We were so close that when Molly went to the hospital to have her baby, Sy asked me to stay with him at his home.

We'd been drinking, a pre-celebration to the baby's arrival. In the middle of the night I went downstairs to get something to eat. I found a chocolate cake with green icing on it. I ate three slices. It was delicious. When Molly came home, I asked her where she had got that cake with the green icing.

"Oh, it was old," said Molly. "The icing had molded."

After the baby was born, Sy asked me how he could get the most publicity for his newborn child. I told him I would release it to the *Hollywood Reporter* and *Daily Variety* for their birth sections, and to Harrison Carroll at the *Examiner*. The next day Sy got a call from Army.

"I thought we were friends, Sy."

"We are," said Sy.

"And you don't give me your child's birth announcement? You call that friendship?"

Sy became flustered. "Well, Jay Bernstein told me."

After that Army never put the names of my clients in his column.

Chapter 19

THE ROYAL
TREATMENT

Cary Grant was on the board of directors of Fabergé. When he called me, it was a replay of the time Henry Fonda called regarding Peter's trial. I was awed; that's the only way to describe it, for, regardless of my success and the myriad famous people I knew, at heart I was still a fan of the screen stars of old. Cary Grant was one of the great ones, and although he had retired from acting he was still very much alive, active in the corporate world and a vibrant personality.

"Jay, I was speaking to Prince Charles," he began, and no one my age could miss the inflections of his voice. "*Jew*-day, *Jew*-day, *Jew*-day," kept ringing in my mind as he spoke, although he never really said that line in a motion picture. "The Prince would very much like Farrah to be one of the co-masters of ceremonies at a forthcoming event for the Queen, to be held at Albert Hall," he continued. "It will be very exclusive—no mere dukes and duchesses—but the elite of European royalty and top international political leaders: kings, queens and presidents."

I was excited, but when I told Farrah she said, "No, I don't want to do it." She was afraid of making a fool of herself. They hadn't taught her in school in Texas how to meet a queen. I would have to persuade her, and it would take time.

Grant kept calling. "We really need her," he said.

At last she acquiesced, if for no other reason than my persistence.

To me, after having discovered her and engineered her career, Farrah's appearance before the queen as an actual participant in the ceremony was a larger honor than winning an Oscar. When you create a star, you want your star on the highest pedestal attainable. I did not think she could top it.

In the appearance deal, which for once I desisted in asking for extra perks, we were given two tickets for Farrah's parents and two for my parents. The good news was that my parents were going to be in London at the precise time of the event, on a buying trip for their store. I was excited because I wanted them to see my own Oscar, which was Farrah.

We flew first-class on a jumbo jet. By the time we were airborne, Farrah was napping, curled up comfortably in her seat. I looked around. Sitting beyond us and across the aisle was none other than the influential media mogul Sir Lew Grade. I went over to him. For a dinner in his honor in New York, I had once miraculously managed—overnight—to attract Hollywood's glitziest stars, from Burt Lancaster to Robert Mitchum to Charlotte Rampling to Goldie Hawn to Tom Jones to John Lennon.

Lew and I chatted a moment, mostly about Farrah. When I saw that she was awake, I said to him, "Would you like to meet her?"

"I would love to."

After I introduced him, he said to Farrah, "I'm just reading a script that you'd be perfect in. Would you care to read it?"

Lew extracted a screenplay from his briefcase. After another five minutes of talk, we all settled in for the long flight. Lew went back to his seat, but every once in a while he looked over his shoulder to see if Farrah was reading.

"This is different," she whispered, "but I don't know if it's for me."

It was a futuristic space film, a genre neither of us was in tune with, but Farrah liked the emotional aspect of the character she would be playing. "Why don't you read it?" she asked.

I did. She was right; it wasn't necessarily her kind of story, but her character had promise. "Maybe it can be fixed," she said. "Maybe we should consider it."

"Lew doesn't realize you've been blacklisted," I told her. "He doesn't know we lost *Foul Play* and *Coma*. We've got to do something, until the atmosphere clears in Hollywood."

"Talk to him," said Farrah.

I went over and sat down by Lew. "Here's the deal," I told him. "We've had so many offers that it's hard to sift through them all. But Farrah likes your story. She'll do it if we can close a deal before this plane lands, before its wheels touch down."

"Go on," said Lew. "I'm interested."

"Farrah chooses the leading man, someone like Kirk Douglas." I threw in Douglas because we were seeing him the next evening. Then I mentioned some perks.

Lew didn't blink. When I finished the list of perks, all of them coming off the top of my head except for Farrah's sauna, he said, "Okay. How much?"

"$750,000."

He looked at me, blinked a couple of times and said, "Okay. We have a deal."

That's how *Saturn 3* came into existence, through linguistic subterfuge. What I didn't know was that Lew was giving me more fluff than I was giving him. The screenplay wasn't even his property. It belonged to, of all people, Elliott Kastner, who had asked Lew to read it, hoping he would be interested in financing it. The next day in London, Lew optioned the property from Kastner.

Farrah and I had suites at the Dorchester. Lee was in Canada prepping for *Agency*, the fourth picture I had put together for him in a year's time. When my parents arrived, they stayed at the Inn on the Park. My mother called. At the last moment, she had decided to bring her assistant buyer, Mary Nobody. "You'll have to get an extra ticket for us," she said.

"That's impossible," I told her. "I can't call the queen of England and ask for an extra seat at a function where they're not even letting Prince Hamlet attend!"

"If you don't get us a third seat, then we're not going."

I thought she was bluffing. The event went off, with two cold, empty seats at my parents' table. They were probably watching television at their hotel, only one mile away. But that was the nature of my mother.

Part of Farrah's responsibility was introducing some Slavic aristocrats from Eastern Europe. Albert Hall had no teleprompters, and she kept fumbling through the names during rehearsal. After we left the hall, I had some cue cards made that spelled the names phonetically.

When we returned for the real event, however, Farrah panicked. She came up with a stomach attack. "I need to go backstage," she moaned. I found a dressing room in the back of the hall where I sat her down.

"I can't do it," she said. "I'm sick. Tell them I can't do it."

First it was my mother; now it was Farrah. "Okay," I said, shrugging, "but first I'm going to find a doctor and see if there's anything he can give you that will help you regain your composure." I was thinking of the Fernet Branca that Bill Holden had given me at the Rome airport, a real cure-all. I had some in my room. I dashed away. When I returned, Farrah was worse.

"Tell them I can't do it, Jay," she moaned. "Just go tell them."

"I found a doctor," I said, "and he gave me some medicine." I poured a tumbler full of the foul-smelling herbal mix, 40 percent of which was alcohol. "He said for you to drink this, and if you don't feel better in fifteen minutes, then I should take you back to the hotel."

Farrah was under pressure, and she knew it. She downed the Fernet Branca in one big chugalug. Her face screwed up, but ten minutes later she was feeling better; twenty minutes later she was on a cloud. She was tipsy, of course, but she didn't realize it.

"How do you feel?"

"Better. Much better," she said, fairly floating.

"Then go break a leg."

Everything went off perfectly, due first to the Fernet Branca and second to the cue cards. Farrah pronounced the names as if she were a Slav.

At the dinner following the ceremony, Farrah, her parents and I were seated at a table with some of the royal family. Jim Fawcett, Farrah's father, a stereotypical good ol' boy from Texas, began some heavy-duty drinking. He was sitting next to Prince Charles and his language was definitely down-home. First he dropped the royal title; then he reduced the Prince's first name to a diminutive. Between spasms of laughter, the future king of England became Chuck, usually with a hospitable Texas slap on his back.

We flew back to the States in the Fabergé jet. Farrah sat with her secretary and I sat with Cary Grant. I had the same feeling I'd experienced when I first met Alan Ladd. We chatted amiably, and I asked him, "Who today could best play the movie roles you played?"

He hardly mulled it over before saying, "Either Dustin Hoffman or Richard Dreyfuss."

In Hollywood a few nights later, I ran into Dreyfuss at a party. When I told him what Cary Grant had said, he glowed. Today, when I see him, he always says, "Tell the Cary Grant story, Jay. Please tell the Cary Grant story!"

I was reasonably certain *Three's Company*—the Americanized version of *Man About the House*—would never be shown in Europe because of the difference in their humor and our humor. Yet I wanted Suzanne to be recognized in Europe, particularly in the United Kingdom, as an up-and-coming star. I placed an emphasis on Britain because most European production money was coming from England.

While in London with Farrah, I learned of a movie script called *Yesterday's Hero*, about World Cup soccer. Jackie Collins, Joan's sister, had written it before she became the female Harold Robbins. Elliott Kastner was going to produce the movie, and the word I got was that he had cast Ian McShane and Lesley Ann Warren in the leading roles.

Jackie had once stayed briefly with Leslie Parrish and me. I called Jackie, whose husband owned Tramp, a famous London nightclub, and made an appointment to see her there.

Jackie was charming, attractive and enthusiastic. When she told me Lesley Ann Warren had not yet been signed to do the movie, I became extremely interested in it as a European vehicle for Suzanne. "Look," said Jackie, "you need to talk to Elliott."

I had dealt with Elliot so many times in the past that I felt we were in the same fraternity. An American who spent a great deal of time abroad, he was a man I could talk with on a serious level. I tracked him down and said, "Elliott, I want to sell you Suzanne Somers for the lead female role in *Yesterday's Hero*."

He could not have been nicer or more blunt as he drove home the limitations of American television abroad. "Jay, I've never heard of Suzanne Somers, and we already have someone in mind."

Elliott had made two dozen movies, but he was a better dealmaker than he was a packager. Most of his movies had been forgettable, and few had profited from television syndication.

"Suzanne is a television star in the States," I told him, "and she can make you a lot of money with a television sale after your movie runs out of steam at the box office."

"I'll keep her in mind," said Elliott.

Back in the States, I closed an $800,000 deal for Suzanne with Ace Hardware for a series of TV commercials. The structure of the deal was laden with conditions—all mine. My major criterion was that Suzanne would never be photographed with hardware. She did a song-and-dance routine with background dancers, then the camera cut to the hardware pitchman.

Next I went to Vegas to see if I could make a deal for a Suzanne Somers nightclub act. I took Alan Hamel with me. In Suzanne's memoir, *After the Fall*, she gave Alan credit for virtually every deal I made for her, which was absurd. One's memory often fails, but it doesn't fail on every recollection. I didn't mind, though, because everyone I negotiated with realized Alan had no expertise in dealmaking.

In Vegas, Alan knew nothing and nobody. I knew the power players who could move things because I'd represented so many singers and entertainers who performed there. It probably didn't hurt that I'd lost a couple of million dollars gambling. At that time, many of the casinos were still influenced if not controlled by the mob, although nobody ran around saying so. Howard Hughes had made his Vegas power grab from his suite at the Desert Inn, purchasing hotels and other properties, and although the industry was in transition, the old players of debatable virtue still counted.

I sought out Bernie Rothkopf at the MGM Grand, and Alan sat in a chair listening while I pitched Bernie. In Vegas you dealt business on a different level. In contrast to what Suzanne later wrote, I cut a deal while Alan looked on like a simpleton with no experience, which is exactly what he was at the time. I hold nothing against Suzanne, because I'm sure Alan rewrote the experience for her. But here's what happened:

"Bernie, I'd like to book Suzanne Somers at the MGM Grand."

Like Elliott Kastner, Bernie said, "I've never heard of her."

His ignorance was more forgivable than Elliott's. With the exception of fight matches, the only television monitors the casino guys watched were the ones that homed in on gamblers at the slot machines and gaming tables.

"She's a big television star," I continued, "with a variety of talents. She'll be a tremendous hit here."

He shrugged. "Get me a tape showcasing what she can do, and I'll take a look."

Alan and I left. I took Suzanne's Ace Hardware commercial, snipped off the beginning and the end, and went back to see Bernie Rothkopf. I played the tape. Bernie liked what he saw. "Okay," he said, "I'll give the girl a week at $150,000."

I remembered Alan Ladd telling me how his wife, Sue, had sold him to A-picture producers for less money than she charged B producers. "No," I said to Bernie. From the corner of my eye I saw Alan flinch at my words.

"That's my top offer. Not a dime more," said Bernie.

"I don't want one-fifty for one week," I told him. "I want fifty a week ... but I want three weeks at three different times."

I was not speaking out of turn. I knew the history of other celebrities who had tried Vegas. Telly Savalas, Lynda Carter, Richard Chamberlain, even Ronald Reagan—all had short, lucrative runs, but then it was over. None was invited back. It took time to build a following in Vegas, which I felt Suzanne could do with enough bookings.

Like Farrah, Suzanne had guts, a prerequisite to major stardom. But her courage was of a different sort—she was extroverted and Farrah was introverted. Although Suzanne had never sung and danced in front of a live audience, she wanted to try it, knowing it wouldn't be much different from performing in front of a studio audience when *Three's Company* was taped after a week of rehearsals.

Bernie bought my offer, and we signed a deal for Suzanne to perform live at the MGM Grand Hotel, starting sometime in the near future.

I took Suzanne to dinner at La Scala. It was the place to see stars, and now that she was one of the biggest, I wanted her to celebrate. It was not unusual to see Henry Kissinger at the first table, Paul Newman at the second and an important producer at the third.

We pulled up in my James Bond Aston Martin. The valets went hopping like rabbits when they saw Suzanne. The maître d' met us at the desk and asked us to wait a moment. As usual, the place was packed. Sitting at the number one table were Natalie Wood and Sir Laurence Olivier. I asked Suzanne to excuse me for a moment and went over to the table.

I'd known Natalie for years, but I'd never met Olivier. I knew that Suzanne, like any actor, would leap at the chance to meet the British thespian. He was God. Natalie smiled and introduced me to Olivier. After a moment of small talk, I asked her if she had ever met Suzanne.

"No, but I'd love to!"

"May I bring her over?"

"Oh, please do, Jay!"

I brought Suzanne over and introduced her. She was nearest Olivier and I thought I'd let her talk to him while Natalie and I chatted. Natalie and I got into a tête-à-tête; I was leaning close to her, my back to Suzanne. After a couple of minutes, I glanced over my shoulder; Suzanne was no longer there. I looked around; she was standing at the end of the bar like a pale ghost. I quickly bid adieu and went to her.

"What's wrong?" I asked.

She was near tears. "He told me to fuck off," she said.

Like all celebrities, Olivier had a side to him that wasn't reflected on the screen. To him, Suzanne could have been a member of a film crew. He didn't give a damn that she was a famous sitcom star. He didn't watch

American television. He was Laurence Olivier, and when you were Laurence Olivier you could be rude to anyone with impunity. Suzanne was upset, but when we got to our table she rebounded. The truth is, she was the most popular star in the restaurant, and there was nothing Olivier could do about it.

Chapter 20

JET-SETTING

The late seventies and the entire eighties decade brought me many amazing experiences both professionally and personally; however, the lines of exactly what was "professional" and what was "personal" became very blurred indeed. I represented Susan Saint James on and off for several years during the late seventies and early eighties, first as her publicist and then as her manager. She had been a television star in the sixties in *Fame Is the Name of the Game*, with Anthony Franciosa, and in *McMillan and Wife*, with Rock Hudson. Susan had a tendency to fall in love with her leading man. When she discovered Hudson wasn't amenable to man-woman romance, she fell in love with and married her makeup artist, which wasn't amenable to Hudson.

That Susan fell in love with her makeup man wasn't unusual. An actress is with her makeup artist constantly. He's the first person she sees in the morning; he gets to know her without makeup. The problem with Susan's marriage was that she made her new husband her manager, and there's a big gap between managing and putting on makeup. Susan became so much trouble that she was fired. *McMillan and Wife* was suddenly *McMillan*.

Getting fired from a television show is a profound event, particularly when the person fired is a star. Overnight Susan became poisonous to producers; word went out that she was too difficult. She was represented by a big agency that wasn't helping her find work, yet they were asking her for exorbitant sums of money as if she were television dynamite. She wasn't. She was a competent actress with a bad reputation. Susan and her husband were desperate, so desperate that she signed with me, a person philosophically alien to her lifestyle. And then they got divorced.

We made a strange combination. Susan was a flower child, a vegetarian, and an animal lover who detested meat and leather products; she thought of herself as a "natural girl" and she shunned the accoutrements of glamour, such as deodorant. I think she even stopped shaving her armpits. I was as far removed from the hippie lifestyle as a person could be; I thought they were idiots. I was a hunter, a heavy-duty meat eater, and I lived in a house in Stone Canyon full of stuffed animals I had killed on safaris. The only thing Susan and I had in common was that neither of us wore makeup. She was always voicing her insecurities. I got tired of listening to her complaints and starting searching for work for her.

Susan was ambivalent about acting. She wanted to be a star, but she also wanted to stay at home with her kids. When she was in her work mode, I got her a role in a Peter Fonda picture, *Outlaw Blues*, filmed in Texas. A couple of weeks into the production, I flew to Austin to see how things were going. Susan was head over heels in love with Peter. After the movie wrapped, Peter went back to his wife and Susan came back to my place in Stone Canyon with a broken heart. I had affairs with her just to keep her happy when her movies were over and her lovers went back to wives or girlfriends. I became her sexual therapist, physically as well as psychologically. It never failed. She fell in love on every movie, was rejected when the film wrapped, and then she came to Stone Canyon to cry on my shoulder and sleep in my bed until the next production. I learned to break up with the girl I was going out with just before Susan's picture wrapped on location.

Mel Simon financed *Love at First Bite*, which I packaged with George Hamilton and Susan. Mel had not met her, so I threw a big dinner party so they could meet. Susan wore her "natural" look, which meant no makeup. Mel was horrified. The next morning he told me to fire her. He was willing to pay her in full, but he wanted an actress of glamour and beauty to play against Hamilton.

After Mel left for Indianapolis, I remembered a photograph I had of Susan and me taken at the world premiere of *Julia*, the Jane Fonda–Jason Robards film about the love affair between Lillian Hellman and Dashiell Hammett. She was gorgeous. I had my art people cut me out and make a dummy *Glamour* magazine cover using Susan. Then I hopped on a plane and trailed Mel to the Midwest. I showed him the phony picture cover and explained that Susan had made a bad decision by not wearing makeup to dinner. Mel relented.

The movie went forward and Susan promptly fell in love with George Hamilton. After the movie wrapped, of course, George was no longer interested in her. As usual, she came back to Stone Canyon with a broken heart, and we renewed our affair.

Next, she was cast in her first starring role in a TV movie, *Night Cries*, with William Conrad. Suddenly I could mount a movie around Susan Saint James. The final movie we did together was *How to Beat the High Cost of Living* in 1980. Although I packaged it, I did not take a screen credit. It was someone else's movie.

How to Beat the High Cost of Living was the story of three housewives who, discovering that a million dollars was floating around a shopping mall, plotted to steal it. We cast Jane Curtin of *Saturday Night Live* as the second girl, but after Susan's $350,000 and Jane's $300,000, we didn't have enough money left in the budget to get a third actress with star power.

I heard about a talented young actress who couldn't get a job. But during due diligence, I was told she didn't have talent after all. Suspicious, I went to see a movie she was in. Rumor had it she had rejected the sexual overtures of a director who then starting disparaging her talent. The movie was *King Kong*; the actress was Jessica Lange. I hired her for $10,000 to play the third housewife.

The big-screen movies I placed Susan Saint James in were independent productions with major studio distribution. Unless an indie film takes off on its own, the majors aren't going to spend much money to exploit it through advertising, so you're starting out in a hole with a steep climb up a sheer face. Susan's movies were good, but they didn't propel her to stardom.

I came across a pilot script for a potential television series called *Kate & Allie*. One of the two leads was perfect for Susan's personality and talent. The story pitted a liberal woman (Susan) against a conservative woman (Jane Curtin). I can honestly say there would never have been a *Kate & Allie* had there not been a Jay Bernstein. Susan had real drawing power on television. I went to the producers and sold her as the talent they needed. The rest is history.

During hiatus from *Kate & Allie*, I put Susan in an NBC movie-of-the-week, *Desperate Women*, a remake of the 1956 Clark Gable movie *The King and Four Queens*. Susan had enough cachet with independent productions that I could pick the male lead to play against her. It was a payoff picture rather than a starmaker. I wasn't representing Robert Redford or Paul Newman—I had to make do with what I had. That's one reason I didn't put my name on the screen as an executive producer. I was playing the money game.

Susan finally got tired of being stabbed in the back by wayward lovers. I was pleased because I thought she had come to understand her problem. Her solution, however, was absurd, and her timing was out of kilter. She decided she didn't want to do any more movies. This was after she had signed to do *Desperate Women*, assuming the role previously played by Eleanor Parker.

The project was strictly about money. The fact that I signed Dan Haggerty for the Gable role was an indication that none of us thought we were going to make a great movie. Most important, though, as I explained to Susan, it was a movie in which there was little likelihood of her falling in love with her leading man. Haggerty was famous as Grizzly Adams, a role far removed from anything Gable ever played.

A week before we were scheduled to begin production, Susan jumped off a fence and injured her knee. She did it on purpose. She was pleased, even with her pain, because now she wouldn't have to do the movie. Angry, I took her to a doctor.

"It's bad," he said. "It's a real injury."

Susan grinned.

"How long will it take to heal?" I asked.

"Four to five weeks," the doctor answered.

"What can you do that will allow her to work for thirty days, starting immediately?"

The doctor mentioned some new steroid shots.

"No way," said Susan.

"Give her a shot," I told the doctor.

"No way," Susan repeated.

I vented my anger. "Dammit, Susan, you've got a network contract. I'm not going to let you pull this. If you do, you'll ruin your career!"

She acquiesced. The doctor gave her two shots and a bucket of medicine.

Relieved, I hauled her back to my car and started for Stone Canyon. We were halfway home when she said, "I've got another problem."

I wasn't concerned with a new problem because I now knew we could make the picture. "Oh, yeah?" I said. "What is it?"

"I'm pregnant."

I almost crashed the car.

The next day I took her to another doctor; a week later we started the movie.

I was right—Susan didn't fall in love with Dan Haggerty. Rather, she fell in love with Haggerty's buddy, Stephen Stills, of Crosby, Stills & Nash, when he visited the location set. They had a torrid affair. When the movie wrapped, she moved in with him near my house in Stone Canyon. I was glad; I could have a real girlfriend again.

A month later, Susan called me, in tears. She had broken up with Stills. He, and his bodyguards—it seemed all pop musicians and rockers had a legion of security people—wouldn't let her in the house to get her clothes and things.

"Calm down, Susan," I told her. "I'll get your clothes."

I strapped on a holstered belt with two .45s, set a cowboy hat at a rakish angle on my head and went to Stephen's house. I knocked on the door. It opened. Two burly bodyguards who looked like army tanks stood on the threshold.

"Are we gonna have a shoot-out here?" I asked, placing my hands on the handles of my six-shooters. "Or is the girl going to get her stuff?"

Susan got her clothes back.

The whirlwind of activity continued. Farrah went to London to make *Saturn 3*. *Sunburn* was in postproduction. Suzanne was riding high as Chrissy in *Three's Company*, but chomping at the bit to make theatrical movies and perform in nightclubs, and Lee was prepping to do *Agency* in Canada. Each day rolled into the next. I flew to Canada. Lee liked to play between workdays. Work, play—it was all the same to me. Everything was connected.

I got a bead on some movie money in Manila. The two of us took off for the Philippines. The money didn't come through, and we hurried back to Canada, where *Agency* was ready to go into production. Robert Mitchum was the star, but Lee had equal billing, his name beside Mitchum's on the same line. He was excited about working with Mitchum. He said they had once been drinking buddies.

I had first met Mitchum in the sixties through Mike Connors, a friend of his. Mike and I went to Stephanino's to have a drink with Mitchum. He was already there, knocking down drinks like bowling pins. In less than an hour he had three to my one. I was afraid of getting drunk and making an ass of myself. Mitchum seemed as sober as when we arrived. "Let's have another drink," he said.

"That's okay with me," I said. He'd been reminiscing, and I wanted him to continue.

More drinks arrived, and I said, "What was it like working with Kirk Douglas?" They had recently co-starred in *The Way West*.

"It's real interesting to work with a movie star," said Mitchum, after he mulled over my question. "It takes Kirk thirty minutes to dive off a diving board. He has to get up there and pose. He's gotta make sure everybody sees that dimple." He laughed under his breath. "Yep, it's an interesting experience to work with a movie star."

I told Lee the story. He laughed and said he knew Mitchum front and back. He decided to play a joke on Mitchum, become Red Buttons. That was Lee's sense of humor—playacting.

The day Mitchum arrived, Lee donned a chauffeur's uniform and drove to the airport to pick him up. He went through a chauffeur's routine, the Six Million Dollar Man acting out another role. He met Mitchum at the gate, wearing his black chauffeur's hat. Mitchum said hello.

Lee loaded Mitchum's bags and opened the limousine door for him. Finally, he exposed his true identity. The joke backfired. Mitchum had absolutely no fucking idea who Lee was. When they got to the hotel, Mitchum gave him twenty dollars. *Agency* was just another job to Mitchum. He wouldn't know *The Six Million Dollar Man* from *The Threepenny Opera*.

Years later, Carrie Mitchum, Robert's granddaughter, became a friend of mine. She was in *The Bold and the Beautiful*, an afternoon soap opera. I had an avuncular relationship with her that on two occasions resulted in fisticuffs.

The first was at the Bistro in Beverly Hills. She was with a guy who was playing with her more than she wanted to be played with. He was making fun of a tattoo on her ankle. She looked at me, signaling "help" with her eyes. I went to their table and asked the guy to stop. He said, "Go fuck yourself!" I didn't want to do that, so we had a fight. The result was that he stopped harassing Carrie.

Another night I was at the Heartbreak Café, a new place on La Brea Avenue. Carrie was there, and a bar hound was hassling her. Carrie asked him to leave her alone. He didn't, so I asked him to stop bothering her.

"Go fuck yourself!" he said.

Again, I didn't want to do that. Rather, I picked up a bowl of salad and slammed it against the side of his head as hard as I could. He stopped bothering Carrie.

The next day the restaurant manager left a message for me to please call him. My alert signal sounded. I smelled a lawsuit. Hesitantly, I returned the call.

"We're changing our menu," the manager said. "Would you mind if we listed a 'Jay Bernstein Tossed Salad'?"

After that, Carrie always said I was her Sir Lancelot.

In 1980, I was forty-two years old, financially successful, yet I didn't own my own house. In fact, I had never owned a house. I had missed two golden investment opportunities, Richard Donner's house at Sunset Plaza above the Strip and Elvis Presley's place in Stone Canyon, because I couldn't afford them due to gambling debts. I could have had Dick's house for $118,000 and Presley's for $220,000. Within a few years each was worth millions.

A realtor called me. He was representing a mountainside home built by Carole Lombard before she married Clark Gable. I was interested, not because it was a good investment (it wasn't), but because of its history. Lombard was still married to William Powell when she built it in the 1930s; then she divorced Powell and became Gable's lover. She and Gable lived in it for one year before they married and moved to Gable's ranch in the Valley. So it was the house where Gable fucked Lombard.

I went to see it. It was an architectural feat, five stories built in Spanish style on a virtual cliff. It rambled up, down and all around. There was a bedroom on the top floor, a bedroom on the bottom floor. The main floor was terraced; the staircase was spiral; the house had a small indoor-outdoor swimming pool. The views were magnificent. From one direction, you could see the skyscrapers in downtown Los Angeles. From another, West Hollywood, Beverly Hills and Century City. To the west, the beach cities, Santa Monica and Manhattan Beach, and the Pacific Ocean. Yet it was almost walking distance from the Beverly Hills Hotel and the Polo Lounge.

The place was in need of major repairs, but I bought it anyway. I thought the ghosts of Lombard and Gable might inspire me. They didn't, but Bren Simon, Mel's wife, did. She was an internationally recognized decorator and designer who took on the task of renovation. She inspired me to work harder, because during her six months' work on the house I didn't receive one bill. I calculated that I owed her another $500,000 on top of the purchase price, which was frightening. When at last she finished and I moved in, I received the bill in the mail. It was my birthday, and the bill was in the form of a card gifting me with the renovation.

With a new home, I felt I had finally arrived. The house was now Gable-like rather than Lombard-like, with room aplenty for my memorabilia, paintings and trophies from hunting safaris. It became my headquarters for business as well as pleasure, which for all practical purposes were still one and the same. One task was left unfinished, though. Carole's pool, hardly larger than a fishpond, was too small for real swimming. I turned it into the largest Jacuzzi in the country, with forty jets surrounding a water fountain. It was perfect; it was Hollywood.

For months the scandal sheets had been predicting a Fawcett-Majors breakup. Nobody took it seriously except Lee and Farrah. All was not well in paradise—they had hardly seen each other in a year. Then Farrah called me from London. She was being stalked by two men on motorcycles. Finally, bobbies confronted them. They were private eyes, they said, spying for an undisclosed client. Farrah didn't say it, but she intimated they worked for Lee.

Saturn 3 wasn't going well. Stanley Donen, originally a consulting producer, took over as director. He was one of the greats (*Singin' in the Rain, Charade, Two for the Road*), but when directors are changed midstream something is awry. It was beyond Donen's control. There was no chemistry between Farrah and Kirk Douglas. She was in every scene, Kirk was in every scene, and Harvey Keitel was in almost every scene. Three actors confined to a cubicle in outer space. Kirk was too old to play a space cadet; Farrah was too beautiful. Keitel could play anything, but *Saturn 3* wasn't his cricket game.

In California, summer turned into Indian summer. In Canada, Lee was cold. In London, winter turned to spring. In Utah, the weather was unpredictable. I was in Utah with Suzanne and Alan. She was guest-hosting a National Cheerleaders television special.

Third parties are a manager's nightmare. A woman client always has a boyfriend or husband watching from the wings. He always tells her he's a genius. Some of it comes from macho necessity, the alpha male thing; some of it comes from ignorance, sometimes stupidity. Pillow talk, however, gives him an advantage.

With Farrah it was Lee, but once she told me to get him some movies, he was pretty much out of the management picture, busy with his own career. With Suzanne there was Alan Hamel, although Alan was smart enough to realize, at least in the beginning, that management was beyond his realm of experience. Management required strategy as well as tactics. It was long-term thinking. On Sunday Alan thought of Monday, the next day; I thought of the Monday a year from now.

Since Suzanne wanted to be Farrah's equal, I had a great relationship with her and Alan at the outset. They not only treated me as a family member, but they demanded my time socially. They wanted to go everywhere I went, be seen with me constantly; when I evaded them to give my time to Farrah, their disappointment was evident.

Suzanne had a driving ambition to succeed. She never questioned my judgment, always willing to do what I asked of her, which was one reason she became an overnight sensation. I was petrified, however, of the possibility of walking into a room and finding both Suzanne and Farrah present. I had learned much about the ego of stars, beginning with a Las Vegas steam-room episode with Sammy Davis, Jr., and Vic Damone, when Vic fired me because I spoke to Sammy first.

I don't know how I did it, but I managed to keep Farrah and Suzanne at a distance. Not once during the years I managed them both did they ever meet. I worked at the separation because I didn't want to face the complications a meeting would engender. But in Utah, I was with Suzanne and Alan in their suite when Farrah tracked me down by telephone. Suzanne answered the call and then handed me the phone. Her face was pale, expressionless.

Farrah was upset; she wanted me to drop everything and fly to London. I was in a quandary, not wanting to show favoritism to either actress, listening to Farrah's complaints and demands while Suzanne and

Alan were listening to me. It was disconcerting, but I stumbled through the conversation without offending anyone.

By the time I arrived in London, Farrah's spirits had changed from low to high. I stayed only long enough to have another fight with the Fabergé people, a big one. They wanted Farrah to go to Paris and other European cities to promote Farrah Fawcett Fabergé Shampoo. They were adamant. Diplomacy was dead because Farrah's contract was coming to an end. Fabergé had the leverage. With me, they threatened to not renew Farrah's contract; with Farrah, they dangled a carrot: perfume in addition to shampoo.

I explained to Farrah the problem I was having with them. She shrugged and feigned naïveté. "Can you fix it where I can approve the scent of the perfume?"

I wasn't against Fabergé. The company had helped make Farrah wealthy, but it was her screen potential that would sustain her future. And that part of my plan had not gone well. *Somebody* had been only moderately successful. *Sunburn* had not been released; if it didn't open well, Paramount would drop it like a hot coal. Farrah's movie career might go down the tubes, because secretly neither of us had faith in *Saturn 3*. It was now a money picture, incapable of exploiting Farrah's assets. These were facts and speculations we avoided discussing.

Stanley Donen, Farrah's new director, was staying at the Dorchester. He was married to Yvette Mimieux, the beautiful actress with Einstein's brain. I ran into her at the hotel. As we talked, I decided to pull a joke on Stanley. Yvette was amenable; we colluded.

When Stanley came home from the set, he found Yvette and me in bed together. It was a take-off on the old joke about the three most horrific words in the world when you're making love: "Darling, I'm home!"

Yvette and I, under the bedcovers, made sounds of wild passion. Stanley glanced in the bedroom without comment, then went into the parlor and mixed a drink. We made more sounds, then paused. We heard the tinkle of ice in a glass. We made more sounds, then paused again. After a minute Donen called out, "Bernstein, will you get the fuck out of here? I'm tired!"

Suzanne and Alan were still in Salt Lake City. When I checked into the hotel, I had a message to call Elliott Kastner in London. I didn't think it was important, so I didn't return the call.

We flew to Las Vegas to take in the Ann-Margret show. The desk clerk at the MGM Grand gave me eleven messages from Elliott. I went to my suite and called him. He was exhausted and nervous, which translated into desperation. He was a week away from his opening shot on *Yesterday's Hero.*

"I was in London a couple of days ago," I said.

"Why didn't you call me?" He didn't give me time to answer. "I checked out your girl. I'm interested in using her in my picture."

"What happened to Lesley Ann?" I asked.

"We had an argument. I want to go with Suzanne. Otherwise I'm in trouble."

"How much were you going to pay Lesley Ann?"

"Seventy-five thousand for three weeks' work."

"Send me the script," I said. "I'll talk with Suzanne."

Two days later, I received the script. I read it and gave it to Suzanne. She thought it was interesting. On a scale of ten, it was a five; Alan said it was a two.

"Look, Alan, Suzanne needs to do a movie in Europe. It's important for her career."

"Forget it," he said. "It's a piece of shit!"

I called Elliott. "She and her husband don't want to do it, and I can't talk them into it," I told him. I suggested Lynda Carter.

"Jay, I need *your* girl."

"The only way I could possibly talk them into it would be—I'm embarrassed to tell you how much money it would take to keep them from refusing."

"How much?" he asked.

"One hundred thousand a week with a three-week guarantee."

The phone clicked in my ear, but three hours later Elliott called back. "Okay, I'll go with your girl for three hundred grand."

"I'll get back to you, Elliott."

I chased down Suzanne and Alan. Alan still didn't want to do it.

"For Christ's sake, Alan, this is not only a financial windfall but it will give Suzanne exposure in Europe."

He began to argue with me. I lost my temper and shouted him down. Finally he agreed, but with conditions: "We want everything paid for. First-class plane fare, the best hotel suite, unlimited dining-room expenses. Everything! And we want the money in cold, hard cash!"

I went to my room and called Elliott. "She'll do it."

The next day Suzanne and Alan boarded a plane for London and I flew to Los Angeles. Over the next few days, I talked to them several times. All seemed to be going well. Apparently, the minute they arrived Alan began hounding Elliott for Suzanne's money, in cash. At last Elliott delivered, all crisp bills in paper sacks. Then, two weeks into the production, Alan called me. "We're coming back today."

"What? I thought you still had a week of shooting."

"The picture will have to wait. We have to go back to do an Ace Hardware commercial." After negotiating the hardware commercial, I had turned the project over to Alan.

I was flabbergasted. "Alan, you can't leave in the middle of a production."

"Watch us," he said sharply. "Call Elliott and tell him." He hung up.

Elliott closed shop for ten days. It cost him a fortune because he had to keep his cast and crew on payroll. He didn't speak to me for two years, until he needed another actress, Catherine Hicks, whom I was representing.

I never knew for certain, but Elliott must have presold *Yesterday's Hero*, because when it finished he gave Suzanne a Rolls-Royce. That was the good news. The bad news was that it belonged to Elliott's ex-wife. When she discovered her car was gone, she sued him.

Chapter 21

FIRED
BY FARRAH

In 1979, I packaged Suzanne's first and last movie for theatrical release in the United States. Alan and I were executive producers.

Nothing Personal was about a college professor (Donald Sutherland) who was trying to stop a corporation from slaughtering baby seals. His co-conspirator was a young lawyer (Suzanne) who attempted to help him. It was essentially an inane romantic comedy.

Suzanne had a tendency to exaggerate everything. A couple of years later, when ABC's *20/20* produced a profile about me, she told a story that was far-fetched but whose roots almost set off a war between animal preservationists and me.

The film was scheduled to begin production in Ontario during the week of my birthday. Somebody threw a big party for me in Beverly Hills and I flew to Canada the following day. My clothes were in two pieces of beautiful new luggage my mother had sent me.

I arrived at the hotel without fanfare, but the second the bellboy entered the lobby with my luggage a buzz began to bounce off the walls like an echo growing louder. I had no idea the whispers were about me, but I definitely heard the hum of the mantra. "They're made out of sealskin," it said repetitively. "They're made of sealskin."

The subject of the gossip was my new luggage, which I thought was made of pony, a natural fabric commensurate with my mother's particular high-fashion eccentricity. It wasn't. The pieces were made out of sealskin.

Now here I was executive producing an eco-picture with a storyline about two people trying to save the world's baby seals from the slaughter of greedy and ruthless furriers. My luggage wasn't exactly the image I wanted to present. And Suzanne didn't help.

She told people I had arrived with sixteen pieces of luggage, like a modern-day Marco Polo intent on gaining attention of press and photographers. It was absurd. Even Elizabeth Taylor hardly traveled with sixteen pieces of luggage. The press took it in nevertheless, and to this day I think Suzanne believes I brought sealskin luggage by design.

Nothing Personal had a nude scene between the two leads. Suzanne and Donald weren't inclined to disrobe, so we decided to cast their doubles locally. The director seemed excited about the casting session, which made me suspicious. I thought he was a little kinky, although my opinion was strictly intuitive. When one of the wannabes asked me what was "really" going to happen, her suspicion prompted me to attend the session, which was to be held in a hotel suite.

When I arrived, several young women were parading back and forth in their birthday suits. They all seemed delighted to be displaying their bodies, including the girl who had approached me earlier. I was amazed at how many women wanted to play Suzanne in the nude. We were only paying a hundred dollars and their faces would not be seen in the film, but there was a bevy of them nevertheless.

During the flesh parade I was called to the telephone. It was my insurance lawyer. "We've got a problem," he said, referring to the John Gavin libel suit.

The suit had been lingering for years, revolving around Joyce Haber, who was Hedda Hopper's replacement at the *Times* and a woman full of malice. Joyce was a cunt. She was a talented, educated person whose success transmogrified her into a monster. It was a shame, because Joyce was more talented as a writer than Hedda or Louella ever were. Success, however, went to her head. She was the most divisive writer I ever knew—she glorified in hurting people.

Joyce, like a self-appointed arbiter of social class, divided the industry into two groups, people of importance and people of unimportance. Her decisions were arbitrary, and they bothered me. Half of my clients were young and ambitious, often without significant credentials. They were B-list people, according to Joyce. The A-list people were the rich and powerful.

When I had parties I mixed my successful guests and less successful guests. It was my way of letting some of my wannabes rub elbows with movers and shakers, and on more than one occasion the mix helped move a client up the ladder of success. When I moved into Elvis Presley's former Bel Air mansion in Stone Canyon, I went so far as to hand out cards at my housewarming party as the guests arrived. The card read: "You are definitely on the A list!"

Although I didn't like Joyce, I needed her, especially after she became the most powerful columnist writing about the industry. It was not easy for me to get along with her, but I did my best, often giving her tips on stories totally unrelated to my clients.

One of my icons when I was a youth was Betty Grable. In a publicity stunt, Twentieth Century-Fox insured her legs for a million dollars. Her World War II pinup poster was the cat's meow. Every teenage boy had one hanging on his wall. She was the masturbator's delight. I remember seeing reproductions of the image on the fuselages of bombers and fighter aircraft. It was a dorsal shot of the blond bombshell in a white, one-piece bathing suit looking back at the camera over her shoulder. Her hair was piled high. Unbeknownst to the viewer, she was pregnant. When the photographer saw Grable's condition, he had said, "Forget it, Betty. Come back when you're not pregnant."

She didn't want to come back. "No, let's get something," she said. "Let's try an over-the-shoulder shot." It worked. It was one of the sexiest photographs ever taken. The subsequent poster became an important part of America's popular cultural history.

In 1973, Grable was hospitalized in Santa Monica. She was fifty years old, already a legend. Her friends told her she was going to be okay; the doctors told her she was going to be okay. Joyce Haber didn't. Joyce wrote the truth: "Betty Grable is dying of cancer." When Betty read the news, she plunged into the abyss and died a few days later.

So Joyce was not a nice person, yet she had a column that I needed space in.

One of my corporate clients was John DeLorean, the charismatic head of Chevrolet, the man who later tried to start his own auto-manufacturing plant and was destroyed in the process by an FBI sting operation concerning cocaine, a crime of which he was acquitted.

One night at dinner, DeLorean told me that actor John Gavin had recently been caught shacking up with Dolly Cole, the wife of the president of General Motors. I didn't think anything about the story until I next saw Joyce Haber. I wanted something in her column. "If you'll use the piece on my client," I said, "I'll give you some hot gossip." We swapped stories. The next day the Gavin-Cole story ran in her column.

Giving Joyce Haber a rumor became a casus belli, first between John Gavin and Joyce Haber, then Joyce Haber and the *Times*, and then John Gavin and me. Gavin, because of his friendship with Dolly Cole or because Dolly Cole was so beside herself, had the power of General Motors' advertising dollars behind him. They threatened to boycott the *Times* until Joyce revealed her source. *The Los Angeles Times* did not defend its columnist—Joyce was given an ultimatum. Either she revealed her source or she was fired. She revealed her source—me—and then got fired anyway. With that, Gavin changed the direction of his attack: he sued me for a million dollars. Newspapers had a field day. One of the New York papers displayed a picture of me on the front page with the corresponding headline: "Top PR Man Named Slanderer."

My lawyer told me not to worry about it, but I did, immensely. For forty days I was in a storm of mental anguish. I was Noah ensconced in his ark, hoping the rain would stop. It didn't. My business manager informed me that I was not insured, even though I was paying a small fortune for insurance. A few days later my insurance company dittoed his judgment. I saw my little empire falling apart. It wasn't that John Gavin was such a big name, but he was bigger then than now, and the truth is, I was embroiled over an untruth, which wasn't good for anybody, especially a publicist. I didn't know what to do.

I was having lunch at Scandia one day with Harold Abeles on totally unrelated business, but my anguish was such that I couldn't keep from bringing up the impending case. Harold and I had been friends since the beginning of my career.

"Don't you have insurance?" asked Harold.

"Yes, but it doesn't cover this type of suit."

"Let me see the policy," he said.

I took it from my briefcase, and Harold perused it for a few minutes. He looked up. "Who said you aren't covered?"

"The insurance people."

"They're lying. You're covered."

I was relieved, but not acquitted. The suit continued. I did my best to avoid John Gavin. I knew I could never explain to him what really happened. The truth seemed so banal. What would I say? That John DeLorean gave me the story and I passed it on to Joyce Haber? That it was Joyce who didn't verify the story? By not doing so, I went through a half-dozen years of hell. My explanation would not have satisfied John Gavin. As far as he was concerned, I should not have given Joyce the story in the first place. But then John wasn't in the publicity business, where there was give and take between flack and columnist.

So, flashing back to the future, I now had my insurance lawyer on the phone, ordering me to come immediately to goddamn Detroit to resolve this ridiculous thing.

"Jay! You're scheduled in court Monday morning in Detroit."

"Detroit! Are you nuts?"

He explained that the company lawyer handling my case had left the firm and the paperwork had been passing desultorily from secretary to secretary. No one had been available to challenge the change of venue, which now was in the backyard of General Motors. Finally someone suggested, "Maybe we should tell Bernstein."

"I can't be there," I told him. "I'm making a motion picture. Right now

I'm in the midst of casting and shooting an insert in Canada. Monday is impossible. I have to be in Los Angeles where Farrah is shooting her first *Charlie's Angels* special!"

He got another lawyer on the phone. Between the two of them they managed to assuage my feelings. They assured me that once the judge in Detroit realized the change of venue was their fault, he would postpone and delay the proceedings. "Don't worry about it, Jay. We'll handle it."

When I went back to the room full of naked nubiles, the director had chosen the body double he best liked. I didn't think she looked remotely like Suzanne, but then I had never seen Suzanne in less than a bathing suit.

The following Monday, when I was at Twentieth Century-Fox with Farrah, the judge in Detroit was telling my lawyers, "If Jay Bernstein thinks he is too important to be in my court in Detroit, then I find him guilty as charged." He awarded John Gavin $280,000.

I was embarrassed by the denouement of the suit, and I was determined to avoid John Gavin. I did, for a year or so. Then I was in an elevator in Century City. The door opened and Gavin stepped in. It was just the two of us. I tried to avert my eyes, but it was useless. When I took a glance, he was staring at me. We descended in silence a moment, and then he said, "I hope you learned your lesson."

I said nothing. What was there to say?

Twenty-five years after the fact, which was recently, I saw Gavin for the first time since the elevator incident. We were seated at the same table at a benefit. When I looked, Gavin was again staring at me. I averted my eyes and wrote him a note, to wit: "John, it's been twenty-five years. Will you please accept my apology and forgive me?" I folded it and passed it down the table. After a moment, I dared give him another glance. He stared, then nodded yes.

After the court settlement, I had gone to visit a friend at St. John's Hospital in Santa Monica. As I was waiting for an elevator, a nurse trundled a patient to the door in a wheelchair. She was having trouble, so I helped her. When I glanced at the patient, I felt I recognized her. At first, I thought she was an aging movie star; then I realized she was Joyce Haber, aged beyond her years.

She was suffering from cancer, and between the disease and her alcoholism she had deteriorated almost beyond recognition. When the elevator stopped again, I helped the nurse pull the wheelchair into the corridor. Joyce looked at me, but it was obvious that senility had set in. She could have been looking at a tree trunk for all she knew. As the nurse pushed her away, I stared after her, considering how quirky life can be. She had once been a woman of great power and influence; now she was reduced to a withered old lady.

I was compatible with most actors, unless they were intellectuals. The problem with intellectual actors is that they think too much. They're dying and the doctor gives them a choice: take the green pill or the red pill. They have to have an explanation first, and then they have to think about it. Donald Sutherland was an intellectual.

When he signed with me as a management client, he was making $500,000 per picture. I doubled his salary to make *Nothing Personal* with Suzanne. It wasn't a very good movie, but no one started out with the intention of making it bad—it just happened. For me, it was a way to get Suzanne a theatrical release as opposed to more television productions, and for Donald—well, he didn't give any of his million back.

After *Nothing Personal*, Sutherland was offered a leading role in *Excalibur*. He wanted to do it because he thought it was intellectual and prestigious, which it was. Before he signed, we were offered a smaller picture for less money but with a piece of the gross. I persuaded him to take the latter, which initiated his endless complaint.

"This picture is glorified television," he said, apparently referring to his co-stars, Mary Tyler Moore and Judd Hirsch, both of whom had made their marks in TV.

I tried to ignore him, which wasn't easy. When Donald thought he had a case, he was without mercy. "I've got a director who's never directed, a boring story that might fit CBS's Tuesday lineup and a cast of lesser players nobody's ever heard of!"

His tirade was endless. Halfway through the production he fired me because I had persuaded him to bypass *Excalibur*, which was in production in England, starring Nicol Williamson. Frankly, I was relieved; it was good riddance for us both.

The story, however, did not end. The little picture I had talked him into went on to garner six Academy Award nominations for which it won four Oscars: Best Picture, Best Director, Best Supporting Actor and Best Screenplay. It was *Ordinary People*, and Sutherland's cut of the gross was in the millions. Robert Redford directed and Timothy Hutton took the Best Supporting Actor award.

That still wasn't the end of the story. Sutherland took his profits and ran, without paying me my share. I threatened a suit, and we settled out of court, which I'm sure Sutherland is still grousing about.

Everything was hectic. I was flying back and forth from one production to another, while managing several actors. Lee and I were back in Manila, preparing to fly to Canada. Farrah called. She wanted Lee to come back to Los Angeles. She complained that they had seen each other only ten days in one year. Lee, always quick to take credit but never one to be faulted, blamed me for the estrangement. I was the one who had put together his movie deals, thus I was the culprit. I remembered the day Farrah said, "Jay, unless you can get Lee some movies, too, I can't do any more movies." I had found him five, including the forthcoming *The Last Chase*, another Canadian production to be filmed in Ontario. Not bad negotiating for a Jew without horns.

As I recall, we flew to Los Angeles for a few days and then Lee went back to Canada. He had some looping to do for *Agency*, and he wanted to see the locations for *The Last Chase*. Because of tax incentives, Canada had become a haven for movie productions, and both Vancouver and Toronto were now Hollywood satellites. The locations for *The Last Chase* were near Caledon, a few miles from Toronto. Another company was filming *Circle of Two* with Tatum O'Neal and Richard Burton. I caught up with Lee in Canada.

Ryan O'Neal showed up to visit Tatum, and called on Lee at our hotel.

Through the years, after Ryan had threatened to kill me, I had done my best to keep some distance from him. He and Lee had remained friends, or so thought Lee. We were still working on the Philippine deal and needed to go back to Manila. I remember Lee asking Ryan, when the latter was getting ready to return to Los Angeles, "Do me a favor, Ryan. Farrah is upset with me for not being home, but Jay and I have to go to Manila again. Can you give her a call and take her to dinner or something?"

Ryan agreed to help his buddy out. Whether he called Farrah when he returned, I don't know, but he obviously called her at some point. I do not believe, however, that Ryan was the reason Farrah and Lee broke up. The seed had been planted long before Lee asked Ryan to give Farrah a call. A relationship between two actors is the most difficult in the world, particularly when both are stars. In my judgment, the primary problem in the Majors-Fawcett relationship was that they seldom saw each other. They simply grew apart.

I was with Lee in his suite in Manila when Farrah told him, via telephone, that she wanted a separation. He was devastated. Fearing he was going to jump from his fourth-floor terrace, I coaxed him away from the balustrade. Lee and Farrah had been married ten years with many ups and downs and myriad threats, but this time Farrah was serious and Lee knew it. She wasn't asking for a divorce, but even legal estrangement was almost too much for Lee to handle. Meanwhile, neither Lee nor Farrah wanted the breach to become public. My task was to make sure the press didn't pick up on it until they sorted things out. I flew back to L.A.

Farrah had changed dramatically in five years. The naïve little girl from Texas no longer existed. She was an experienced Hollywood woman now—smart, savvy and growing tough.

I had become her alter ego. She didn't like giving interviews, so I gave them for her. It finally got to be too much for Farrah. We were doing a photo shoot at my home when she overheard me giving a telephone interview in another room. I had become Farrah. I said, "I get up in the morning and go jogging, and then I play racquetball. And then I do this and I do that."

Farrah didn't like what she heard. Later she cornered me. "I heard you give that interview as if you were me."

"Well, you hate to give interviews," I said. "I'm just making it easier for you."

She made a face. "It's crazy, Jay. It's like we're in the Twilight Zone."

It was true. Sometimes I didn't know if I was Jay or Farrah, and the same was true of her. In retrospect, it was a pivotal moment. Farrah had been dependent on men all her life. Her father had been a strict disciplinarian, and then she had come to California and immediately met Lee. She had never been independent. The men in her life had guided her every move. She looked to men to make decisions, as if they were carrying suitcases too heavy for her to lift. She had counted on Lee for years, but now I had taken over his decision making. Of course, I thought I was building her into something she had never been—a role model, a legend, a living symbol of the best things in American life: baseball, apple pie and Chevrolet. I had pushed her beyond her limit, because Farrah was not ambitious. It was me—I was ambitious for her. Now that was changing.

The release date for *Sunburn* was approaching; we had a seven-city promotional tour in front of us. The press was clambering as ever, wanting stories. The *Los Angeles Times* called, wanting to interview Farrah about the movie. I said yes.

The *Times'* Charles Champlin was the most likable, personable and smartest of the Los Angeles film critics. He was a real journalist who took his business seriously. I'd had good rapport with him for years.

Farrah and I met Champlin on a bright, sunny afternoon at the Polo Lounge at the Beverly Hills Hotel. It was Tuesday; he was writing for the *Times'* Sunday entertainment magazine. A pleasant man, prematurely gray at the temples, he exuded warmth and a genuine admiration for Farrah. The first thing he asked was, "How is Lee doing?"

"Wonderful," said Farrah. She glanced at me, determined that her private life was going to remain a secret, with me caught in the middle like a punching bag. I shrugged and nodded.

Farrah giggled and exuded a lot of verbiage about how much she missed Lee and how well he was doing in Canada on his shoot and how she wished he could be with her on the forthcoming tour for *Sunburn* and how they talked to each other on the phone every day, gushing on and on ad infinitum, Lee and Farrah, two lovesick puppies.

Champlin believed her, and I wanted to. Their lives were not running smoothly, but maybe there was still room for patches on the old inner tube. It was a good interview.

We left the next morning for Dallas, the first of seven cities. Farrah seemed remote, caught up in her thoughts. She slept until it was almost time to touch down at Dallas/Fort Worth International. We had been given the "Fasten your seat belts" announcement when Farrah said, "Before we have our press conference, I want you to announce that Lee and I have separated."

What? The first thing that came to my mind was the Champlin piece for Sunday. After *Somebody Killed Her Husband*, which some critics had tabbed as "Somebody Killed Her Career," we needed some good press to get *Sunburn* off and running. Champlin was going to be one pissed-off journalist. Worse, he was a journalist with clout; he could kill a movie.

"What about all the lovey-dovey stuff you told Champlin?"

"He'll have to change his story."

In my years with Farrah, there were few times when she wouldn't listen to my advice; this was one of them. Her mind was made up; it wasn't going to change. I began to think of ways to handle the press.

We landed, and I called the AP and UP. I put out a tersely worded statement confirming that Farrah Fawcett and Lee Majors had separated: "For the past two years their careers have interfered with their marriage. They have been like ships passing at sea, pausing only to exchange mail. This is a trial separation, not a divorce; they hope reconciliation can be attained."

I was right about Champlin. When he heard that Farrah and Lee were separating, he felt betrayed. He had to rewrite his story, which had been a blissful portrayal of the Fawcett-Majors marriage. Farrah had almost made a fool of him. It did not bode well for *Sunburn*.

Thirty reporters were waiting in a conference room at our hotel in Dallas. Two dozen more were tied in by telephone from other cities. I told them questions about Farrah's marriage were off-limits, and then Farrah came out. The first question was about her marriage. She began to cry. I handled the rest of the questions, and then we dashed back to the airport. The next stop was Atlanta.

One of the flight attendants was almost as pretty as Farrah. Farrah saw that I was enamored. "Why don't you go talk to her?" she asked.

I made up an excuse not to. I didn't want to be rejected in front of Farrah. It was a three-hour flight. When Farrah went to sleep, I slipped out of my seat and approached the attendant. Her name was Kathy Dutler; she was in her early twenties. My fear of failure was unfounded—we hit it off immediately, joking and laughing. Atlanta was her termination point. "Why don't you hang out with us while we're in town?" I said.

Kathy joined us the next day, which was the beginning of a relationship between us. She had an apartment in Chicago, her home base, but she flew in and out of Los Angeles a great deal.

We finished the tour in ten days. Farrah cried a lot. The first press-conference question was always "What about you and Lee?" We avoided it, often with Farrah running offstage, escaping and leaving me to answer the rest of the questions.

Sunburn opened as we completed the promotional tour. The first bad news was Charles Champlin's review. It was devastating. He was still upset over Farrah's deceit regarding her breakup with Lee. (Champlin later told me he actually enjoyed the film.) His review was all Paramount needed. They pulled the film after three days.

We were in a dilemma. We had two independent movies behind us, one moderately successful and the second pulled from distribution, with a third on the horizon. Part of my job was to keep my clients working, but three hitless movies in a row wouldn't help Farrah's future. It was evident she couldn't carry a theatrical movie. She would never go to the Super Bowl unless she could finish a season. Right now, I was having trouble keeping her in the game.

We had a second feature deal lined up with John Daly and Hemdale Films, *Strictly Business*. Roger Moore was set to co-star. When *Sunburn* was pulled, Moore walked. Then Farrah and I walked, giving up her

$800,000 salary and my $100,000 fee as executive producer. Farrah's future as a film star did not look good.

Bubble gum and hustle had not worked. We had made the films because no offers had been forthcoming from the studios after the Spelling-Goldberg suit. I told Farrah the truth: "We didn't pick *Somebody*, *Sunburn* and *Saturn* over offers from Fox, Universal and Warner Bros. We took what we could get. You haven't been getting bad reviews, Farrah; the movies have," which was true.

Farrah understood. She was tough and resilient. I began to put together a new plan, still convinced she could become a legend like Harlow and Monroe, without having to die at midnight. We would have to bypass movies for a while. I thought a Broadway play could be a starting point, followed by a Kazan-type, art-house movie. The main emphasis would be to showcase her talent, which had become evident even to the critics who blasted our movies. As I vented my thoughts, Farrah said nothing. Unbeknownst to me, I was chasing moonbeams.

After we got back to L.A., I received a belated birthday card in the mail: "Dear Jay, I love you and happy birthday two months late, August 7, 1979. En route was one of my most fun and fascinating trips ever, the Sunburn tour. You are my favorite traveling companion—Farrah."

The gossip sheets reported that she was dating Ryan O'Neal.

August ended, September passed. One October morning, Farrah called me. She wanted to know if I could meet her at the Bagel Nosh, a small restaurant in Beverly Hills. We sat across from each other chewing bagels. The atmosphere was distinctly foggy.

"Jay, I'm concerned because the movies haven't done very well."

"It's funny," I said. "We didn't do them to make gobs of money, but you're rich now."

"Richard Barrie says my new Fabergé contract will have a condition."

"Like what?" I answered, as if I didn't know.

"They won't renew it if you are my manager."

I did not say anything. Barrie had bypassed me because he knew I would bring a stiff bargain to the Fabergé table. I observed Farrah. When I had become her manager, she was the second-billed Angel. The number of lucrative contracts I had negotiated for her in the interim was too many to calculate, but she was now a bona fide multimillionaire.

"What do you think I should do?" she asked.

"You're asking me a silly question, Farrah," I said calmly. "You already know what you're going to do."

She did not know what to say. The silence was suddenly funereal. Without another word, I got up and left.

Chapter 22

THREE'S
NOT COMPANY

Most stars have a closet they don't want opened because it's full of skeletons. Actors become actors because they don't want to be themselves; they want to be someone else. During a production, an actor often personifies the role he is playing off-camera as well as on—it's more than make-believe to him. Sometimes an actor adopts a role and keeps it long after the movie is finished. The baggage an actor brings to Hollywood is usually rooted in childhood, often in a dysfunctional family. Suzanne Somers had more skeletons in her closet than a natural-history museum.

Her father was an abusive alcoholic, a sick man. I don't think he physically abused his children, but mental scars are often worse than physical ones. Suzanne had more scars than the victim of a lion attack; you just couldn't see them. She hated being Suzy Mahoney from San Bruno, California, and the only way to escape her past was to become Suzanne Somers, star of television, movies and stage.

When a good publicist or a good manager knows everything about his client he is prepared to counter past history when it is dredged up. Suzanne was incapable of letting anyone in on her dark secrets until they were revealed publicly, which was like treading on thin ice over a big, cold, deep lake. It was a dangerous game, but Suzanne had a problem differentiating truth from fiction. She wanted to bury the past and live happily in the made-up world of the present.

In late 1979, I received a call from a reporter at the *National Enquirer*. The pulp weekly was running a cover story on a hot-check scam Suzanne had been caught up in ten years earlier. She had been arrested, and now the *Enquirer* was using her mug shot on its front page. Suzanne was at the height of her popularity in *Three's Company*. No doubt the article could damage her public image, but I was equally concerned about her fragile ego.

I called Suzanne and told her what was in the works.

"What are you going to do?" She was frantic. "You've got to save my career!"

"This time you're going to have to do it yourself," I said.

"What do you mean?"

"Here's what I want you to do," I continued. "I want you to call Vernon Scott at United Press. He's a good man and generally sympathetic. Tell him you want to meet with him personally. When you do, here's what I want you to tell him."

I gave her the following story: Suzanne was a single mother. She was struggling. Her child was sick. She was due a modeling check that didn't come in the mail. She had to have medicine for her son, but she had no money. No one would help her—she was alone in the world. She wrote a bad check for the medicine, then another. They bounced, but she couldn't cover them. She didn't care. Her son's health came first. If the *National Enquirer* wanted to capitalize on her misfortune as a struggling single mother with a sick child, so be it. If she had to do the same thing over again, she would.

Vernon Scott put the story on the United Press wire. It ran around the world. The tabloids had a field day for a couple of weeks, but UP's subscribers were mainstream newspapers. They were legitimate; the tabloids weren't. Viewers of *Three's Company* who loved Chrissy Snow, Suzanne's character, came to her defense, responding with letters to editors and to ABC. It was a cakewalk. I never asked Suzanne the true story, just as I had never asked Farrah about her being charged and convicted of petty theft; I didn't want to know.

A few weeks later I scheduled Suzanne for a Barbara Walters

interview. To be featured in one of Barbara's well-produced specials was the epitome of celebrity, a milestone. It meant Suzanne had really made it. Walters didn't interview wannabes or has-beens. Alan was against it; he didn't think Suzanne could handle herself. I thought he was nuts. After the hot-check story, I felt Suzanne could handle anything.

She could and did, although the Walters interview was not without controversy. Halfway into the session Barbara handed Suzanne a ten-year-old nude photo taken by a professional photographer. "I have to ask you, Suzanne—why did you do this?"

Caught by surprise, Suzanne turned ten shades of red, but once she regained her composure she handled herself admirably. She harked back to the poverty theme: mother alone and son sick. It was plausible because almost every girl who does a nude layout, then and now, is desperate for cash. Suzanne ended the Walters session by reading one of her poems. It was poignant, and she was perfect.

The downside to the nude-photograph revelation was that Hugh Hefner bought the series for *Playboy*. "What are you going to do, Jay?" Suzanne was frantic again.

I knew Hefner, which meant I knew he was tough. He didn't give a shit about a woman's feelings if it meant an increase in *Playboy* sales.

First, I did the obvious. I threatened to sue if Hef published the photos, a ploy that would come to nothing if I didn't have a better angle than hurt feelings. We made some press hay out it ("Poor Suzanne Somers. Why don't they just leave her alone?"), but it wasn't enough. *Playboy* published the photographs. By today's standards they were tame, but this was 1980.

The first backlash came from Ace Hardware. They suspended Suzanne's commercials and put out a Mickey Mouse press release about the company's morals. Had it not been for the money involved, I would have laughed. But money *was* involved. I had to come up with an angle, a counterpunch.

I had arranged for Suzanne to be National Campaign Chairperson and Telethon Hostess of the 1980 Easter Seals campaign. Again she was walking on thin ice; it wouldn't look good for her to be fired from a charity, particularly because of nude photographs. I called Hefner.

"Hef, I need help," I told him. "Suzanne is being squeezed. Her career is at stake, while you're reaping rewards from a mistake she made years ago. I don't want to sue you, because I know we would lose. But it would still cost you a couple of hundred thousand dollars in legal fees. Why don't you settle with us for fifty grand, and we'll give the money to the Easter Seal Society."

Hef, being smart and experienced, agreed. We settled. I made a big deal out of giving the proceeds to Easter Seals, including my commission. As I recall, Hef paid Suzanne with a diamond ring he said was worth $50,000. I don't know if she gave it to the charity, but she kept her position as Campaign Chairperson. A few days later Ace Hardware lifted its ban on Suzanne's commercials. All was well in the Hamel household.

Unlike the early days when I first became Suzanne's manager, I was now seldom alone with her. Alan wouldn't allow it. Pillow talk wasn't enough for him. He had to be involved in every conversation between Suzanne and me. He didn't see me as a threat to his marriage as much as he feared that somehow he would be overshadowed.

Unbeknownst to Alan, Suzanne and I met once a week at her beauty salon, Vidal Sassoon's. While she got coiffed, manicured and pedicured, I got a haircut. It was the only time we could talk confidentially.

One day, aware of my depression over having been fired by Farrah, Suzanne said, "I have a present for you that will cheer you up."

She gave me a gift box. I opened it. Inside was a silver medallion with the inscription "Mr. Mean, I love you . . . Suzanne." I looked at her.

"If you ever think I'm going to fire you, just rub the medallion," she said. "I'm not like Farrah, Jay. I'll never fire you."

I hugged her. She had lifted my spirits, but only momentarily. I knew Alan was unaware of the gift, as well as her promise. Otherwise, she would have given it to me in front of him.

Kathy Dutler had become my anchor. She lived with me as much as possible, and I was back and forth from Los Angeles to Chicago when she couldn't be in Hollywood. Spring passed uneventfully. Suzanne opened her nightclub act at Harrah's Lake Tahoe. She called and invited me to fly up on June 7. "We've modified the show," she told me. "Why don't you come and see it?"

I was excited. June 7 was my birthday. By this time I had given Marsha Yanchuck, my secretary, to Suzanne. Marsha had been with me thirteen years, but when the pressure became too much I asked Suzanne to hire her. She knew how important my birthday was to me. Jumping to a conclusion, I called Kathy in Chicago. "You've got to come," I said. "Suzanne is giving me a surprise party in Tahoe."

Kathy was on call for flights all over the nation, but she managed to take a twenty-four-hour break to be with me one night at Lake Tahoe. She flew into LAX on my birthday, and we caught a puddle-jumper north.

We got to Tahoe just in time to go to the show, where Suzanne and Alan had reserved front-row seats for us. Marsha was there. She wished me happy birthday. I made notes on some of the flaws in Suzanne's performance, but my mind was really on the postshow party.

At the end of the show, Alan said, "Come on," and we followed him into the hotel kitchen, where Suzanne was waiting for us. Neither of them mentioned my birthday. The conversation was all about the show, which they thought was the greatest performance since Hamlet's soliloquy. From there we went the back way up to their suite. I felt good, knowing when the door opened a host of people would suddenly cry, "Happy birthday, Jay!" I held my breath.

Alan opened the door; Kathy and I followed Suzanne in. The room was empty.

My heart fell, but I didn't say anything. Five minutes later we heard a rap at the door. I suspected again that this was going to be it, the moment of surprise. Alan opened the door. A single room-service valet rolled in a table set for two.

"Why don't we get together tomorrow for lunch?" said Alan.

"Okay, sure," I answered.

"Have a good time tonight," said Suzanne.

I was more than disappointed—I was in a state of shock. How dare they! I had just saved Suzanne's career, not once but twice. Kathy and I did not go to our suite. We drove around the lake. I finally pulled over and began to cry. I cried for thirty minutes.

Two weeks later, Kathy and I broke up.

Tony Thomopoulos was the new president of ABC Television. Suzanne, Alan and I were joining him for dinner at Michael's Restaurant. Linda Thompson, my date, was meeting us there. I went to Suzanne's house for cocktails first. She and Alan were annoyed because I was running late. I sensed their irritation was about more than my belatedness.

After clinking glasses, Suzanne grew serious. "Jay, Alan and I have been discussing my future. You've done everything for my career that you could possibly do, and we both appreciate it."

She paused. Blood was curdling in my face because I realized what was coming. She continued: "We think it's time for Alan to become my manager."

To say that I exploded would be an understatement. I erupted like a volcano. Suzanne wrote in her memoir that I pulled a sword from my walking stick and swung it through the air; she also said she never thought for an instant I would harm them. She was wrong on both counts. I didn't have a sword, just my stick, but I wanted to slay them like dragons.

After a few minutes I calmed down, but my mind was racing. We drove in separate cars to Michael's in Santa Monica. We were an hour late for dinner. I had hoped to repair my relationship with ABC through Thomopoulos, but that was now wishful thinking. I'd been blackballed so long that it seemed normal.

Linda, who had been Elvis Presley's inamorata during his prime, was waiting with Tony and his wife. I confess I ignored her. I couldn't keep my eyes off Suzanne, who I stared at with laser-like intensity. My gaze unnerved her, which was my intention.

Tony ordered an expensive bottle of red wine. It was not just bad but terrible. It wasn't tainted—it was lousy. I told the sommelier.

"I'm sorry," he said. "It's usually a great wine. I'll get you another bottle of it."

"Please do," said Suzanne.

"Why would we want another bottle of the same bad wine?" I asked.

"Oh, Jay!" protested Suzanne.

Thomopoulos probably thought I was setting the stage for Act I, but we were already deep into Act II. It was a miserable evening.

When we left the restaurant, I felt as if I were in a vacuum. The valet brought my car. When we got in, Linda said, "I can't go out with you anymore, Jay."

I looked at her, as if it were important. "Why?" I asked.

"You remind me too much of Elvis."

Chapter 23

HOLLYWOOD HELL

Absent Farrah and Suzanne, my life went into a tailspin. What few clients I had left, I let slip away. All of them fired me. I held no hard feelings; I wasn't doing anything for them anyway. It was as if I had no energy, no desire to wheel and deal.

My reputation had caught up with me. I dated dozens of beautiful girls, but I was never sure if they were interested in Jay Bernstein the man or Jay Bernstein the starmaker.

I met a young woman named Joan at the Polo Lounge. We had one date. It was fun. She said she didn't know who I was. "Can we do this again?" she asked.

I gave her my number and she called the next night. She was at a well-known producer's house in Beverly Hills. She wanted me to come over. Her voice was sexy, enticing.

I drove over to the house thinking about Joan. She was a beautiful girl, twenty-three, maybe twenty-four. She looked like a model, except for her bustline. She was bountifully endowed. Full of erotic dreams, I drove over to the house.

Nobody answered the door. I listened; I could hear noises inside—not voices, not laughter, just sounds. The door was unlocked, so I went in. It was an elegant house, big and rambling. I followed the sounds into a den. What I saw was weird.

Three girls were nude, each wearing a dog collar. One was walking in a circle and the other two were crawling, making barking sounds. Joan was not one of them. "What in hell are you doing?" I asked.

"Don't worry," said one of the girls. "We get paid for it."

I heard more noises and went into the next room. The well-known producer was there. It was as if I were his cousin. "Hi, Jay, come in. Partake." He was watching another girl wearing only a dog collar. She was down on her hands and knees slurping from a dog bowl.

"Where's Joan?" I asked.

The man shrugged, his eyes intent upon the girl. "Around here somewhere."

I got the hell out of there. I never saw Joan again, but she called me the next day. "Where did you go last night? He told me you were there."

"I'm not into kinky stuff like that," I told her.

"I'm not either," she said, "but he's promised to put me in a movie."

I didn't say anything; it wasn't worth my time. The raw side of Hollywood did not appeal to me. It was an element that appealed to gossips, and it always got blown out of proportion to the detriment of the industry. I resented it, yet I continued my descent into Hollywood hell.

I was still in the doldrums when I got a call from a friend of Ronald Reagan. It was during the presidential campaign of 1980. He wanted to know if I would be interested in managing Patti Davis, the candidate's daughter.

Patti, who had taken her mother's maiden name, had been struggling for years to find a career in Hollywood. Except for the fact that her father was a national figure, Patti was like thousands of other would-be actors— she had found little success. Her parents, as well as other members of the Reagan election team, were concerned about Patti's liberal views. I was quietly asked to represent her, ostensibly to advance her career but also with implicit instructions to control her publicity. The Reagan people considered Patti a loose cannon, a young rebel who often spouted views contrary to her father's positions.

Patti's career in Hollywood was not floundering; it didn't exist. In

seven years she had managed to gain just two credits. The press latched on to our relationship like leeches. A trade paper wrote in typical Hollywood lingo: "Hot shot agent puts Reagan's daughter on road to stardom. . . . [Patti is] being groomed by veteran Jay Bernstein [who says] the statuesque 28-year-old daughter has special star quality." With that kind of publicity, failure was not an option.

Patti's advantage was the precise element of her potential that she resented. She was Reagan's daughter, yet she didn't want to use her legal moniker as a career stimulus. Her attitude was admirable, but she was being naïve. That she was the daughter of her father was inescapable, especially after Reagan became president.

She was a so-so actor, but talent is only part of the recipe for success. She needed a top talent agent also. Throughout my career I have been tagged as an agent, but I never was, although a manager's duties often overlap other fields. I sought out Norman Brokaw at the William Morris Agency, where I continued to have a good—even symbiotic—working relationship. Overnight we put her to work. Said *Time* magazine: "Patti is just about the hottest name in town, appearing on TV's *Vega$ . . . Fantasy Island . . .* [and] *CHiPs*."

As far as the family was concerned, my involvement with Patti was meant to give her something to do aside from making public pronouncements, especially espousing her view on nuclear weapons. It worked, because when a young person begins to break barriers in Hollywood, life changes. The world looks different from how it did when you were in the unemployment line.

If I was initially hired to keep Patti busy, my efforts did not long remain in that single domain. Nancy Reagan called me infrequently, but when she did call she usually had questions about other aspects of public relations. After one of the presidential debates, she was curious about her husband's performance. "I thought he was shooting from the hip," I told her. "He didn't do his homework, what I call 'due diligence.'" Nancy seemed to agree, although I saw no improvement during the next debate.

Patti and I became friends. In the early days we got along famously. To quench her thirst for liberal talk, I kept her working. After the TV serial roles, I set up a deal for her to do an NBC Movie of the Week. She was cast as the female lead against Gregory Harrison in a teleplay about the Chippendales, the famous male dancers—or infamous, depending on one's perspective. It wasn't Shakespeare, but then Shakespeare never drew a television audience. It was an easy sale because the executives at NBC knew Reagan's daughter would attract a large audience.

When Reagan became president-elect, Patti asked me to be her date for the inauguration. I said yes, I would be delighted. Meanwhile, I introduced her to some of the young up-and-coming actors I knew. One night when I had to take my client Melissa Sue Anderson to a social function, I set up a date for Patti with Timothy Hutton, my old friend Jim's son. Patti fell in lust. A few days later she called me: "Jay, would you mind if I take Timothy to the inauguration instead of you?" I didn't mind, and she made arrangements to take Tim.

A week before the inauguration, Timothy had second thoughts. He was a Democrat, and he didn't think the idea of escorting Patti was so cool after all. He said he didn't want to look like George Hamilton, who had dated Linda Bird Johnson back in the sixties. He bowed out, and Patti called me. "Jay, I want you to be my escort after all. Will you?"

Actually I had been excited about going the first time she'd asked me, but now I had reservations. Patti was too protean. "Patti, I'll commit to take you if you promise you're not going to change your mind at the last minute," I told her. "I've got a lot of stuff to do, and the press will want to go through me to get information about you. I don't want to tell them something that's subject to change on a whim." She promised there would be no further changes.

The Air Force was sending a plane. For security purposes we had an entire floor reserved at a Washington, D.C., hotel. One of Reagan's campaign aides scheduled a photo session for us with her parents. I started feeding the press pre-inauguration stories about Patti, in which I included myself. I announced on *Good Morning America* that I would be Patti's date and escort for all events. The day before we were supposed to leave, Patti called me.

"Jay, I've been thinking." She began to hem and haw without saying anything of importance. She didn't have to; I knew what she wanted to say.

"Get to the point, Patti."

"I've decided to go alone. I mean, you're still invited to the inauguration and the parties and all, but I think I should fly to Washington by myself."

"And how am I supposed to get there? By stagecoach? And where am I supposed to stay? Every hotel in Washington, D.C., is booked out by now, Patti."

She talked around the issue until I grew tired of it.

"Fuck you," I said, and hung up.

Patti and I didn't speak again for a long time, although I continued to manage her career. I was angry as well as embarrassed. Essentially, she was dumping me publicly, and now I would have to deal with all the newspeople who had reported that I was going to be her escort.

I speculated as to why I'd been dumped. Perhaps it was because I represented an image the Reagans were trying to avoid. It was the same when JFK switched from Sinatra's house to Bing Crosby's house before his visit to Palm Springs. Sinatra had the wrong image; he was no longer valuable to Kennedy. I wore a beard, carried a walking stick and was a show-business mover and shaker named Bernstein. Somebody in the Reagan coterie had decided my image was not what he or she wanted to portray. Now that Ronnie was president, it was time to avoid the Hollywood stuff, the flamboyant stuff and the Jewish stuff. Maybe that's why Nancy Reagan was so nice to me later.

I was really down in the dumps. My biggest clients were starting to disappear, and it seemed that so, too, was a lot of money. I wasn't exactly sure what my accountants thought of me, but I thought I had a really good relationship with all my accountants, who worked with Union Bank. By most standards I was rich, a millionaire on the low end of the scale, but wealthy enough that I no longer watched my money with scrutiny. My accountant was a young man named David Flynn. When David went into partnership with Ed Trabner, it seemed like a good idea. Ed handled a number of established stars, including Red Buttons and Gig Young. David had several up-and-coming stars, including Farrah and Lee, who I'd sent to him. Their firm quickly became a powerhouse, representing stars like Paul Newman, Goldie Hawn and Warren Beatty.

Once Flynn and Trabner became my business managers, I didn't give them much thought. They had a blue-chip clientele, which included me somewhere down the list among the $2 and $3 million group, and I felt secure. All seemed well; then weird things began to happen. I started getting calls from businesses I owed money to, a hundred dollars here and a thousand there. "Mr. Bernstein, could you please pay this outstanding bill? It's been four months," or "Mr. Bernstein, we've billed you time and again. We would hate to turn your bill over for collection."

I called Union Bank to check my accounts: savings, investments and checking. Collectively they were $1 million short. Not only was nothing there, but also I was in debt $500,000. It seemed someone had embezzled my hard-earned fortune. I was bankrupt, and to top it off, Union Bank wasn't very cooperative.

It was one of the most horrible periods of my life. I had lost Farrah and Suzanne, and with them my energy. I was playing a game with myself, feigning retirement. I was in the process of building a big terrace deck off the second floor of the Carole Lombard home; suddenly I didn't have money for the construction workers. My life was a mess, but I kept plodding along as if everything was fine.

I had booked Patti Davis on *The Dinah Shore Show*. I went to the studio to see the taping, but Patti wasn't there; furthermore, she wasn't on the guest list. When I discovered she had been bumped from the show, I was angry. How do you bump the daughter of the president of the United States? I went to the casting director to find out what the hell was going on.

"She was canceled, Jay."

"Canceled? By whom?"

"Well . . . by you."

I didn't remember doing it. I had no idea why I would have canceled Patti, but it was there on the log. Suddenly Hoyle was more than a cliché;

nothing was working accordingly. It was time to have a long talk with my best friend: me. The conversation went like this: "If you don't know what you're doing, then maybe it's time to check out." I had always been a winner; suddenly I felt like an abject loser.

I went home, packed a bag, took my .38 and six shells, and drove away. I went to a bookstore and bought two new biographies of Susan Hayward. Then I got a few tins of Russian caviar and two bottles of Russian vodka. By the time I finished shopping, I had ten hundred dollar bills and a handful of credit cards to my name. But where was I going?

The Beverly Hills and the Beverly Wilshire Hotels were out of the question. I did not want to run into someone I knew who would say, "Hey, Jay! Did you hear? I put a deal together at Columbia!"

"That's great. Congratulations."

"And what about you? What are you up to?"

"I'm on my way to commit suicide."

"That's great, Jay! See you later!"

Instead, I went to the Beverly Crest, a three-star high-rise at Pico Boulevard and Beverly Drive, a few blocks south of downtown Beverly Hills. A Japanese clerk was behind the desk.

"I want a full suite," I told him.

"You have reservation?"

"No."

"No reservation, no suite. No rooms vayable."

I didn't want to fool with this guy. "How much is a suite?" I asked.

"Four hundred dorras."

I put six hundred dollar bills on the counter.

He looked at the money and said, "No room vayable."

I placed another two bills on the counter.

"No rooms."

I lay down two more bills, and asked, "Have you got a broom closet?"

"No rooms vayable."

When he turned down a thousand dollars, I knew I couldn't bribe him to open the sushi bar a half-hour early.

I drove down Pico Boulevard toward the ocean. Off on a side street

I saw a high-rise Ramada Inn. I took a small suite on the ninth floor. The building reminded me of my first apartment in the Mexican hood. It wasn't the place I had pictured in my mind for suicide. I thought of Edward G. Robinson's pleasant death scene in *Soylent Green*. I put off my death until the next day. I went to bed and began to read one of Susan Hayward's biographies.

I was ensconced in the room for two days trying to work myself up to committing suicide. When I realized it wasn't working, I called my answering service. One of the messages was from Kathy Dutler in Chicago. She was upset; her sister had given birth to a stillborn child. I decided to put off suicide for a while longer and go to Chicago.

It was the same as usual at O'Hare International, cold and windy. Kathy met me. She was cold, too, having seen her sister's baby dead at birth. I tried to soothe her feelings, but it didn't work. I stayed one night and flew back to Los Angeles.

Since I was still alive, I honored a luncheon engagement with Michael Roshkind, vice-chairman of Motown. Mike knew I wasn't myself. He began to quiz me. I told him everything—Farrah, Suzanne, Kathy, the embezzlement, even my botched suicide. "I don't want anything from you, Mike. I'm not a good businessman, and I don't know what to do."

"Let's go to the bank. I'll loan you a half-million dollars."

"Sure," I said, "and what will I put up as collateral?"

"I'll take a mortgage on your home."

"I already have a mortgage."

"Then I'll take a second mortgage."

"I have a second mortgage, too."

"Then I'll take a third mortgage."

"There isn't such a thing, Mike."

"Look, I don't have time for this, Jay." He stood up. "Don't fight it. Let's go to the bank. I'll loan you a half-million, and you can pay me back when you get the money."

"Will the offer still be open if I call you tomorrow?" I asked.

Mike laughed. "Sure. Call me tomorrow." And he left.

The next morning, I thought, "If Mike has that much faith in me, then I should have faith in myself." Then I went to Vegas.

For a reason beyond my comprehension, I took on a partner. I was still depressed, although I had overcome my flirtation with suicide. Vegas is the worst place in the world to resolve one's problems, unless you hit big at the tables, which I didn't. I was on the phone with my lawyer, Larry Thompson. Suddenly I said, "How would you like to be my partner?"

"Let's do it," he said, and that was it.

It had never occurred to me to have a partner. Larry said he would make me rich if I would make him famous. "Okay," and suddenly we became the Bernstein-Thompson Entertainment Complex. We became the hottest management team in town, except I was the one who was signing the talent. I brought in Linda Evans, William Shatner, Steve Gutenberg, Donna Mills—about three dozen clients. Drew Barrymore was the only person Larry Thompson ever signed during our partnership.

It turned out we were not compatible. Larry was a brilliant lawyer, an excellent negotiator and a good man, but I felt from the beginning that he was in the business for money. I did not fault his attitude, but my motivation was achievement. We were sure to clash. The one thing Larry did, for which I will be forever grateful, is get my bank account straightened out. He discovered the improprieties and I got my money back. I was rich again.

Chapter 24

SPELLING RELIEF FOR CAPTAIN KIRK

Regardless of my disaffection for Patti Davis, her father's presidency gave me a new mind-set. I felt that society would change—it was cleanup time. Wyatt Earp would come back to straighten things out. After the inauguration fiasco, I started working hard to get a Mickey Spillane project off the ground. The national mood had changed dramatically, and patriotism had reached a fever pitch. People were tired of the Carter years of malaise. I thought they were ready for action and justice, and so did Bud Grant, president of CBS Television Entertainment. Bud gave me the go-ahead for a two-hour movie based on Mickey Spillane's fictional detective Mike Hammer.

Mickey and I had stayed in touch. To a degree we had become alter egos. Working together we developed a storyline that screenwriter Calvin Clements Jr. wove into a teleplay. It was simple, retaining the 1940s film noir flavor of Mickey's original Hammer novels. Mike's best friend is killed, and in the process of solving the murder he untangles a web of corruption between the New York mob and political officials.

Networks seldom finance 100 percent of the budget, so I needed a financing partner. An independent producer usually goes to a major studio for his deficit. The studio hopes for a series spin-off, from which it will eventually recoup its money when the show goes into syndication years later. In the case of *Margin for Murder*, I had guidance from Steve Mills, head of movies at CBS. Steve, more than any other network executive in my experience, tried to help fledgling producers. He sent me to Robert Hamner, an independent moviemaker who not only became my co-executive producer but also secured Columbia Studios Television as our partner.

CBS wanted Kevin Dobson to play Mike Hammer. I did not know Kevin, but he was a seasoned television actor with myriad credits. He was currently co-starring in *Knot's Landing*, a nighttime soap hit. Fortunately, Kevin was on hiatus between seasons. He accepted the role. For the role of Velda, Hammer's girl Friday, we chose Cindy Pickett.

We went into production at the Burbank Studios, but I was not a hands-on executive producer. Hamner did the yeoman chores, for which he was extremely competent. I went to the set often, but usually with advice on how I thought we could make the picture better. My reputation as a perfectionist and a star manager, however, grated on lesser souls. It should not have surprised anyone that I would speak to our "stars" about the possibility of my managing them, since Larry and I now had two dozen well-publicized clients.

One day I had a long and pleasant conversation with Dobson. The next day a security guard forbade me from entering the set. I was taken aback. "Why?"

The guard shrugged. "Orders from headquarters," he said.

I went to see Herman Rush, president of Columbia Television Pictures. I did not know Herman well, although later I would find him to be one of the better executives in the industry. He shrugged. "Columbia hasn't barred you, Jay, it's the network."

Craig Rumar and Larry Kubick, Dobson's agents, were afraid I would sign their client to a management contract. They had gone to CBS with a threat: if I went to the set again, Kevin would not work until I left. Whoa!

I let the threat pass. Bob Hamner was de facto executive producer, and I had more important things to do. But I didn't forget the incident. One hundred-plus people were involved in the production. Not one of them would be employed had it not been for me, and suddenly I was anathema on the set. Well, two could play that game. I would wait for a more opportune time to take my revenge.

Margin for Murder aired on October 15, 1981. It was good; better yet, it got viewer numbers, the bottom line in television. Judith Crist, reviewing it in *TV Guide*, rated it sixth in her ten best list of TV movies for 1981. A San Francisco reviewer summed up Mike Hammer's philosophy accurately: "Do unto others before they can do it to you." The climate of the country had changed. I knew Mickey Spillane's Mike Hammer was not a one-time shot.

I now had two professional roles—manager and producer—and they were not necessarily compatible. Both, however, were time-consuming. I had little time left for new clients and became selective about who I signed.

I was in the parking lot of the Century Plaza Hotel in Century City, going to a dinner function for musicians and singers, many of whom I had previously represented. A weird-looking black guy in a tuxedo started following me. I hurried my walk. He called after me, "You're Jay Bernstein, aren't you? I'm a singer, and I'd give anything in the world if you would represent me."

I stopped and looked at him more closely. He wasn't Tyrone Power, he wasn't Alan Ladd and he wasn't Clint Eastwood. He wasn't Harry Belafonte or Sidney Poitier, either. I thought he was goofy, a strange-looking dude in a tuxedo. He made me nervous.

"I'm not taking music clients anymore," I told him, "but I know a guy named Ken Craigen. He's the best in the business. Talk to him, and tell him I sent you."

I went on to the function and forgot about the guy.

About a year later I was driving on Sunset Boulevard. My eyes held on a big billboard. There in bold colors was a picture of the guy who had accosted me. "Merry Christmas Hollywood, From Lionel Richie and Ken Craigen," read the message. Geezus, I thought. I hadn't given him two minutes. I hadn't given him enough time to tell me his story.

Many years later, I was in front of my house in the Hollywood Hills. It was dusk and I was in my paranoid mode; I was packing a .38. A black Mercedes with blackout windows pulled up and stopped. One of the windows started to roll down. I reached for my gun, thinking it might be a hit.

"Don't shoot, Jay. Don't shoot!" The window came down and a man's head popped out. "It's just me, Jay—Lionel."

By that time, Lionel Richie was as successful as you could get. We chatted a few minutes. "I'm curious," I said. "How much in commissions do you think I passed up by not representing you?"

Lionel thought for a moment. "I don't know . . . probably around ten million."

When I signed Persis Khambatta, I felt I could take her to the heights of stardom. A former Miss India, Persis was one of the most exotically beautiful women in the world. When she landed the role of Lieutenant Ilia in *Star Trek: The Motion Picture*, I thought her career would soar. It did not, but that was in the future.

Persis and her *Star Trek* co-star, William Shatner, were selected to present the Documentary Feature Oscar at the 1980 Academy Awards presentation at the Dorothy Chandler Pavilion. Persis, always nervous, wanted me to go with her to the rehearsal the day before the event.

There, Shatner and I struck up a conversation. He was concerned about his career. *Star Trek* the television series was done, but Bill was afraid the new motion picture would stigmatize him further as Captain Kirk. It was a box-office success, and no one knew better than Bill that a sequel was in the works. He felt caught up in a quandary—he was a star attached to a single character.

"Why don't you let me manage your career?" I asked him.

"What could you do for me?"

"Look," I said, "I can't make you any bigger than what you are as Captain Kirk, but I can expand your industry participation."

Bill was interested in hearing me out.

"First, I'll find a television series in which you play a character far removed from *Star Trek*; it will be your second career. And two, I'll let people know who Bill Shatner is as opposed to Captain Kirk. Being Bill Shatner will be your third career."

I signed him. Aaron Spelling gave Bill his second career as T.J. Hooker, a police sergeant in the series of the same name. His co-star was Heather Locklear. It was a big hit.

As to removing Bill from his Captain Kirk image, the record speaks for itself.

Aaron Spelling's perspective was always from a producer's standpoint, which surprised me because he had started as an actor.

"I'll never do another show without an ensemble cast," he once told me. "I learned that when I was making *The Rookies*. Unfortunately, I had to fire Michael Cole, but after he left, the show was still *The Rookies*. My cast was large enough to cover the absence of one actor. I don't think the audience ever missed Michael."

Mod Squad and *S.W.A.T.* were ensemble pieces. Then Aaron did *Starsky & Hutch*, with just two stars. I represented Paul Michael Glaser, who played Hutch. Paul started making trouble because he wanted to become a director.

One night we met Aaron for a drink at the Polo Lounge. Aaron wasn't in the mood to discuss issues with an intransigent actor. "Look, Michael," he said, "I can always rename the show *Starsky & Smith*."

Aaron did several more ensemble shows, all successful. He produced *Family*, *Dynasty* and *The Colbys*, series where he could fire an actor and replace him without a hiccup in the production schedule.

I remembered everything Aaron said, and then Bill Shatner became *T.J. Hooker*. As the time approached for Bill's contract to be renegotiated, Aaron didn't want to talk about it. I advised Bill to keep his cool and not ripple the waters. Finally Aaron made a lowball offer, and Bill's back suddenly went out. I had Aaron in a fix, and he knew it. Bill got a good contract.

Bill's contract put us both on cloud nine. And going a few rounds with Aaron and coming out the champ made my heart sing. It was a great time to celebrate, but there wasn't time for celebration—I was racing against the clock to make some big deadlines. One of them was the Golden Globe Awards at the Beverly Hilton Hotel, a real yawn-fest I never looked forward to. This particular year was no exception. As usual the program was too long and attendees spent a great deal of time running back and forth between the ballroom and the bar. Finally it was over. My date and I were talking to Elliott Gould at the valet curb. I had a plastic glass of champagne. When my Aston Martin pulled up, I gave my glass to the valet driver and said goodbye to Elliott.

"Drive carefully," he said. "The police are cracking down on partygoers."

The previous week the mayor had announced an ultimatum on driving under the influence. No one was immune. The police had promptly arrested Johnny Carson, Dean Martin and F. Lee Bailey for alleged drunk driving.

We drove a block and a half before we heard sirens. I looked in the rearview mirror and saw Star Wars: two police cruisers with blinking red cherries and three motorcycle cops like little space jets. I pulled over. There were seven cops. One of them looked at my driver's license and said, "You're the starmaker, right?"

They huddled, whispering. Then they made me do the walk routine. I had to place one foot directly in front of the other, moving along like a clown. I did it without incident, but they weren't finished. "What test do you want, Starmaker?" asked one of the cops. "Breath, urine or blood?"

Without thinking, I said, "Blood."

They handcuffed me and told my girlfriend to take my car home. As I was being escorted away, I yelled over my shoulder, "Call Bob Shapiro!" She nodded. Then I was placed in the backseat of a cruiser and chauffeured to Cedars-Sinai Hospital, a mile away.

A nurse took a vial of blood from my arm. Then I was retired in handcuffs to a waiting room, where I sat quietly, motorcycle cops standing at attention left and right. A young woman came up to me. "Aren't you Jay Bernstein?"

"Yes, I am," I answered.

She wanted my autograph. The two cops rolled their eyes and took off my handcuffs. I scribbled my name on a piece of paper and gave it to the woman. The cops handcuffed me again. All this while I'm sitting in my tuxedo in a hospital waiting room.

An hour passed. I was certain I did not have enough alcohol in my system to be considered intoxicated. If I did, I would be sober by the time the cops got the test results. I suspected they were letting me stew, hoping it would unnerve me. It didn't. I began to stare at the cops as if they were targets. They averted their eyes. At last the arresting officer returned. "Mr. Bernstein, did you take any medication today?"

"Yes, a Valium."

They took me to the Beverly Hills City Jail, ten minutes away, where they placed me in a small holding cell with a wiry little fellow who kept saying, "I didn't kill him. I didn't kill nobody." It was winter. The man was wearing a short-sleeved shirt open to his waist. He kept repeating his mantra. I thought, "I don't need this!" All I'd done was take a prescription Valium.

"I didn't kill nobody," said the murder suspect. Then he yelled, "I'm fucking cold!"

A jail keep issued wool blankets. I lay down on a bench, but the blanket was so scratchy my hands and neck began to itch.

"I didn't kill nobody!"

I needed to relieve myself. I looked around; the cell had no facility. I banged on the bars and joined the murderer in yelling. The jail keep returned and asked what I wanted.

"I need to relieve myself, and this fellow needs a goddamned sleeping pill!"

He unlocked the cell and took me down the hallway to a urinal contraption recessed in the wall. As I did my thing, he stood behind me as if afraid I might make a sudden break for freedom. A black flush knob was set oddly in the wall to the left of the urinal. When I finished, being a gentleman, I pushed it. A spout of water shot out like a geyser, drowning my clothes. It was a drinking fountain gone awry.

I was escorted back to the cell, my tuxedo dripping, my shoes wet, my upper body soaked. As the door slammed behind me, my lunatic cellmate screamed, "I didn't kill him! I didn't kill nobody!"

At 4:47 a.m., Bob Shapiro got me released. There were no charges against me. I was not a star, but I'd just tasted one of the negatives of stardom.

Chapter 25

HIRINGS
AND FIRINGS

Dr. Joyce Brothers and I were having lunch at the Bistro. We were friends. I had been her entertainment consultant for years. We were reminiscing when she suddenly said, "Today, with modern medicine and technology, with diets and fitness centers, with birth control, a woman is still young at forty. Why don't you take on that issue?"

I laughed. "I wouldn't have a clue as to how to do it, Joyce."

"Well, you did it with Farrah and Suzanne. You made them role models at thirty. Why don't you do the same thing with a woman who's forty?"

Three months later I was at a cocktail party in Bel Air. Vincente Minnelli and I were talking about my next Mickey Spillane project. Vincente was a big Mike Hammer fan. I looked across the room and saw Bo Derek. She glowed. After the movie *10*, she had become the reigning queen of beauty. She had recently married John Derek, Linda Evans' ex-husband. Bo was hot—I wanted to talk to her. I excused myself to Vincente and sought her out. I found her, except she wasn't Bo; she was Linda Evans. What struck me was Linda's resemblance to Bo, yet Linda was pushing forty and Bo was twenty-five. Suddenly Joyce Brothers' idea about making a role model of a middle-aged woman came to the fore.

I'd represented Linda as a publicist back in the sixties when she co-starred in *The Big Valley*. She hadn't changed. She was still quiet and shy.

She had continued to work throughout the seventies, but had never established an identity—most people didn't know who she was. She recently had been cast in a new series, *Dynasty*, and was as gorgeous as ever.

"Linda, how would you like it if men would rather go to bed with you than with Bo?"

She looked at me quizzically, but I could tell I'd struck an emotional chord. "What do you mean?" she asked.

I explained to her my perception of the new woman of the eighties, which Joyce had given me. "Middle-aged women have diets, exercise programs, cosmetics, leisure time, but they don't have anybody to look up to. I'd like to make you their role model, the perfect forty-year-old woman."

She didn't know what to say. My comment caught her by surprise, but she didn't have to say anything. The sparkle in her eyes said it all. The idea played to her ego. Linda was thirty-eight. Today everybody takes for granted that middle age is a primetime of life, but in 1981 being a woman Linda's age was very close to being old.

"Linda, you can do a great service to women by helping them realize that life isn't over after they turn thirty. By being the perfect forty-year-old, you can demonstrate to women that glamour and beauty and happiness are just beginning for them."

I signed her with high hopes and the help of Aaron Spelling. I emphasized to her the importance of striking a game plan and sticking with it. Linda would become America's role model just as she approached her fortieth birthday. I saw her as the mature sex symbol America was clamoring for. The campaign was simple: "Women over forty have a future." And Linda had the perfect face and figure to represent them.

I began a newspaper and magazine campaign. The idea snowballed. One major newspaper said, "Forty-year-old women are going to love Jay Bernstein." The writer missed the point—forty-year-old women were going to love Linda Evans.

During the Golden Age of Hollywood, stars usually played themselves. Gable was Gable and Bogart was Bogart. Method acting had not captured Hollywood's imagination. Linda Evans was a new experience for me. She wasn't anything like the characters she played. In real life she was passive, without ambition and easily manipulated. She didn't have the rage stardom required. She often took the advice of the last person she spoke to.

A successful campaign requires a modicum of control. Manager and client have to follow the plan without deviation. As I guided Linda's career into new realms, her talent agent and her business manager became upset. They had been pulling her strings for years, but now they felt left out. No matter that my campaign had worked. Linda told ABC's *20/20* interviewer, "Probably, if it weren't for Jay, I would be leading a much more obscure life, because I don't go after things. It's not my nature; it's not how I think, and I know that he will take me step by step."

Her comment opened a dam. At every turn thereafter her coterie of advisers tried to veto my ideas. Even her boyfriend got in the act. Their main worry seemed not to be Linda's success as much as their fear that I would get a cut of the action.

Linda had just finished TV shows in Italy and Australia and she had one in the hopper for the Orient. With a little fine-tuning I saw an opportunity to make her an international star, as opposed to what she was: a working actress. Her shyness helped give her an image of grace and dignity, but her greatest asset was that she knew how to act.

I knew I was on the right track when the press began picking up my message. In retrospect, it was easy to promote Linda. A shift in demographics was already underway with the maturation of the baby boomers, and Linda was one of them. She was the perfect star for them to emulate.

Unfortunately, Linda and I did not have a good relationship. It wasn't her fault. She lived in a spiritual netherworld and I lived in a very mundane, down-to-earth world. She dealt with God; I dealt with people. Her agent kept trying to pull her strings, and Linda was not strong enough to hold them in place.

Stan Herman, a Beverly Hills real-estate magnate, was one of Linda's ex-husbands. He was a better friend of mine than Linda was. Stan was an alchemist, a philosopher-scientist who lived his life to the fullest, experimenting with everything. He told me about overdosing on a drug he called "Holy Ghost." He actually died—one of those near-death experiences—before being resuscitated. The drug left him feeling exalted, full of confidence.

I was not into drugs except for an occasional puff of pot and medicinal Valium. I knew nothing about them. Stan said Holy Ghost was a strange cross between arsenic and cocaine, or heroin and arsenic, something like that. He said he had gone to Ma Maison high on the drug. He felt all-powerful. "I felt I could step on the entire restaurant with one big foot like the Jolly Green Giant," he said. "I could crush all the plastic people."

With Stan high on the drug, he and Linda went to dinner at El Cielo. Stan's sensations were still alive. He said, "Linda, I know you won't believe this because you are so spiritual, but I feel like General Stan Herman, and I'm here to save the entire world." She started crying. Concerned, Stan said, "Don't cry, darling. It's a happy feeling, not a sad feeling."

"You don't understand," cried Linda. "I'm crying because I feel like that every day!"

The first goal of starmaking is to place the spotlight on your client. Take Kristy McNichol. When I became her manager she was fifth-billed in *Family* under Sada Thompson, James Broderick, Gary Frank and Meredith Baxter Birney, all strong actors. Once I put the spotlight on her, however, producers began to take notice. It was the same with Farrah and Suzanne, a ploy I learned in my PR days. The poster was my first angle with Farrah; she was a combination of Betty Grable and Rita Hayworth. Suzanne was Marilyn and Judy Holliday. I was giving the media an image they could identify with. For Linda Evans, I chose Grace Kelly.

It was as if one were an Aston Martin, another a Lamborghini, and the other two a Rolls-Royce and a Cadillac convertible—but I was the engine for all of them. That was my career, putting my clients on the main drag and moving them through the traffic. I took bubblegum stars like Bobbie Sherman, the Jackson Five, the Osmond Brothers, the Lennon Sisters and put them in the spotlight. What eventually happened with Farrah was that I edged into the spotlight *with* her. It was the same with

Suzanne and Linda, and later, when Stacy Keach went to jail, I had to virtually replace him in the spotlight to save his career.

When I was invited to be on NBC's *Current Affair* magazine program, the spotlight was supposed to be on my accomplishments. Rather than promoting myself, I promoted Linda as the perfect forty-year-old. The spotlight shifted to Linda.

When I came up with a book idea for Linda, her advisers advanced on me like a small army, demanding I sign away any interest in the project. Eventually, of course, I recognized how easy it was for them to pull Linda's strings. With the exception of Farrah, I had never spent a great deal of time with my clients. I wasn't a babysitter. I was an idea man who turned ideas into realities. Ultimately I was excluded from virtually every deal Linda got after she became the perfect forty-year-old: television, books, fitness centers, perfume. I estimate her income jumped to the range of $5 or $6 million a year. During the entire time I managed Linda, I received a grand total of $42,000. It was hardly worth my time.

After the *Current Affair* show I was at a party in Beverly Hills. John Forsythe told me, "God, Linda thinks the world of you. Yesterday she said so many beautiful things about you—that you are a wonderful person and that she has a great relationship with you."

When I got home that night, Linda had left a message. She wanted to see me on the *Dynasty* set the next day. I didn't like to go to sets. Marty Baum, one of the better agents in the business, had once told me, "If you go to a set, don't linger, because first of all you'll hold up production, and then before you know it you'll be running around getting coffee for your client. Stars have to let other people know that they're in charge."

The fact that Linda wanted me on her set smelled of trouble, but I went. She was in her dressing room. The meeting was short, sour and to the point. "Jay," she said, "I always thought it was you who did all the wonderful things that made my career suddenly blossom. But I've been talking to God, and He told me that you were just His instrument."

Joan Collins, her co-star in *Dynasty*, was no fool. After Linda fired me, Joan took over Linda's role as the perfect forty-year-old. Linda didn't know how to keep her place, nor did her agent. They didn't understand image maintenance.

Getting fired by Linda was not the same as getting fired by Farrah and Suzanne. It was bittersweet, but I was getting used to it. Before, on a scale of pain from one to ten, termination had been a definite ten. Gradually I had come to expect it, so getting fired by Linda was down the scale. The pain wasn't as wrenching as in times past.

Getting fired—it hurts. It hurts very badly. However, the truth is, I did not like all my clients. When you have over 600 clients, it's difficult to like them all. With those I disliked it was strictly business, nothing more, but I tried to serve their needs equally with clients I did like. Two of my all-time favorites were Angie Dickinson and Dionne Warwick.

Angie was hip. She understood publicity as well as the best of them. She usually turned one interview into two. Halfway into a dialogue with a journalist she would suddenly look at her watch and say, "Oh, I'm out of time. Can we finish this later?" The reporter generally ran with what he had, called Angie a few months later, and they would start anew. When getting one's story or profile in "Calendar," the *Los Angeles Times* Sunday insert, was considered the zenith of publicity success for most actors, there seemed to be a piece featuring Angie every six months.

But she was feisty, too, sensitive and quick-tempered. Early at a party at my house one night, Angie and I were outside on a terrace, smoking. I don't remember what prompted my remark, but I said, "Angie, I love you, even though you're a pain in the ass." She laughed without comment and we went back inside.

A few days later she sent me my walking papers. A note read: "I don't think a publicist who thinks I'm a pain in his ass should be representing me." I waited until I felt she had calmed down, called her and persuaded her to continue with my services. But that wasn't the end of it.

Another time my billing department sent a statement to Angie "Dickenson" instead of "Dickinson." She promptly posted a letter: "If my publicist doesn't know how to spell my name, then he's not really interested in me. You're fired." I called her and got her back again.

Then she married Burt Bacharach. Because of Angie, Burt became my client, and I did his campaign for *Butch Cassidy and the Sundance Kid*. He won two Oscars, one for original score and another for the song "Raindrops Keep Fallin' on My Head," which he wrote with his partner Hal David. I worked hard for Burt, and he was grateful for my effort without realizing he was one of those few clients I didn't like.

It was through Burt that I got Dionne Warwick. Dionne had been my neighbor when I lived at Sammy's house. She was one of the nicest people I'd ever met. We became friends, just as Angie and I were friends, but in a different way. I trusted Dionne absolutely.

Unfortunately, after Angie became Mrs. Burt Bacharach she was shuffled to the shadows. Then Burt and Hal David had a fight and severed their partnership. Dionne had a contract with them, and when Burt and Hal went their separate ways, they owed her two albums. For whatever reason, they couldn't or wouldn't fulfill their obligation to Dionne, so she sued them.

I soon got a call from Burt. "I want you to stop representing Dionne Warwick."

"Burt, I don't want to get in the middle of your business, but I don't want you to get in the middle of mine, either. Dionne is a client, and she'll remain a client."

"Then fuck you, Jay. You're fired!"

The first client who fired me was Arthur O'Connell, the two-time Oscar nominee for supporting roles in *Picnic* and *Anatomy of a Murder*. It was many years ago, but it's noteworthy. He simply sent me a letter of termination. I was devastated. Tears welled up in my eyes.

"What's wrong?" asked my girlfriend, Leslie.

I couldn't tell her. I took the firing as a personal affront, a rejection. "It's nothing," I said.

I went outside and walked in the rain to hide my tears. To me it was like breaking up with a girlfriend and knowing she would go out and find a new guy. I was not experienced enough to accept the reality of the publicist-client relationship.

Over the next thirty years every actor I represented eventually fired me. Usually it was because of finances. Actors, even the best of them, seldom work. They are insecure, often paranoid. It was hard for them to realize that public relations, media exposure, helped get them jobs. The PR man is the last person hired and the first person fired. He's low man on the totem pole.

When I got back to the house, I called Arthur. He didn't answer. I called him again; no answer. I called him a dozen times over the next few days, and then I sent him a letter. He didn't respond. Later I saw him at a restaurant, but he ignored me. I then realized I could not be a friend of ex-clients. I didn't have time for them. I was incapable of separating my business life from my social life—they were the same to me. When someone fired me, I thought, "Fuck him! He doesn't think he needs me, so I don't need him!"

One friendship that was unbreakable was the one I had with client Nick Adams. Nick was like me—he had so much passion and enthusiasm for projects he believed in that it was strangely intoxicating. I respected that very much and I understood it. Back in 1961, ABC canceled *The Rebel*. The series was not a failure; it got caught up in industry politics. Andrew Fenady, the show's creator, had developed a pilot spin-off called *The Yank*, about the post–Civil War life of a doctor who had participated in the war. After ABC offered Fenady an unsatisfactory short-run commitment, he took the project to NBC. That's when ABC pulled the plug on *The Rebel*. "Disloyalty" needed to be punished.

Nick, certain of stardom and ever the hustler, seemed unconcerned by *The Rebel*'s demise. I thought maybe he had the secret formula, because he put together a three-picture, big-screen deal at MGM. The first was *Twilight of Honor*, with Nick billed below Richard Chamberlain and above Claude Rains and Joey Heatherton. He seemed to be on a roll. "It's gonna be one of the best movies ever made," Nick proclaimed. "My performance is brilliant."

Having never gone to the set, I took Nick's critique at face value, even though I realized he could pump his performances into over-expanding balloons. I wasn't bothered by it, since egomania was the norm in Hollywood rather than the exception. Besides, Nick was a good actor, and growing better. Every time I saw him, he was super-enthusiastic. "*Twilight* is gonna make me a movie star!"

There was no reason not to believe Nick, because it happened every day. Unknown actors shooting to stardom was commonplace, and here was Nick with an advantage. He was a bona-fide television star with an audience waiting out there for his first big movie hit. "I'm telling you, Jay," he said, "my performance is Oscar caliber. You gotta do something!"

He convinced me. "Okay," I told him, "let's put together a campaign."

I engineered the best public-relations promotion I had done up to that time, although without ever realizing it was for the wrong reasons. It was more than a campaign—it was a crusade. If Nick thought he was that good, then I was determined to get him an Oscar nod.

The Academy was broken down into divisions—actors, directors, cinematographers and so forth. Except for balloting for Best Picture, the voting went by categories. Actors voted exclusively for actors. My first objective was to obtain a list of Academy actor members and their telephone numbers. I did, and then I put Nick on the telephone.

"Hello, is this Myrna Loy? Miss Loy, I can't tell you how brilliant I thought you were in the *Thin Man* movies. Just brilliant! Your performances have always been my inspiration."

"Who did you say you are?"

"Nick Adams, the actor. You may have seen me on television as Johnny Yuma in the hit series *The Rebel*. I've just made a movie called *Twilight of Honor*, and I'm hoping to get nominated for an Academy Award as Best Supporting Actor."

"I wish you luck, Mr. Adams."

"Please, Miss Loy, it's Nick to you."

"What was the name of the movie . . . uh, Nick?"

"*Twilight of Honor.*"

"I'll consider voting for you."

Nick called every member of the actors' branch of the Academy, with an emphasis on the older members, because I knew their chances of screening Nick's picture were next to nil. The idea was to implant two names in their minds: Nick Adams and *Twilight of Honor*.

I placed several sophisticated full-page ads, thousands of dollars' worth, in the *Hollywood Reporter* and *Daily Variety* promoting Nick's nomination. A witch's brew was being stirred. Although trade advertising is commonplace today, back then Nick's ads drew more than a frown. Some of the hard-line, conservative Academy members thought we were demeaning their profession by reducing acting to a low common denominator. What we were really doing was getting Nick's name out there, making it a conversation piece.

The campaign worked. In January, Nick was chosen as one of the five nominees for Best Supporting Actor—and that's when troubles for me really began. I went to a screening of the movie, which I should have done weeks earlier. I remember squirming in my seat, because it was so-so at best. What was worse, Nick was no longer in it. He had been sent to the cutting-room floor, except for some reaction shots. I was stunned. All his action shots, including an attempted suicide scene he had raved about, were gone.

Strangely, Nick was not the least offended by his role being cut to shreds. He was already an Oscar nominee and determined to win the statuette, regardless. If I knew we were in trouble, Nick did not. He wouldn't listen. On the eve of the ceremony he asked me to buy three cases of Dom Pérignon for a celebration party at his home. Wisely, I did not make the investment. He did not win; only a half-dozen people showed up for his party. We drank cheap wine.

Nick was blacklisted by the studios for his impudence. I thought it would pass quickly, but it didn't. MGM forgot about Nick's three-picture contract, and he never worked in a major motion picture again. It broke his heart. Hollywood is a tough business and dreams don't always come true. But I loved Nick, I really did. He was my great pal, and to this day I miss him dearly and am very close to his family.

If I thought the pain wasn't so bad now, I had only to wait around a second or two before a nightmare would come to haunt me as I was fully awake.

It started with a very strange phone call from Larry Thompson's wife. Larry who? Well, Larry Thompson was my "partner," I was once told.

Larry and I had been partners only a couple of years when that haunting call came. "We're going to celebrate Larry's birthday at Ma Maison, and I want you to come. It's going to be fun—black tie and all that. Would you get up and say something nice about him?" Something just didn't feel right, but I couldn't exactly pinpoint what.

Ma Maison was the place where stars lunched and dined. I had my own table there, next to Greg Bautzer, the famous celebrity lawyer. I knew the layout of the restaurant like I knew the palm of my hand. It was small, haphazard in design, with one private room upstairs that could accommodate a party of perhaps twelve. I thought Larry's birthday party would be there.

Already bad blood existed between us. When ABC did its *20/20* profile of me, Larry split at the seams. It was more than simple jealousy; he actually thought he should have been featured as my equal because we had a partnership. He wanted half of all the action, including publicity that came my way because of who I was and what I'd done. *20/20* was not an isolated event; it was a near culmination of our polarization. There had been intimations before, but I had ignored them.

When I started to pull into the Ma Maison parking lot, I was in for a surprise. A huge tent had replaced it, with enough tables to seat the Ringling Bros. Circus. After I found a parking place on the street, my date and I entered the outer tent foyer. Cameras were going click, click, click. The first person I saw was our new client, little Drew Barrymore, a mere child who had just starred in *E.T.: The Extra-Terrestrial.* Larry held her hand; they were posing, or at least Larry was, for the paparazzi.

I stood in the shadows feeling like Margo Channing, the Bette Davis character in *All About Eve*. Then I led my date into the main tent room where there were three hundred people. I looked around. ABC had a table, CBS, NBC; there was a Paramount table, a Warner Bros. table, a Columbia table.

It was the worst night of my life. I had to sit there while the Bernstein-Thompson clients marched individually to the podium and gave Larry a testimonial. Of course, they had been put upon to do it, with the exception of little Drew. We had thirty-three clients and I had signed thirty-two of them. I felt as if I had been slapped in the face or, worse, kicked in the ass. All those clients I had signed were paying tribute to my partner because they thought it was a favor to me. With every passing moment, I sunk deeper into the psyche of Margo Channing. It was like I had stepped out for a moment and didn't get back for the play.

Entering a partnership with Larry was a mistake from the outset. I had been in the business ten years longer than he, and I'd become high-profile, partly because I sought it and partly because it just came. I had a bona fide reputation as a starmaker; Larry was a lawyer with a low-profile music-industry background. I was in the business for achievement; Larry was in it for money. At least that was my impression. He was an excellent lawyer, but I thought his drive to make money was much greater than his drive to take care of his clients.

We were partners for the run of our contract, ten years, but after that night we rarely spoke again. We split the clients and the profits, and that was it. Larry handled the money, which was fine, because he was honest. We just no longer spoke to each other.

After my Hollywood "nightmare," I took off and went to Paris with a girl-friend. We were staying at the Hôtel de Crillon, where I ran into Terence Young in a hallway. Terence owed me several thousand dollars, dating back to *The Klansman*, when I was his publicist. We chatted amiably in the corridor. I didn't mention the money. Business is business and friend-ship is friendship. There's a time and a place for everything.

Good to see you, Terence. Good to see you, Jay. We parted. My girl-friend and I went to the Georges V, where we ran into Jack Nicholson. He invited us up to his room. We started drinking champagne and smoking pot. We drank and smoked for fourteen straight hours in Jack's suite at the Georges V.

Jack's career seemed on the downslide. His movies—*The Shining* and *The Postman Always Rings Twice*—weren't doing well at the box office. We were up all night, talking about the industry. I gave Jack my advice, unsolicited. He wasn't interested, at least overtly.

"The audience doesn't identify with you when you play weird characters," I told him. "Do something like *Chinatown* again, where the audience identifies you as the leading man, or do something in which you are not the star; if it fails, it's someone else's fault, not yours."

"I don't give a shit what the audience thinks," he said. "I'll do what I want to do, when I want to do it. I don't think like you, Jay. I don't think like that at all."

Jack was a free spirit. He had no responsibility to anyone or anything but himself and his own sanity. He was the guy with no money in his pocket, just his lawyer's telephone number. He didn't get paranoid, like say, Warren Beatty, his good friend who worried when he started losing a little hair on his head and his ass dropped a notch. Jack didn't give a shit; that's what he told me while we were drinking champagne and smoking pot for fourteen straight hours. Jack wasn't handsome like Warren. But he was virile, and he turned his virility into attractiveness.

Jack stopped listening to me. We drank and smoked. I stopped talking because I thought it was going in one ear and out the other. Finally we left. Back at the Crillon, there was a message for me from Terence Young. "It was good seeing you, Jay," accompanied by a case of Rose Cristal. Business was business and friendship was friendship.

We went back to the States, time passed, and Terence Young still had not paid me. I had a subpoena that couldn't be delivered because he lived in Europe.

One day, I was waiting for a table at El Padrino at the Beverly Wilshire Hotel. It was noon. I glanced at the reservation book and saw Young's name. He had a dinner reservation.

That afternoon I hired a celebrity look-alike. She was a copy of Jane Fonda. That night I sent her to El Padrino. When Terence arrived, the maître d' told him Jane Fonda would like to meet him. Terence leaped up and went to her table. After he introduced himself, "Jane" served him the papers. "This is from Jay Bernstein," she said, and then walked out.

I got my money.

The next year Jack Nicholson did *Terms of Endearment*, playing second to Shirley MacLaine, the picture's real star. He won an Oscar for Best

Supporting Actor. Then he directed and starred in *The Two Jakes*, a sequel to *Chinatown*, although it was less critically acclaimed. Mainstream movies.

Perhaps he had listened to me, after all.

A few months went by and I was getting back into the swing of things. I was prepared for anything, but then, sure enough, Tatum O'Neal calls and wants to know if I would become her personal manager. I was surprised. She had been living with her father and Farrah, whose romance had blossomed into a tabloid fiesta, and Ryan had been guiding her career. I was suspicious. It was public knowledge that Tatum disliked Farrah, and I didn't want to get embroiled in a family feud.

"Tatum, your father and I are not the best of friends," I told her.

"I've moved in with my mother, Joanna Moore, whom you know."

Her mother, of course, was the root cause of my problems with Ryan, dating back to when he threatened to kill me because I had dated Joanna. I was uneasy, but Tatum was persistent.

She certainly had credentials for superstardom. At nineteen she was an accomplished actress with a strong resumé, which included being the youngest Oscar recipient, for Best Supporting Actress in *Paper Moon*. Yet I was still hesitant. I was afraid her mother had put her up to calling me to spite Ryan.

Tatum and I talked back and forth several times, and then we met for lunch. She was a beautiful young woman, ready to make the transition from child star to mature actress. She reminded me of Elizabeth Taylor—not physically, but artistically. I finally relented and signed her. I had a queasy feeling, knowing that when Ryan discovered I was her new manager he was going to explode. He did, although I was not present for the eruption.

Ultimately it came to naught, my managing Tatum. Exterior forces were too strong. Tatum was caught in a tug-of-war, pulled at one end of the rope by Ryan and at the other by her mother. Drugs came into play, as they often do with children of successful but dysfunctional parents. Then she married John McEnroe, the fiery tennis star; I thought he was a surrogate for Ryan.

Meanwhile I was without a housekeeper. With the exception of my chauffeur (I had only two in twenty years), my staff was evanescent. People came and went so quickly I hardly knew who worked for me. Part of it was my fault; part of it was the pressure of the business, which was conducted to a great extent in my home.

When I hired Delmy Tochez, a Salvadoran immigrant with a broken accent, I thought I was getting a housekeeper. What I got was a woman of all seasons. She became more than my girl Friday; she became my girl Monday through Sunday, seven days a week, and my most trusted confidante. Eventually she became the de facto manager of both my estate and my affairs. Although Delmy was younger than me, she became my surrogate mother. I affectionately called her Mama. I truly love Delmy. Without Delmy's friendship, companionship, loyalty, integrity and savvy, I would have been lost in this life. She is my godsend.

HAMMER
TIME

I was at midlife. It wasn't a crisis, but I had choices to make. I could either quit or find another rainbow. I decided to go for it.

My resumé listed several hours of television credits as an executive producer: the *Wild Wild West* telemovies, the ongoing *Bring 'Em Back Alive* series; Mickey Spillane's *Margin for Murder*. In each case I had been the idea man, the packager and overseer, the mover and shaker of financing, but I had not been a hands-on producer. I decided to change that. I wanted to shape my next project from the mold of my own imagination and philosophy.

The character of Mike Hammer was forever in my thoughts. Politically I was a traditionalist, which was different from being a conservative. In my mind the last national hero had been a woman, Farrah Fawcett. The women's lib movement had tried to reduce men to a secondary role in society and family. Athletes seemed to be out on strike half the time. General Westmoreland's lies had eliminated military leaders as national heroes. Politicians were still drowning in the muck of the Nixon years. Musicians had green hair and wore body armor. I didn't like any of it.

My old-fashioned ideas were wrapped up in men as leaders, heroes and mythical figures. Yet we were losing our manhood. We had become subservient to political correctness. In screen stories, evil now won out over good. The antihero reigned supreme. I saw in Mike Hammer a means to change that way of thinking, if only slightly. I wanted to revert to the truth of evolution, where for a million years men had been aggressive and women had been receptive; when men were warriors and women were domestic goddesses. I wanted to project the image of a take-charge man whose soul was committed to the protection of women and the fight against evil, not for money or material gain, but because it was right. The Mike Hammer philosophy was simple: revenge for injustices committed against good people.

We had gone from a permissive society to an ultra-permissive society. When the transition had begun in the postwar forties, Mike Hammer did something about it in Mickey Spillane's books. I didn't want Hammer to be wishy-washy. I wanted him to take over when government failed society. Criminals might beat the system in many of the new television shows, but in mine I wanted Mike Hammer to win out, regardless. I wanted to go back to Mickey's prototype, a man who loved women and sex because it was man's nature. I wanted women to be beautiful again, not the flat-chested androgynes being presented by extreme women's libbers, clothes designers and style magazines. I knew tons of women, had affairs with hundreds of them, and not a single one sought to be Twiggy instead of sexy. No, the women I knew wanted to be treated like women. So something was wrong with the way the media was projecting the image of women. I wanted to change that, and I wanted to use Mike Hammer as my catalyst. It was not a new idea, of course; Clint Eastwood had shown there was still a huge audience for a one-man-vigilante-lover through his Dirty Harry character, but Clint was doing movies. I wanted to hit the vast television audience. I wanted them to say, "Mike Hammer might be unorthodox, old-fashioned, even immoral by today's standards, but he's right." While the networks were trying to give the public what they thought it wanted, I wanted to give it what I thought it needed. I saw myself as the keeper of the flame.

On January 6, 1983, the *Hollywood Reporter* ran a front-page story: "Jay Bernstein Productions has finalized a deal to produce 'Murder Me, Murder You' as a telefeature in association with Columbia Pictures TV for

CBS. . . . 'Murder Me' is from an original script by Bill Stratton and will be directed by Gary Nelson, with Lew Gallo producing. . . . The current project marks Bernstein's fourth time as executive producer of a telefeature. . . . The increased moves into production will not preclude Bernstein's partnership with Larry Thompson in what he called 'our selective management business.' . . . Recent signings by the duo include Tatum O'Neal, Catherine Bach and Stephen Macht. They join a client roster that includes William Shatner, Bruce Boxleitner, Cicely Tyson, Linda Evans, Gil Gerard, Robert Blake, Catherine Hicks, Jeff Conaway, Drew Barrymore and Donna Mills."

The *Hollywood Reporter* had enough facts to lift anyone's spirits, but what it left out what I was most excited about. Bud Grant had said, "Jay, if you can make Hammer successful again as a television movie, then you can take it into a series."

I went to see Mickey at his home in South Carolina. He lived at Murrell's Inlet, about ten miles south of Myrtle Beach, in the middle of nowhere. His house was an unpretentious abode on the ocean. It had a Jag sitting in the driveway and a boat on the water out back. "I'm not rich," said Mickey, "but I don't owe a dime. The bank can't take my house because they don't hold a mortgage. My car's paid for. I'm just a working writer, but I get paid for it. I don't have a yacht, just a fishing boat, but unlike the big fiberglass jobs with all the fancy fixtures mine really fishes."

For Mickey, Murrell's Inlet was ideal. He could lose himself in his work without fear of being bothered by his neighbors. The little town was still a village; when he first moved there its population was 750. People said, "What do you do for a living?"

"I'm a writer," answered Mickey.

"But what do you do for a living?" they repeated.

That's when he knew he had found a home.

He was working on a children's book, which caught me by surprise. Mickey Spillane, the creator of Mike Hammer, doing a children's book?

"I don't make any money out of it, but my publisher challenged me to do it. Anybody can write a detective story, but a children's book? Now, that's something else."

Mickey and I worked out a step sheet to a new Hammer teleplay. Originally Mickey's Hammer was a veteran of World War II, but we updated his military experience, making him a Vietnam vet, while retaining his 1950s view of life. That was important. I wanted people to get back to an ethic we were losing. Back in Hollywood, Bill Stratton did an excellent job of capturing the essence of the ideas Mickey and I came up with.

When a producer has an agenda, his project usually fails. You can't hit people with a sledgehammer to get your point across. The audience knows what you're up to and usually switches channels. I didn't want to use a sledgehammer, but I did want to make some subtle points. *Mickey Spillane's Murder Me, Murder You* was entertainment, and I always kept that in mind. Hammer wasn't Sherlock Holmes. He worked on hunches and instinct; he was Everyman. I wanted to project three basic things: criminals brought to justice, men who were men, and women who were women.

I did not have an actor in mind to play Mike Hammer. I knew only that he wouldn't be Kevin Dobson. The network strongly suggested Stacy Keach. I didn't know Stacy, but I remembered his performance in a John Huston–directed boxing movie, *Fat City*, made ten years earlier. Ray Stark, the movie's producer, had told me, "I knew *Fat City* was a loser when it won first prize at Cannes. It was just too artsy-craftsy."

I wasn't looking for artsy-craftsy. Also I was concerned about Stacy's background. He was a trained Shakespearean actor. I was in the television business, not in theatrical arts. After word came down the network pike, I checked out Stacy's resumé more thoroughly. He'd been in two recent movies, *Roadgames*, with Jamie Lee Curtis, and *Cheech and Chong's Nice Dreams*. He'd also starred in a major CBS Civil War miniseries, *The Blue and the Gray*, the reason the network was high on him.

We met in my office at Columbia, then located at the Burbank Studios. "Have you ever read any of Mickey Spillane's books?" I asked.

Stacy laughed. "When I was in junior high the word circulated that some guy named Spillane was writing stuff that nobody else would touch. Hot sex scenes and violence. Naturally, his books became black-market items. One night I fell asleep before hiding *Kiss Me Deadly*. My mother found it on my bed the next morning. All hell broke loose. When I told her a friend had loaned it to me, she said I needed new friends!"

We chatted further. I expressed my mind-set: "The public is fed up with the 'me generation.' It wants a 'we generation,' stars it can respect and look up to, on-screen and off."

Stacy agreed. By the time he left my office he was the new Mike Hammer. He could shed his lackluster "good actor" image and become a "star personality," combining adventure with humor and romance. I thought Mike Hammer would change Stacy's image from a character lead to a leading man. It was a case of the right actor in the right role at the right time. Mike Hammer fit Stacy Keach like a glove.

Our story was simple. Hammer discovers he has a daughter (Lisa Blount) whose mother (Michelle Phillips) is his ex-lover and the only woman he ever loved. The troubled girl is missing, and the trail Hammer follows to find her leads to some typically awkward situations. Bill Stratton had done an excellent job in retaining the snappy flavor of Hammer's one-liners. What violence we had was necessary to the story, not gratuitous. The humor came from the women. It was a fun mystery with a Mickey Spillane twist at the end. No one could guess who the murderer was until Mike Hammer knew.

Aside from Hammer, the two most important roles were Velda, Hammer's secretary and girl Friday in Mickey's novels, and Pat Chambers, the NYPD police captain. I cast Tanya Roberts as Velda. *Charlie's Angels* had just been canceled, which meant I had worked with the first Angel, Farrah, and now I would work with the last, Tanya. I had known Tanya since Suzanne Somers' first starring role in *Zuma Beach*. I cast Don Stroud as Chambers. It was Don's first good-guy role after playing a hundred villains. He was like Charles Bronson, Walter Matthau, Lee Marvin and Anthony Quinn—all villains before their careers took off. Now it was Don's turn to be a good guy.

As for Stacy, he had a distinctive look, but he wasn't Robert Redford. I knew what to do. I surrounded him with beautiful women that I named the "Hammerettes." I sometimes interviewed seventy girls to cast one that might have a single line. By the time I finished, we had fifteen of the most beautiful women in the world. I hung an eight-by-ten publicity glossy of Stacy surrounded by five Hammerettes in my office; never once did a visitor fail to mention it. Women would say, "Oh, I'd like to meet him!" The psychological message was simple: if a woman wanted Stacy, then three more might want him; if five wanted him, then another twenty would want him.

If Stacy was going to be a hero, he had to look like a hero. When I first met him, he was overweight. Mike Hammer was mean, lean and athletic, the toughest of all private eyes. Stacy tried to lose weight but nothing worked. I tracked down a trainer who had worked with John Travolta and Sylvester Stallone. After five workouts Stacy said to me, "I hate your guts."

"Think of it this way," I told him. "It's better to hate me now than to hate yourself later."

By the time we began shooting, he was a rock. He looked like Superman.

Wardrobe was another problem. I sent Stacy and our production manager on a shopping spree to find Mike Hammer clothes. When they returned, Stacy looked like James Bond. I flipped. "Oh, no!" I said. "Hammer is like Columbo. Chic he isn't."

Stacy got another set of clothes. Instead of letting the wardrobe people hang up his suit when Stacy took it off, I had them shove it in the drawer of the desk in the Mike Hammer office. Stacy hated wearing wrinkled clothes, but for me the more wrinkles the better. Mickey Spillane's Mike Hammer was not a clotheshorse; he also wasn't a slob, but he was unpretentious.

I spent seven days a week on Hammer. I'd been working in the industry so long that my life had become a movie itself. I went to bed late and was up early. The first sound I heard when my eyes popped open was the smack of a clapboard and a director saying, "Action!" Some people couldn't take it. Most people are attracted to Hollywood glamour, but making a motion picture entails much more. Glamour is the icing; we were making the cake. It required sacrifice, a reality many people are unwilling to accept.

Director Gary Nelson brought the production in on schedule and within budget. When I saw the assembled movie, it was apparent that we had something. To promote *Murder Me, Murder You*, I put together a multi-city tour for Mickey, Stacy and me. Mickey, now in his mid-sixties, had a recognizable image because of his beer commercials, and Stacy was Stacy. We wore Mike Hammer snap-brim hats. Stacy was a consummate actor, so I knew he would do well with the press. It was Mickey, however, who stole his thunder. At one press conference a reporter asked if Mike Hammer was an anachronism in the 1980s. Mickey fired back: "Wait a minute. I'm here, ain't I? I just got married a couple of months ago and my wife is thirty-seven. What you see in me standing here isn't some old anachronism creeping around. Believe me, I can still pull my own weight."

A few critics disqualified Hammer as a hero because he liked girls. They said he was sexist, which was fine with me. I liked girls also, as did the rest of America's red-blooded males. Teenage boys and young men had not bought 12 million Farrah Fawcett posters because they thought she looked like a woman wrestler; it was her sexuality that appealed to them.

Murder Me, Murder You was scheduled to air at nine p.m., April 9, 1983. It was pitted against *Fantasy Island* on Saturday night. I wanted a big rating. I wanted to beat *Fantasy Island*, but more important, I wanted to beat Aaron Spelling, who produced it. I did.

I was always enamored of the Academy Awards, even though I realized from my own experience that the process of choosing nominees and winners could be manipulated. To me the ceremony was the most glamorous show on earth and the singular event where moviegoers from around the world could participate vicariously in the phenomenon known as Hollywood. I gave short shrift to other awards presentations, and I attended or didn't attend depending on whether I had a client up for an honor or not.

The Emmy Awards for prime-time programming between July 1, 1982, and June 30, 1983, were presented at the Pasadena Civic Auditorium on September 18, 1983. *Murder Me, Murder You* received only one nomination, which disappointed me. I was pleased, however, when cinematographer nominee Gayne Rescher was announced as the winner. That is, until he gave his acceptance speech. He made a terse comment, something to the effect of "I want to thank everybody," and that was it; he walked off the stage. Everybody? Who in hell was everybody?

The next morning I called the Academy of Television Arts & Sciences. After identifying myself, I told the guy at the other end, "I'm upset about last night's awards. I want the Academy to give Emmys to Stacy Keach and to my line producers Lew Gallo and John Anderson."

"You want what?" the guy asked snidely.

"I've had my lawyers research your bible," I continued. "It says you can give Emmys for contributions. I want those Emmys based on your regulations, and I'm going to fight for them."

"That's unheard of!"

"Read your Academy bible. My cinematographer received an Emmy last night and he didn't have the courtesy to acknowledge a living soul responsible for *Murder Me, Murder You*. I can assure you, other people were more important to the project than he was! So I want three—no, make it five—Emmys for contributions, as your rule states. Larry Thompson and me, executive producers, Anderson and Gallo, producers, and Stacy Keach, who is Mike Hammer incarnate." I hung up.

Two days later the same guy called me back. "We'll make a deal with you," he said. "We'll give you the Emmys, but on the condition that you won't tell anyone how you got them."

"Naturally I won't."

"This will be a first, and it will be a last, because we're going to amend the rule book, so this will never happen again."

Five Emmy plaques for special contributions were issued. Of course, I had never read the Academy's rules and regulations in my life, but neither had anyone else. It was over a thousand pages.

Bud Grant of CBS was a man of his word. When *Murder Me, Murder You* got the numbers, he okayed another Mike Hammer movie to be followed by a midseason replacement series.

But no project is problem-free. During the writing phase of *More Than Murder*, my writer quit with the teleplay only two-thirds finished. Time was of the essence—I finished the script myself. I didn't take credit for it, but the experience was cool. After we went into episodes, I wrote three of the Mike Hammer scripts.

The cultural climate had changed since my first Mike Hammer movie with Kevin Dobson. Times required a reinvention of Hammer. I wanted his character to be a cross between Dirty Harry and James Bond, and I wanted the stories to be hard-hitting. I didn't want a watered-down show. I wanted to do something John Wayne fans would admire, while watching a lot of gorgeous women.

Tanya Roberts was no longer available. She was now Sheena, Queen of the Jungle. Tanya had been a good Velda, but this time I wanted an actress who fit my exact vision of Hammer's secretary. I initiated a national Velda search, always a good idea for generating publicity.

We'd been casting six weeks, but still no Velda. I was getting nervous. Then Tim Flack, my casting director, brought in a girl who was perfect. She was Lindsay Bloom, a voluptuous dark-haired beauty with perfect breasts, a thin waist, the right weight—everything I wanted. "She's Velda!" I told Tim.

He laughed. Lindsay had auditioned five weeks before and I had rejected her. She had been a chubby blonde with a southern accent, not the type of woman I had in mind. But Tim thought her personality matched what I wanted, so in the interim he got Lindsay a trainer (she lost twenty-two pounds), dyed her hair black and got her voice right. Then he brought her back, knowing he had created the vision I had described to him.

The casting couch is part of Hollywood lore. No doubt many young women have given sexual favors to producers and directors in hopes of getting parts in movies, but it seldom works.

I'm aware of only three people who accomplished their goals by sleeping with someone. Two of them are women, and each attained a level of stardom before descending to a lower plateau. (Both have roles in this book, but legal considerations keep me from identifying them.)

One of them was extremely selective, bedding a director to get her first major movie role; then bedding a star to get her second major role (she upstaged him in their movie); and then she made room in her boudoir for a producer, securing her third starring role. All three movies were hits. She stayed on top for fifteen years, until gravity took its toll.

The second actress was less discreet. She bedded everyone she could—usually producers, directors and writers of B movies—until one of the movies vaulted to the top and became a box-office hit. For a fleeting moment she was a hot item. She made two more big-budget movies, but both failed, sending her back down the ladder.

The third casting-couch veteran slept with his producer to get an acting role; then he slept with his producer to get a writing job; finally he slept with his producer to get a directing job. In each case the successful aspirant was Jay Bernstein, but so was the producer. By sleeping with myself, I became a member of the Writer's Guild, the Director's Guild and the Screen Actors Guild.

Every person who has ever told a lie is an actor, which means all of us are actors, to one degree or another. Occasionally acting is elevated to an art form. Following World War II, a shift to true art took place, first on the stage and then in movies, motivated by the Russian theater director Stanislavski and enhanced by American director and acting teacher Lee Strasberg, among others. From the new school came the likes of Marlon Brando, Montgomery Clift, James Dean, Paul Newman and a host of lesser names—lesser only because they did not receive star status. A movie star and a movie artist are not synonymous, although true artists sometimes become stars, like those mentioned above.

By the mid-eighties, I had been representing actors for twenty-five years, yet every actor I knew told me I didn't understand actors and acting. Thus I decided to become an actor, temporarily. Tawdry as my means were, I cast myself, which Columbia Studios didn't look upon favorably. We were fifty-fifty partners, but they didn't want me in my own movie. Why? Because they thought I would get a bad laugh. That's when *I* laughed. How many of our 40 million viewers would know who the hell I was?

However, the Columbia execs were adamant. I had to fight my own studio to get a part in my own movie. But I was determined. I went to my lawyers and had them peruse my contract with a microscope. Then I bypassed the studio and got permission from CBS, which had final authority. The episode left a bad taste in my mouth because I realized Columbia was no longer a risk-taker. The hierarchy was changing; the new people got nervous when anyone wanted to do something different. As executive producer, I set my acting salary at half scale, just enough to pay my way into the Screen Actors Guild.

I hired an acting coach who didn't teach me anything I didn't already know. I'd been acting all my life. I wanted to make my character a cross between Charles Revson and Hugh Hefner. After I had my role down pat, I added a couple of props; I carried a white cat à la Leslie Parrish and used one of my trademark walking sticks.

On the day my scene was shot I was nervous, but I tried not to show it. I was in the first ten minutes of the movie, and then I got killed, riddled with machine-gun bullets. It was fun, but it was also my first and last effort acting in front of a camera. I had more fun acting the role of Jay Bernstein.

The Hammerettes provided comedy in otherwise hard-hitting stories. I wasn't concerned about the feminist movement, although I realized we would lose hardcore libbers from our audience. Hammerette cleavage had everything to do with me, not Mickey, Stacy or anyone else. It was my preference because I thought women's bodies were beautiful and something to be admired. Since I was the executive producer, I had the power to give the viewers cleavage, and I did. It didn't take a genius to realize we were not playing the Hammerettes as serious entities. Even diehard feminists couldn't make that mistake. We were being silly, offering comic relief.

For casting purposes, I invented the pencil test. I needed approximately seven beautiful girls in each episode, and I wanted them to have real breasts. Silicone implants didn't work for the costumes; the gap in cleavage was too wide. False boobs looked false. The pencil test wasn't politically correct, and today I would probably be arrested for it. Women executives at the network hated it, but none of them would have passed the test anyway. It was simple but foolproof. I would take a pencil and drop it between an actress's breasts; if the breasts were firm and close enough to hold it, she was hired. If the pencil slipped through, she got paid, but I didn't use her. When reporters asked if I was the one who gave the tests, I said, "Well, somebody has to do it!"

I cast a lot of the non-recurring roles out of the trunk of my car. I would go to parties and bump into people. Susan Strasberg asked me one night if I could help her; she had just moved out from New York and she was without representation. "Come to the studio in the morning," I told her. "I've got a part for you." I did the same thing with Dick Van Patten and a dozen other actors. I was limited by Columbia's stingy budget—I could only pay $2,500 for a guest appearance, far less than most series paid, but I could get them to do it for me.

Sharon Stone was a struggling actress with savvy. She knew how to go after a part and she wanted badly to be cast in one of the Mike Hammer episodes. She was a bright, beautiful, sexy young woman, and if you didn't believe she was bright, beautiful and sexy, all you had to do was ask her. She never stopped selling herself, which is what an unknown has to do.

"Your thighs are too big," I told her.

My criticism didn't faze her. The word no didn't exist in Sharon's vocabulary. I finally relented and gave her the part of the villain in an episode entitled "A Shot in the Dark." Of the guest stars, she got third billing below Delta Burke.

The filming went well until the final scene—the demise of Sharon's character. She had to fall into a vat of black oil, which was really colored water. Sharon balked.

"I'm not doing it," she said. "I'm not jumping into a pool of anything."

"What? The scene is critical to the story, Sharon. You knew you had to do this when you took the job!"

"I don't care," she said. "I'm not going to ruin my hair."

"But you have to!"

"I don't have to do anything," she said, and walked off the set.

We had to scramble to find a Sharon look-alike. I was angry. She wasn't remotely the star; she was just getting her career off the ground. Furthermore I was scheduled to attend a triple-A dinner party that evening in honor of Steven Spielberg.

Two hours later, after immense overtime costs, we finally had a stunt double in place, wigged and costumed, who could play Sharon's role as long as the camera didn't show her face. We got the shot, and it was a wrap.

I arrived at the Spielberg dinner party an hour late, found my seat and looked around. Seated at the head table next to Steven was Sharon, aglow in the limelight of the evening. Her hair looked great. She obviously thought Spielberg was more important than Mike Hammer, but it took her another ten years before she got star billing alongside a major star. And Steven Spielberg was not the director.

When I was handling Farrah, my dentist was always after me to send her to his office. I finally did, and he told me his business doubled after Farrah became a client. Some years later, he asked me if I would recommend him to Sharon Stone, who had become famous for *Basic Instinct*. I didn't want to, but he kept after me. Then I ran into Sharon at an Academy Awards party. I used my dentist as a conversation piece.

"He'll do your teeth free of charge," I told her.

She arched her brow. "I'm pleased with the dentist I have, Jay," she said. "And besides, I remember what you once said to me."

"What was that?" I asked curiously.

"You said my thighs were too big!"

Chapter 27

MEN
OF THE
YEAR

"Congratulations, Mr. Bernstein, you've been chosen to receive the David Award."

"What's that?" I asked suspiciously.

"It's our Man of the Year Award," said the caller. He was a member of the Van Nuys chapter of B'nai Brith, located somewhere in the San Fernando Valley.

As usual, I was wary. "Tell me more," I said.

"Some of the past recipients are Ed Asner, Sammy Davis, Jr., and Aaron Spelling."

"Oh?" It was getting interesting. "What do I have to do?"

"Just come to the tribute dinner. Everything else will be taken care of. You won't have to do anything, except say 'Thank you.'"

I knew B'nai Brith was a Jewish international service organization, but that was the extent of my knowledge. The guy kept talking, pitching, like the check was in the mail. Finally I said yes, and regretted it the minute I hung up.

When somebody says you don't have to worry about anything, you'd better worry about everything. I began to wonder why anyone would go to a dinner where Jay Bernstein was the recipient of a Jewish award. If nobody showed up, it would be humiliating. I called back.

"I'll only do it if you also honor Stacy Keach with the same award," I told him.

"But he's not Jewish."

"What difference does that make?" I said. "No Stacy, no Jay."

Telephone calls back and forth. I did some serious thinking between each one. The guy called again: "Okay, we'll give the award to both of you."

"Stacy gets first billing," I said.

"What do you mean?"

"Stacy's name comes before mine, in advertising, press releases, program, everything."

The Valley B'nai Brith probably wished they'd never come up with my name, but they agreed to place Stacy's name before mine. I was not being philanthropic. If the program went down the drain, Stacy would get the blame; if it was successful, I could take as much credit as I wanted to. It was set: Stacy Keach and Jay Bernstein, Men of the Year, 1984.

But the more I thought about it, the more I worried. Who would be the speakers? I hated the idea of B'nai Brith choosing people to praise me, when, if I were to die, they wouldn't take the time to go to my funeral. I called back.

"Why don't we do this thing as a roast? I'll get five people and Stacy can get five people. We'll all sit on the dais, and they can say whatever funny things they come up with."

B'nai Brith agreed, although they really didn't have much choice. My guests were Robert Culp, Robert Conrad, Bruce Boxleitner, Dionne Warwick and Dr. Joyce Brothers. Stacy chose Cheech Marin, Michelle Lee, Michael Crichton, Edward Albert and Ed Flanders.

Next, with the help of Warren Cowan, I got Milton Berle to be the program's master of ceremonies, gratis. Suddenly the B'nai Brith Man of the Year Award program was a Jay Bernstein production.

On the day of our anointment, Mayor Tom Bradley declared "Jay Bernstein and Stacy Keach Day in Los Angeles." It was the only time I took first billing, but now I had a hunch the evening's festivities would be successful.

They were. My parents flew in from Oklahoma City and sat among 1,600 people in the ballroom of the Sheraton Universal Hotel. My final contribution as de facto producer of the event was securing the entertainment. Theodore Bikel did his folk-music routine and Danielle Brisebois, from *All in the Family*, sang. Both were clients of mine.

Not all actresses are little angels. In fact, some are just the opposite. One actress that always had a personal vendetta against Jay Bernstein, so it seems, was Kate Jackson. In those days, the Burbank Studios were divided between Warner Bros. and Columbia, each renting about half of the property. I had an office at Columbia, but Warner Bros. was off-limits to me because of Kate Jackson. *Scarecrow and Mrs. King* was produced there.

When *Scarecrow* entered its third year, I thought enough water had passed under the bridge to venture over to see Bruce Boxleitner. They were shooting on top of a building. When I walked on the set, the first person I saw was Kate Jackson. I smiled and said, "Hi, Kate."

A few minutes later a secretary interrupted my conversation with Bruce. "You're wanted on the telephone, Mr. Bernstein."

I followed her to an office. On the phone was Alan Shayne, my neighbor and the head of Warner Bros. Television. He said curtly, "Jay, get out of there fast."

Frankly, I thought the building was on fire or there was a bomb threat. I hung up and went back to get Bruce, noticing en route that no one else was evacuating the premises. Before I reached Bruce, the secretary caught me again. "You have another call, Mr. Bernstein."

I returned to the office and picked up the telephone. "What's going on, Alan?" I asked. "I thought there was a fire or something."

"It's Kate," he answered. "You're creating a problem by being on her set. She wants you to leave."

After that Kate wouldn't acknowledge Bruce's existence except when the camera was rolling. Her behavior wasn't new to him; they'd had fights before, usually because Bruce wouldn't go along with her when she wanted to fire someone.

Not long after that, Hollywood insiders voted Kate as one of the least likeable actresses in show business. Jaclyn Smith, the third of the original Charlie's Angels, was voted one of the nicest.

Stacy Keach signed for the lead in *Mistral's Daughter*, a big-budget mini-series to be produced in Europe by Steven Krantz. Steve was the husband of Judith Krantz, who wrote the best-selling novel the script was based on. The movie would be shot during hiatus. The cast included Lee Remick, Stefanie Powers, Bob Urich and Timothy Dalton.

We were shooting the final episode of the first season of *Mike Hammer*. Stacy was antsy, eager to get to Marseilles, France, where *Mistral's Daughter* would soon go into production. I let him leave after his final shot, based upon his availability to loop scenes that required him to go to a sound studio. Paris had a good facility, so I foresaw no problems.

It turned out we had considerable looping to record, but Seymour Friedman, head of physical production at Columbia, didn't think much of the Paris studio. He wanted the work done in England. I called Stacy, who made arrangements to fly to London on April 3.

Stacy was a fine actor, which he recognized, but he didn't realize he had become a star. Mike Hammer was to television what James Bond was to movies. Stacy, self-effacing and mild-mannered, didn't get it. He thought of himself as another working actor, faceless and nameless after the job was done. His attitude was a mistake.

Early morning of April 4 my telephone rang . . . and rang. I came out of slumber and looked at my watch. It was after three a.m. and I was groggy. It was someone from Warren Cowan's London office. A dream lingered fitfully in my mind; I tried to shake it.

"Stacy's in jail."

"What!" I sat up.

"He got busted at Heathrow."

"Busted for what?"

"Smuggling cocaine."

"Stacy doesn't use cocaine," I said, and paused. "At least not that I know of."

"Well, he's in jail at Heathrow."

We hung up. I got out of bed and began to pace. Calls started coming in like news bulletins, each with a flash of fact. I slowly pieced them together like a jigsaw puzzle. Stacy and Deborah Steele, his secretary, had flown to London from Marseilles for the looping session at Pinewood Studios. Customs had minutely inspected Stacy's luggage. In his ditty bag they discovered a jerry-rigged can of shaving cream containing 3.5 grams of cocaine. The stash was worth $10,000 on the street; it was a major offense. Stacy and Deborah were placed in holding cells at the airport.

Shit! It was part of a continuum of high-profile busts. Recent Heathrow drug arrests featured an all-star cast, including American actor Tony Perkins and British celebrity wife Linda McCartney, Beatle Paul's mate. On the plus side, Perkins and McCartney had been released after hand slaps and fines. The negative side was the bad publicity. I could see the headlines: Drug Cops Nail Mike Hammer! Crime Buster Keach Busted!

The saga continued. At noon London time, Stacy was in the dock at the Uxbridge Magistrates' Court, adjacent to the airport. He pleaded guilty. The British Crown Prosecutor said he should be locked up and the key thrown away until the trial. The judge was in a more munificent mood, although only slightly. He set bail at $100,000 for Stacy and $15,000 for Debbie—in cash. They were remanded to holding cells while the machinery of their release, namely the machinations of Jay Bernstein, kicked into motion.

The immediate crux was the money. Unlike in America, where the court required 10 percent of the bail, the Brits wanted the whole measure—not nine yards but ten. I didn't have $100,000, certainly not in cash. I talked to Warren Cowan, with subtle hints. He'd been on the horn engaging a British barrister to defend Stacy. When he didn't volunteer to help with the bail, I called Bud Grant. I got the cold shoulder; he said he didn't think CBS could help, which was a diplomatic way of saying CBS *wouldn't* help. I called Herman Rush. Columbia was now owned by Coca-Cola. Surely they could come up with 100 Gs from their British account. Negative.

The question was who needed to help Stacy? The answer was obvious:

Steve Krantz, the producer of *Mistral's Daughter*. Stacy had taken leave from the miniseries for one day; to further delay the production would be costly. I called Steve in Marseilles. It's amazing how showbiz people come up with solutions when the problem affects them directly. The money was wired to London. By one p.m. British time, Stacy was out of jail. A hearing was set for May 16, time enough to finish *Mistral's Daughter* and get a defense in place.

Stacy had not called me, but I contacted the wire services anyway. "Stacy does not use drugs. Quote, unquote," I told them. "Before we went into production with *Mike Hammer*, he told me not to be vigilant about it, but if anyone working the series was known to be using drugs and we had proof, they were to be fired." The idea was to cushion the second day's headlines, to de-emphasize the story of Stacy's arrest with a second, objective account from someone in his inner circle, namely me.

By the time I got the AP off the line, the first light of day was edging over the hill directly below and across from my house. There was nothing to do but wait for Stacy's call. The telephone kept ringing—I had multiple lines. I foiled most of the questions as if I were making croisé moves with a sword, like a fencer in combat. I had nothing more to say until I talked to Stacy.

He called at midmorning my time, about six p.m. London time. He was back at Heathrow, awaiting a flight out to France. He was like the proverbial child caught with his hand in the cookie jar, chock-full of apologies and excuses. He did not admit to being guilty, but I knew he was, which, at the time, seemed suddenly irrelevant.

"Do you think this will affect the series?" he asked.

"I don't think so," I told him. I reminded him of the recent Perkins and McCartney sagas. And there were also the Tony Danza and Vanessa Williams cases. Danza had been found guilty by a jury of his peers for assaulting a bartender at Studio 54 in New York, but his conviction had not affected ABC's production of his new show, *Who's the Boss?* Williams had been forced to resign her Miss America title following publication of sexually explicit photos in *Penthouse* (shades of Suzanne and *Playboy*); yet she had landed a juicy role in NBC's *Partners in Crime*.

"I'm truly sorry it happened," said Stacy sincerely.

"You're my brother, Stacy. I'll stand by you, regardless. We're in this together."

We hung up, but I was concerned. Stacy was really down, depressed. I decided to get a reading from the network and the studio and then fly to France. I needed Stacy to be up when we resumed shooting *Hammer*. Besides, I wanted to thank Steve Krantz for springing him with the bail bond.

Before I left, I met with Bud Grant, who said succinctly, "As far as I'm concerned, if there's a problem, it's between Columbia and Stacy. I'm not going to worry about it." At Columbia the buck was passed to CBS. "If they don't rock the boat, what's there to worry about? It's up to them."

I did not stay long in Marseilles. I went out of a sense of duty. Although Stacy was not my client, he was my star and my friend and I felt obligated to boost his morale. No reason existed to be concerned about his day in court. Without exception, including Stacy, we all thought he would get a slap on the wrist, a fine and be sent his merry way.

Stacy completed *Mistral's Daughter* and appeared in court in London, and a trial date was set for December. He returned to the States and we went back into production on the series. We had completed nine episodes when Stacy voluntarily returned to London with his attorney. I did not go. I saw no reason to—it was a formality, nothing more. Warren Cowan went, hoping to stymie any negative posttrial publicity. We all knew the court would reprimand Stacy and then fine him. It was the amount of his fine that we talked about. None of us took into consideration the blizzard of cocaine stories that was consuming the British press.

When it's noon in London, it's four a.m. in L.A. That's about the time my phone rang. At first, I didn't recognize the voice. It was hysterical, spouting a geyser of emotion.

"Jay, it's horrible! It's horrible!"

"What is? Who is this?"

"It's inconceivable," he continued. "No one expected this, least of all Stacy."

Now I recognized Warren's voice, but his words didn't make sense. "What are you talking about?" I asked.

"They've taken Stacy away!"

I lurched to a sitting position. "Taken Stacy where? Who?"

"He pleaded guilty and the judge sentenced him to nine months in jail! They put him on a bus with bars on the windows, and it took off!"

By now I was standing, trying to absorb the information. I was as dumbfounded as Warren. We hung up. Prison? If the court was trying to make an example of Stacy, it had succeeded. Now I understood the horror in Warren's voice, and my own horror grew equal to his. The sentence was more than a ballbuster for a misguided man; it was a career buster, not only for Stacy and me and a dozen other executives, but for a cast and crew of two hundred. We had done so well, first with the movies and then with the series, now firmly entrenched at ten o'clock on Saturday night. Nine months in jail? Stacy Keach? Mike Hammer? I couldn't believe it.

Three days after Stacy was incarcerated, I was hit by another low blow. I was in Palm Springs. It was morning; I turned on the television set. A reporter on *Good Morning America* was announcing that my home had been firebombed. It was a surreal feeling, standing there, watching television and getting the first news about my own tragedy. I called Delmy. Most of the house had been physically saved, but the smoke damage was extensive. The bomb had been thrown into my garage. My Alan Ladd Rolls-Royce (I had bought it from his estate), the garage and the adjacent kitchen were destroyed. After we hung up, I sat down in a state of semi-shock. I didn't get up again until I saw Mary Hart on television that evening. She looked into the camera and said, "Jay, everybody is looking for you."

I drove to L.A. and checked into a bungalow at the Beverly Hills Hotel. I didn't see my house for six months. I didn't want to. I let Delmy handle the renovation. My thoughts were consumed with saving the Mike Hammer series.

I wired Stacy every day, but he was limited to posting one letter a week. I didn't want him to waste his time on me, so it was a one-way correspondence. When I read that he had been placed in the general criminal population, I put out a phony wire story that he'd been beaten up in jail, hoping it might get the attention of the prison authorities. Nothing happened. Then the playwright and actor Jason Miller tried to visit Stacy, but was disallowed. I put out another story criticizing Britain's treatment of celebrity inmates. This time Stacy was assigned work in the prison library.

Stacy was the first star to be charged, convicted and incarcerated for use of illegal drugs since Robert Mitchum got caught smoking a joint in 1949. Mitchum spent a month at Los Angeles County jail mopping floors, and then he went on to become a major motion-picture star. But Mitchum was Mitchum, a rebel from the outset, the kind of low-key man people liked after World War II. He was a misfit in a society tired of convention.

Stacy's problem was different. People didn't go to movie theaters and pay money to see him. *Mickey Spillane's Mike Hammer* was an invasive television program, and network executives were acutely sensitive to public reactions. Other series had been canceled for less valid reasons, and in the one sacrosanct category of success—ratings—we were just holding our own.

The odds against *Hammer* coming back after Stacy finished his jail sentence were enormous. Jimmy the Greek told me the odds were 1,000 to 1. But I was determined to save the show. My message was simple: Stacy had committed a crime, but he should only pay for it once. That was the American way.

Then CBS announced they were canceling *Hammer*. I countered by running an ad in the trades saying it wasn't canceled but put on hold. I didn't ask for network permission because I knew I wouldn't get it, but the ad put the show in a holding position, like an airplane flying in circles with its nose tilted down. I had to do something more dramatic, and I had to do it fast. I needed to save Stacy's reputation and the show at the same time. I called my PR man and told him to start planning a "Save Mike Hammer Campaign."

"What the hell does that mean?"

"It means I'm going on the road," I told him.

Chapter 28

SAVING STACY

I decided on a personal national campaign, seventeen cities in thirty-five days. It wouldn't be a crusade, because I could no longer make Stacy out to be a hero. And I didn't want to have a confrontation with CBS that would serve no positive purpose. It had to be a pilgrimage. My plan was to get on every radio and television talk show that would have me. While pitching the merits of *Mike Hammer*, I would encourage people to write the network asking to save the series. Columbia Television, my partner, had a vested interest in seeing the show back on the air, so Herman Rush gave me $20,000. I ended up spending another $40,000 out of my own pocket.

The first mistake I made was taking my girlfriend with me. Kristen was twenty-two, starstruck and preferred Hollywood to the pressure of the campaign. The second mistake was telling Stacy I wouldn't smile until he was out of prison. I went six months without smiling, which would end with Kristen and me breaking up. She couldn't handle my dour look. I sent Stacy a telegram Monday through Friday. He's a Gemini, like me, and I wanted to keep him in a positive mood.

I was an evangelical preacher on a country circuit espousing a fundamental gospel: once a man has paid for a crime, he should be allowed to go on with his life. It was a message of understanding. I thought Bud Grant at CBS was the man who would make the final decision on *Hammer*, but then I learned he had passed the buck to Harvey Shephard,

VP in charge of programming. I had lots of moles at the network, and one of the secretaries told me no one was reading the letters stimulated by my campaign; they were sending them to a dead-letter file in a basement warehouse. That pissed me off, so I got Harvey's home address.

I renewed my effort, beseeching TV viewers and radio listeners to write Harvey letters telling how good they felt about Stacy's rehabilitation and how much they missed *Mike Hammer*. On television I had them flash Harvey's home address and on the radio I repeated it a half-dozen times. My goal was to drive Harvey nuts with thousands of letters, enough that he would be forced to seriously consider placing the series back on the air. It was a 24/7 nonstop campaign.

I got sick in Cleveland and considered canceling the rest of the schedule. Yet I thought it was working, so we continued. Kristen was unhappy, and when my money began to run short she was even more unhappy because we had to bypass four-star hotels for cheaper places. It was like driving cross-country without a spare tire.

Chicago was the halfway point of the tour. We were tired when we arrived at O'Hare. I have flat feet and use arch supports in my shoes, but I was wearing slippers. We were walking down the concourse when a man with plastic limbs dashed by and—swoosh!—grabbed three pieces of our luggage without breaking stride, then was gone like a UFO. The luggage he stole contained my arch supports.

I saved Oklahoma City for last. I wanted Kristen to meet my parents, but when we deplaned, no parents were at the gate. I thought maybe they had decided to meet us at the hotel. We caught a cab and drove into the city. No parents were at the hotel. I went to the desk to see if they had left a message. No message. I called them. No answer. Four hours later my father called. My mother had unplugged the telephone because she thought they needed to take a nap before our arrival. I never saw them. I asked my dad to come to the hotel alone, but he said he couldn't. What he really meant was that he wouldn't.

We returned to L.A. just in time for Kristen to break down. She couldn't take it anymore, poor girl; she couldn't handle it. My house was not finished, and we had to check into another hotel, the last thing either of us wanted to do. The next day she was gone.

I leased a mansion in Stone Canyon, three houses from the Bel Air Hotel. It was sumptuous, with a volleyball court and bleachers, a half-size Olympic swimming pool and tennis courts. They meant nothing to me. I still wasn't smiling, nor would I until Stacy was released.

The network gave me no encouragement regarding the future of the show, not a hint. Nobody said, "Congratulations, Jay, you put on a good road show. Maybe you saved *Mike Hammer*." But I didn't need accolades. I had faith, like a Muslim before his execution. I just believed.

Harvey Shephard said he was unmoved by the tons of mail. When *People* asked him how many letters he and CBS had received, he said he didn't know. A CBS insider told me 400,000 people had responded to my message. Whatever Harvey really thought, the series went back on the air May 4 with nine weeks of reruns. I felt vindicated, even when Harvey proclaimed the letters had nothing to do with the decision. Someone somewhere in the CBS hierarchy had noticed them, even if Harvey had not.

Reruns, however, were not what I was after. Rerun audiences are weak compared to audiences watching original programming. Yet the networks were going into the summer season where almost everything aired was a rerun. It was now beyond my control. I could only hope that the summer audience would stick to *Mike Hammer*. It was a ratings game, which made me nervous. After two weeks, we were in third place. Harvey told *People* if the show didn't finish in front of NBC's *Hunter*, the future for *Hammer* looked bleak.

I decided to go see Stacy at Reading Gaol. I had begun to feel guilty. My enthusiasm for *Mike Hammer* had been so intense that it had become my life. I had pushed everyone for perfection, including Stacy. On a normal day I worked seventeen hours, and Stacy had kept up with me every step. I once asked him, "How do you do it? How do you keep up with me?"

"I learned at the Royal Academy of Dramatic Arts in London, when I was studying acting, how to nap five minutes an hour," he said.

Now I realized RADA was a cover for cocaine.

A couple of London newspaper reporters were waiting as I came out of customs at Heathrow. They started firing questions like Roman candles.

"It was my fault," I told them. "I pushed Stacy too hard. I tried to make him stay up with me, but he couldn't do it without some help. I didn't realize it, but he was like a tired truck driver who has to continue his trip. The little cocaine he used was like NoDoz, heavy caffeine. He didn't take it as a recreational drug; he took it to keep up with me, his producer. I drove him too hard." I choked back tears; I didn't want to, but I couldn't help myself.

I checked into the Dorchester. The next day I drove to Reading, a grim, overcrowded Victorian prison about thirty miles from London. When I saw it, I knew why Oscar Wilde had written *De Profundis* while he was jailed there. The place hadn't changed much in eighty-five years.

Stacy had been incarcerated five months. He was limited to one guest per month; I was May. I was ushered into a drab room, much like a set in a television drama about prison life. Several tables neatly checkered the room, occupied by inmates and their guests. Stacy was waiting alone at one of the tables. I hardly recognized him. Reading Gaol had done wonders for his weight, but it was a hell of a way to diet.

Network television executives aren't spineless, but sometimes they're close to it. Back home I "took" a meeting at CBS, pitching hard for the women who wrote letters on behalf of *Mike Hammer*, a quantitative element we had never considered. Everybody thought *Hammer* was a guy show. After lengthy debate, the TV hotshots said okay, they'd give *Mike Hammer* another chance. I felt redeemed. Then they threw me a curve.

"We're not sure if people interested in *Hammer* are interested because of *Hammer* or because of Stacy or because of you, Jay." I don't remember who was speaking; there were too many of them. CBS had more executives than stars. The bottom line was they wanted to test it.

Test *Mike Hammer*? Are you guys out of your fucking minds? I had produced three successful *Hammer* movies and over a dozen series episodes, and they were talking about testing.

"We'll let you do a two-hour movie, *The Return of Mike Hammer*. We'll give you a good time slot. If women want to see *Hammer* continue, then you'll get significant ratings and we'll give you a thirteen-episode trial."

It was more than a curve; it was a trick ball. They were putting me in an eight p.m. slot, the hour women dominated the clicker. Come on! I wanted to keep the women *Hammer* had, but it was still basically a guy show. Guys weren't going to watch the show at eight. They had me at home plate with a stick for a bat; I had to figure out a way to knock the ball out of the park. I left the meeting and set to work on *The Return of Mike Hammer*.

I called Nancy Reagan. It wasn't that I was trying to use her; one couldn't do that. Rather, I tried to influence her efforts to warn kids about the adverse effects of drugs. I had suggested the slogan "Just say no to drugs," which to my surprise became her campaign theme.

After I got him out of prison, my next major concern was the swift rehabilitation of Stacy Keach. I was sincere in my belief that a person should not be stigmatized for life because he made one mistake. That Stacy was a celebrity was both an asset and a liability. Had he not been a television star, his conviction and incarceration already would have been forgotten. But he was famous, and the issue wouldn't go away. Under the circumstances, I thought we should exploit his mistake positively before fame became infamy.

Nancy, fully aware of the trials and tribulations actors had to deal with, helped us considerably, knowingly and unknowingly. Almost by rote, Stacy became the poster child of her own campaign. There's no doubt in my mind that her support of Stacy helped CBS make its decision to give *Mike Hammer* another chance.

When it was announced that Nancy would be honored at an industry dinner for her "Say no to drugs" campaign, I made certain Stacy was invited. The affair was held at the Sheraton Universal Hotel at Universal City, adjacent to the huge Universal Studios complex.

The audience was a who's who of Hollywood. My table was behind Lew Wasserman's and next to Jimmy Stewart's, which meant my efforts in the war on drugs had been sufficient to keep me from being relegated to the bleachers.

Frank Sinatra was tabbed to present Nancy her award, an apt choice after his dynamic performance a few years before as a heroin addict in *The Man with a Golden Arm*. He was in top form. At the podium, he said, "Before I give this award to my friend Nancy Reagan, I first would like to give another award to a man who has more guts than anybody I know. His name is Stacy Keach." He then homed in on Stacy. "And, Stacy, if you ever need anything, just give me a call. My name is Sinatra, S-I-N-A-T-R-A. Stand up and take a bow, Stacy."

Sheepishly, Stacy stood. He received a standing ovation; indeed, the applause was greater than Nancy's when she received her award a minute later. Here was a guy who'd just spent months in a British penitentiary for drug smuggling and now his professional colleagues were honoring him. I was proud. Stacy's life had turned around.

I was a difficult producer. I had no background in producing; I had not worked my way up through the ranks learning the ropes. I made myself a producer the same way I made myself a publicist and a manager—by trial, error and force of will. Looking back, it was my misfortune to hook up with Columbia Studios. They wanted things done on the cheap. I strove for perfection, a difficult goal when your studio is sending you personnel that is sometimes as cheap as the budget.

Some satirists once put together what they named Hammer Lawn, a takeoff on Forest Lawn Cemetery. It had miniature tombstones engraved with the names of producers I fired from the *Mike Hammer* shows. Inexperienced, I didn't know a good producer from a bad producer. I just knew when someone wasn't doing what I wanted them to do. I ran off a lot of bad men, but I ran off some good ones too.

Producing was the third phase of my career, but I didn't really love it, which is what it takes to be successful in Hollywood. It was a thankless job. I had to be in charge of everything, and I never learned to delegate authority. It wasn't like *Sergeants 3*, where there was always time to kill, rehearsal time, preproduction time, production time and postproduction time. Television was a different world. Time meant everything, and the budget was set in concrete.

People published an article on me. Referring to the production of the *Mike Hammer* series, the writer said, "Bernstein was as much fun to have around as Mike Hammer at a mob picnic." He claimed more than twenty-five people, "four of them producers, either left the show or were fired." I didn't argue with his statistics. Fortunately, he interviewed Larry Brody, my supervising producer and top writer. Larry said, "I've worked for monsters, and Jay is only a monster if you haven't encountered the real monsters. He's not a megalomaniac and he doesn't take pleasure in manipulating people. He's a yeller and a screamer. He's also honest, and when an honest man is a yeller and a screamer, you're subject to confrontations. People in this business aren't used to confrontations. They're happier being stabbed in the back."

I wasn't any better on *The Return of Mike Hammer*. I ranted and raved, but I got the movie finished. It was good, but was it good enough to get a rating and go into series? I'd done everything I could, from getting the writers to packaging the talent. It was a strong story. Lauren Hutton was excellent as a counterpoint to Stacy. Short on budget, I persuaded Dionne Warwick, Dabney Coleman, Mickey Rooney and Bruce Boxleitner to play cameos for virtually nothing.

Once finished, however, everything was out of my control; a high rating or a low rating was up to the television audience. They would either like the show or not like it. They would either watch it or click to another channel. My emotional problem was the airdate—it was three months away. I had to wait it out, and as a consequence I fell into a severe depression. I retreated hermit-like into my home.

Stan Moress came by. He was getting ready to leave for Australia. After leaving public relations, he had developed a thriving management business, discovering diversified talents like the Miami Sound Machine and Gloria Estefan. He had not been without personal problems, however, and had succumbed to the pressures of the business. Recently he had been in rehab for drug and alcohol use. Having completed his regimen, he was feeling well and positive. I, of course, was his opposite.

"I'm going to be gone for a while also," I told him.

He was surprised. "Where are you going?"

"I don't know, but I can't handle the pressure anymore. It's too much."

"When are you leaving?"

"Tomorrow, about ten in the morning."

The truth is I didn't know where I was going or what I was going to do. The letdown after all my work to save *Hammer* had overwhelmed me. Was I suicidal? I don't know, but Stan thought I was. I wished him a happy and successful trip to Australia, and he left.

The next morning I packed a bag. I had no plan. I was going to get in my car and drive. I didn't know when or if I was coming back. It all depended on whether *Hammer* was successful or not. My doorbell rang. It was Stan. "You're supposed to be on a plane," I said.

"I'm going with you," he responded.

"I thought you had business in Australia."

"This is more important."

An hour later, we were in my car, Stan behind the wheel. We had no destination. Once we stopped and played miniature golf. In Ojai we checked into a hotel filled with superannuates, which seemed symbolic. We were there ten days. Stan was no longer drinking, but I made up for him. That's all I did—I just sat there and swigged booze. I had no desire to go out; my career, that is, *Hammer*, was out of my hands. I had to wait for its telecast, and then the ratings. One day Stan coaxed me out of my room. We went down to a lake and watched the ducks carouse and float about. It was a depressing time, but I will never forget Stan's patience.

Chapter 29

HOLLYWOOD
HART ACHE

Mary Hart came to Hollywood from South Dakota via Oklahoma City, where she had been a reporter on a syndicated television show called *PM Magazine*. She had a winning personality and television presence that served her well. I first met her when she came to my home with her mentor Danny Williams, an Oklahoma City radio-television celebrity. Danny asked me to represent her, but I wasn't interested. This was before she became the personification of *Entertainment Tonight*.

"She's gonna make it big," nagged Danny, "but she needs guidance."

I had no doubt that Mary was talented, but switching from journalism to entertainment was a heavy-duty task. Over the next eight years I saw her at various functions and she always asked me to become her manager. Each time, I politely turned her down. My attitude changed, however, when my home was firebombed and I saw Mary say nice things about me on television. I was touched, and subsequently signed her to a personal-management contract.

But what to do with her? Mary already had a blossoming career as the hostess of *Entertainment Tonight*. She was well-educated and multi-talented, but making a transition from reading a teleprompter to stardom as an actor or comedian was something of a different order.

My first big idea for Mary came about when her studio constructed a new set for *Entertainment Tonight*. Viewers complained because the new desk design obscured her classy legs. I saw my chance for a huge publicity stunt, with history repeating itself.

I announced that I was going to insure her legs for $2 million with Lloyds of London. Most people thought it was an original idea, but it harked back to Betty Grable, whose publicists at MGM had done the same thing forty years earlier, although for only half the amount. And in the fifties, publicists for Angie Dickinson, before the collapse of the studio system, had done the same for her, again for $1 million. I just doubled the amount.

The idea took off like a rocket. If Mary had been popular before, now she became iconic. The press devoured the story, and her picture, with an emphasis on her legs, was plastered on dozens of magazine covers. It made me nervous, however, because I had never purchased a policy.

I contacted Lloyd's of London, told them what I wanted to do and asked for a price. I had no intentions of buying anything more than a one-day policy, but when I got a quote for twenty-four hours of insurance it was astronomical. I said, "Thanks but no thanks," without informing anyone else, including Mary. We'd already reaped enormous dividends from the idea with no expenditure, and so had Lloyd's. It had been good advertising for them, and free. The press had made such a big deal about Lloyd's of London and their insurance that most people probably thought the company would insure the flies in their kitchen. So I remained mum and watched the story regenerate itself time and again, like a protoplasmic cell. When a representative of Planet Hollywood in Beverly Hills asked if he could hang the policy on the restaurant's wall, I told him I would have to find it first, and never called back.

Mary, as it unfolded, was one of the most difficult clients I ever represented. Neither Farrah nor Suzanne ever questioned my judgment; when I got an idea, I just did it. Alan Hamel might ask me about it later, but he was learning, or trying to. With Mary, however, I had to explain everything in fine, time-consuming detail. Something within her brain— it was more than curiosity—needed to know *why*. She was a pain, and also sneaky, although I'm sure she would not agree with my analysis. We argued a lot, and sometimes yelled at each other.

When you're sick, everybody is suddenly a doctor. When you have

a legal problem, everybody becomes a Robert Shapiro. In management, it's worse. Every Tom, Dick and Harry thinks he knows the pitfalls of the Hollywood jungle better than you do, although not once has he climbed up a tall palm tree to observe the lay of the land. Mary, unfortunately, seemed to listen to every pseudo-guide she came in contact with, particularly her boyfriends. Pillow talk!

Mary, like Suzanne Somers, wanted an all-encompassing career. She wanted a sitcom; she wanted a nightclub act; she wanted it all. I was not averse to her goals. Mary was a naturally talented girl, but it takes more than talent to be super successful, a fact I've reiterated. A career has to be choreographed.

I booked her in Las Vegas, but she went behind my back and made a separate deal with another hotel. Her boyfriend at that time was Henry Bushkin, Johnny Carson's manager. I suspected he was the mastermind behind Mary's actions. Mary, however, wasn't Johnny Carson. She was good on camera for *Entertainment Tonight*, but that type of talent isn't enough for a nightclub act. I wanted her to spend four months rehearsing, because if she failed, her dreams of a show-business career beyond a Paramount soundstage with a quasi-news show would be next to nothing. But no, Mary said she could develop a Vegas act in six weeks. Obviously, she did what she wanted to do. She rehearsed six weeks and opened at the hotel of her choice, rather than the one I had initially chosen. She failed, miserably.

I had misread Mary. She spoke as if she wanted to pursue an acting career, to do something that would take her beyond *Entertainment Tonight*. But that was all talk. Her income was the problem. After I began managing her, her earnings went from about $5,000 a week to $5 million a year. She was making so much money from *ET* that it subverted her other ambitions. As usual, I had made a business mistake when I signed her. I committed to manage Mary for 15 percent of everything she did, except *Entertainment Tonight*. Even when I renegotiated her contract at Paramount, I got nothing from it. I even put her with William Morris, who got 10 percent of her *ET* income, while I got nothing. It was a dumb thing to do, but I had done it before. In this case, however, it was the magnitude of my stupidity that bothered me.

After the insurance ploy, Mary was famous. I was at the height of my career as a producer, with both *Hammer* and *Houston Knights* on CBS, so I made a deal to do a *Mary Hart Show*. I put together a development package at Paramount, where *Entertainment Tonight* was produced. The first year they offered me one lousy treatment that was only two pages long. They knew what I didn't—Mary was no longer crazy to have her own show, and they weren't crazy for her to have one either. After all, Paramount was making a fortune on *ET*.

Our partnership was tumultuous and short-lived. After two years she fired me. I wasn't disappointed. She was rich by then, which gave her the latitude to think she was a genius. And then she sued me for "ruining her career." That was Burt Sugarman's ploy. Burt was not only a smart Hollywood producer, but he had become Mary's husband. Mary owed me about $100,000, and Burt persuaded her to file the suit. He was smart enough to know I would never go to court, and if I did, and won on top of that, it would take years and hundreds of thousands of dollars in a seemingly never-ending pursuit. We settled out of court, but it was hardly worth the effort.

For a brief period, like Arthur at Camelot, I was King of Columbia. I was the only producer on the lot with two ongoing series. In fact, the studio had only one other television project, *Starman*, with Robert Hays. It was hard not to become full of myself. Reaching millions of people every week made me feel powerful and preacher-like. *Mike Hammer* became a showcase for Old Testament justice; he never turned anyone over to the police because I didn't want a Robert Shapiro to get a criminal off on a technicality or a Johnnie Cochran to defeat the prosecution's case with histrionics. After the audience saw that the bad guy was guilty, Hammer killed him. The censors at CBS, always nervous about my shows, told me to make sure the victim drew a gun or knife first. On the other hand, *Houston Knights* was a lesson in the Golden Rule. I started doing what Michael Landon had done in *Highway to Heaven*. I tried to preach New Testament morality. It wasn't bad, being full of myself. Landon was gone, and no one else was preaching.

Unfortunately, Barbara Corday, president of Columbia Television, inserted herself more and more between Herman Rush and me. Had Barbara been a women's libber of the natural ilk, I would have gotten along with her. But she wasn't. She told me more than once that *Mike Hammer* was setting the women's movement back by a decade. I admired female pulchritude; Barbara couldn't stand it.

Barbara's claim to fame was as co-writer and creator of *Cagney & Lacey*, a show that had as much to do with reality as *Mike Hammer* did. They were entertainments, but at least, in my opinion, Hammer harkened to a day when men were men and women were women. To put it bluntly, Barbara gave me a lot of shit.

Suddenly *Hammer* was in trouble. Our ratings began to fall. We were in the wrong time slot; everybody knew it, but no one had the guts to do anything about it. Barbara began to wield her power. We argued about the well-endowed women I used in *Mike Hammer*. She hated the Hammerettes, which were the comic relief in an otherwise hard-hitting detective show. "You've got to get the girls out of the show," she told me. She didn't mean girls; she meant breasts. "You're setting the women's movement back ten years. You're a chauvinist."

"Oh, really?" I answered. "I thought I had helped women gain esteem. Farrah was considered perfect at thirty, after centuries of women being considered over the hill at twenty-five. And I don't think Linda Evans and her fans would agree with you, either. I made her the perfect forty-year-old, remember?"

"You're not going to fill the television screen with big-busted women anymore," she said authoritatively.

I was angry. I didn't like hardcore feminists any more than Barbara liked men. I looked at her, my face flushing red. Her chest was as flat as a board. "If you had tits, you'd know what this was all about!"

I exited, slamming the door so hard I heard pictures falling off the wall.

I did not know Kim LeMasters well. I had always dealt with Bud Grant. When cbs fell to third place among the networks, it became apparent

Bud was on his way out and Kim might be kicked upstairs. I needed to have a good relationship with him, and I wanted to make certain I had some negotiation leverage. I always tried to learn in advance as much as I could about the men and women I had to negotiate with. When I discovered that Kim loved Scotch and the finer things in life, I sent to his home a case of the oldest, most expensive Scotch money could buy. I did it secretly, making sure no one could trace the purchase back to me. I put a simple note with it: "With best wishes, the Phantom." A week later I checked with my courier to see if the Scotch had been accepted. It had.

The next month I sent Kim an expensive watch. It, too, was accepted. Thereafter I sent him a gift every month, always from the Phantom. He once asked me, "Are you the Phantom?"

I screwed up my face. "Am I the *what*?"

He dropped the subject, convinced I wasn't. This went on during the first short season of *Houston Knights*. Not once did Kim decline a gift, all of them expensive items. They amounted to about $10,000.

Then *Hammer* took its plunge, and we all knew it wouldn't survive in the ratings game.

I directed the last episode, "A Face in the Night." I got the job the same way I became an actor, by sleeping with the producer, one Jay Bernstein. And I had to go through the same convoluted exercise to become a director as I did when I became an actor, even when everybody at the studio and the network knew we were making the final episode. None of the big shots wanted me to direct, until I threatened a lawsuit. Then they decided I was the next John Ford.

What did I know about directing? Nothing, except what I had seen other directors do. I bought a book on how to direct, read thirty-two pages and threw it away. Like every job in the motion-picture business, the only way to learn how to do it was on-the-job training.

Seymour Friedman, who oversaw Columbia's television projects, became my mentor. On the first day of shooting he gave me a riding crop, à la Cecil B. DeMille. Every time I yelled "action," I felt embarrassed; and every time I yelled "cut," I inadvertently whipped my thigh with the crop.

By the end of the first day, my thigh was bruised. By the end of the week, it was bloody.

The episode was highly praised, due primarily to Stacy and Mary Frann, our guest star. I was more than pleased; I got on film what I set out to accomplish—dramatic action and production value. I had even tried to give motivation to the extras.

When I received my Directors Guild card, it was my seventh membership in an industry guild or union. I'm aware of only two other people who have as many memberships: Warren Beatty and Woody Allen.

Finished with my first and last directorial job, I turned my attention to *Houston Knights*, which wasn't doing much better in the ratings than was *Hammer*. But it was still new, having premiered as a midseason replacement. Given a chance in the fall, I thought it would get the necessary ratings. I was nervous, however; I saw the possibility of falling from my position as king to that of court jester.

It was the time of year when shows were renewed or canceled. We were on the schedule and off the schedule, swinging back and forth like a pendulum. When I heard finally that *Houston Knights* was not going to be renewed, I caught a plane to New York, where the decisions were made and announced.

It was night when I arrived. I went straight to the Essex House on Central Park, the hotel where Kim LeMasters was staying. He was not there, so I stood vigil in the lobby. I wouldn't leave until I talked to him.

He returned at 2:45 in the morning and didn't seem the least surprised that I was waiting in the lobby of his New York hotel.

"Kim," I said, "we've got to talk."

He looked at his watch, the one I had given him. "Jay, I'm tired. It's almost three in the morning. We'll talk tomorrow."

Tomorrow would be too late. If *Houston Knights* was canceled before I intercepted Kim again, I would be without a series.

"I need three minutes of your time, Kim. Not a second more."

He sighed. "Okay, talk."

"Not here," I said, looking at the late-night stragglers. "I've got to do it privately." He nodded, and we went upstairs to his suite. After he closed the door, I said, "Number one, I'm the Phantom."

He stared at me in silence.

"Number two," I continued, "I never thought it would come to this, but I have silent partners who want *Houston Knights* to stay on the air." I bent my nose with my knuckles in a mob gesture and then slashed my throat with a finger. "If it gets canceled, there's going to be real trouble for everybody."

We stared at each other, measuring reactions. I was calm, cool and acting as serious as I could. Kim was nervous.

"I'll see what I can do," he said.

I left. The next day *Houston Knights* was back on the schedule, renewed for the fall season. I didn't tell my partners, because I didn't have any.

I was in New York, so I called every media connection I had, setting up a summer publicity blitz. Midseason replacements seldom get media play if they don't vault to the top ten, but I had the contacts to put the show in the limelight. I scheduled appearances for the show's stars, Michael Beck and Michael Paré, on *Good Morning America*, *The Today Show*, the CBS *Early Show*, interviews on most of the independent channels, radio stations, and morning and afternoon newspaper interviews. It was a schedule that gives birth to stars.

As soon as I got back to L.A., I invited the two Michaels and their wives for dinner at Chasen's. If they knew we had been given twenty-two new episodes, they didn't act like it. Once we were seated, I gave them the news. "Congratulations!" I said. "*Houston Knights* has been picked up for the fall season!"

I told them about the advance publicity schedule I had set up. The couples looked at each other as if a stillborn child had been delivered. I was disappointed by their reactions, but it didn't curb my enthusiasm. As I continued, Michael Paré's face fell to his feet. I was befuddled. I really liked Michael, but I couldn't figure him.

"What's the problem, Michael?"

"Well, gee, I . . . I've got a movie in Colorado I'm supposed to do."

"Get out of it," I said. "We're talking about the beginning of your future here. You'll make more money on one episode of *Houston Knights* than you'll make on the entire movie."

He nodded, wavering. Then Michael Beck jumped into it. He said to Paré, "You don't have to do this publicity thing. I'm not. I'd rather do summer Shakespeare in the Valley. Columbia and CBS only have me when I'm doing the series." He turned to me. "You only have me when I'm actually working, Jay."

I was incredulous. I'd heard some misguided arguments before, but this was sheer stupidity. Rather than expressing my anger, I gave a sarcastic laugh. I told them, "If you guys are really serious about your careers, and I know you are, then jump on the bandwagon. This is an opportunity of a lifetime!"

Paré, who had a hangdog expression, said, "I'll see what I can do, Jay. I'll see if I can get out of my picture."

Beck started arguing, telling him a television project shouldn't dictate his schedule. "You should do what you want to do, not what they want you to do. They can't make you. Watch me." Then he looked at me. "I'm not doing it, unless you pay me for it."

I was getting pissed off. Obviously Beck realized expenses for him and his wife would be covered, but for me or Columbia or CBS to pay him to promote himself was outrageous. He was staring a gift horse in the mouth, but rather than come to his senses he grew more recalcitrant.

It went back and forth between us, our tempers rising. Then Beck's wife got her two cents in, and I, being the Southern gentleman I am, politely told her to shut the fuck up. That was it. Beck leaped up, fighting mad. He was compelled to protect his wife's honor. He challenged me without realizing I wasn't afraid of man or beast, including a fucking grizzly bear. It was stupid, but it happened.

I leaped up. Like two schoolboys, we got into a shoving match. My antics were well-known at Chasen's—it was one of my favorite restaurants—and already the waiters were scampering about trying to hustle people out of the dining room. The shoving match continued, and then Beck hit me. Naturally, I hit him back. From there we evolved into John

Wayne and Stewart Granger in *North to Alaska*. As with most fights, we both lost.

The next day I sent Beck's wife $500 worth of flowers with a handwritten note. My apology was not sincere, but I tried to make it sound sincere. If Michael and I couldn't get along, the show was in trouble. The flower man was turned back at the gate. I then mailed a copy of the note. I doubt if she read it, much less Michael. It was the beginning of the end for *Houston Knights*.

Paré sided with me, but he wasn't in a position to take a public stand. It wouldn't have made any difference. When you have polarization between two key elements in a production, you've got a problem; this one was insurmountable. It's okay to fight and argue—it happens all the time in the production business—but at the end of the day you have to let go of your hostility. Michael Beck couldn't do that. Like many actors, he was incapable of thinking ahead of the game; he allowed his wife to kill his career.

When we went back into production, Beck started siding with Clyde Phillips, a producer who had been foisted on me. It was Paré and me against Beck and Phillips. Then Barbara Corday got into the act, which meant Columbia Studios, my partner, was against me.

Beck and I never spoke to each other again. When I was on the set, I ignored him; likewise, he ignored me. A plot unfolded, obviously masterminded by Corday. I should have seen it coming, but I was too naïve to realize Barbara would let another series go down the drain just to suit her feminist philosophy.

Chapter 30

BLACKLISTED

I don't remember the exact chronology, but through the years I was on more blacklists than the Hollywood Ten. Of course, after Farrah left *Charlie's Angels*, I was blacklisted at ABC. They said they would never do any of my shows. Guess what? They didn't. I survived because of my relationship with Bud Grant at CBS and Herman Rush at Columbia.

Then Herman was kicked upstairs, and Barbara Corday succeeded him. After my fight with Michael Beck, it didn't take a genius to figure that Barbara would have a new ally in her war against me. I was becoming isolated. When Kim LeMasters asked me to come over to CBS for a meeting in his office, I saw the writing on the wall.

"Michael Beck won't go to work if you're on the lot," he said. "They want you to leave Columbia."

I was vulnerable and I knew it. "That's the name of the tune," I answered philosophically, "but I won't go easily."

It didn't matter that I had created *Houston Knights*; Barbara wanted me off the lot, and if Kim LeMasters of CBS was backing her, then I was gone. Kim explained that I would continue to be paid—$35,000 for each episode—and would still receive my credit as executive producer, but henceforth I was barred from entering the studio premises.

It was unfair. Kim knew it, but he didn't want to argue the issue. The two Bs had got me, Barbara and Beck. Yet I saw an opportunity in the midst of despair.

"Kim, if you're going to back Barbara, then I want you to give me the go-ahead to do a movie you once turned down, *The Diamond Trap*. I don't want it to look as if I can't get work. You know this town. Word spreads like a prairie fire. I don't want to have to play hardball."

I was trying to be nice and threatening at the same time. I was the Phantom speaking. Call it blackmail, but whatever it was, Kim gave me the go-ahead. The project would give me a needed break from the machinations of Hollywood. It would also give me $350,000.

"What about deficit financing?"

"I'll talk to Herman Rush," he said.

I took a 360-degree look at the industry, or rather, at my role in it. I was blackballed at ABC, and nobody was saluting me at NBC. The CAA crowd hated my guts. Army Archerd wouldn't give me a line of coverage in *Daily Variety* even if it were my obituary. And now, because of Barbara Corday, I was on the shit list at Columbia, where I had done four series and twelve television movies. Yet Kim was going to get my old studio to pick up the deficit on *The Diamond Trap*. Hollyweird! It was a ridiculous way to operate, but I didn't argue about the perks. I was still okay because I had CBS, where all of my projects had originated. Other than a few select members of the Hollywood Blacklist during the McCarthy era, I couldn't think of anyone who had survived as many blacklists as me.

The Diamond Trap was a teleplay by David Peckinpah from a book by John Minahan. Steve Mills, head of movies at CBS, had recommended it to me. Kim turned it down the first time I tossed it in the hopper, but now he gave me just enough money to executive produce it, which would not be easy because of the varied and remote locations. The story pivoted around a young woman involved in a diamond heist and two cops trying to solve the crime.

My first chore was to cast it. The actress was the critical role, the drawing card. In those days the maximum pay for a television movie star was $250,000, which I didn't have in my meager budget. I went to Emma

Samms, who I had discovered when I did *More Wild, Wild West*. I tried to persuade her to take the lead for $150,000. She was hesitant because she was doing *Dynasty*.

Around the same time, I ran into Brooke Shields at a party. She and her mother-manager, Teri, were on the West Coast to attend the People's Choice Awards. Brooke was concerned about her career. She had recently graduated from Princeton, and because her last movie, *Brenda Starr*, had been riddled with legal problems, she was considered difficult. Her pre-Princeton price had been $500,000, but now she was having trouble getting work of any kind.

Emma was taking too long to make her decision. Brooke would generate a great deal of publicity for the picture. I went to the People's Choice Awards with a script under my arm and gave it to Teri Shields, telling her I had a green light from CBS and I wanted Brooke. She seemed interested, but she didn't get back to me right away.

Meanwhile the network wanted this actor and the studio wanted that actor, but we couldn't reach an agreement on anyone. Then Teri called me and said Brooke wanted to do the movie. I said great, and meant it. I went to Columbia.

"We don't want her," I was told. "The network doesn't think she can act."

They were passing the buck again. The network had more one-shot amateurs than a high school senior play. Half of their productions wouldn't pass muster at a junior college. That's why they had fallen to number three. I countered, "Would you let Brooke read for the part?"

Brooke was back on the East Coast, but she flew out and read for the part. I figured any girl who had just graduated from Princeton would do a good read if she wanted to. Brooke did, and the director liked her. But Columbia still said no. They couldn't think beyond their five o'clock cocktails.

I didn't tell Brooke the problems I was having. She would have walked away. I went back to Kim, knowing he would have heard about her audition.

"Here's the problem," he said. "Everybody's afraid Brooke will pull an Elizabeth Taylor, hold up the production with demands and cost us a fortune."

"Let's be realistic," I said. "Brooke has been out of the business four years. She needs a comeback. She's not going to pull any stunts. Besides, she's a really nice, responsible young woman."

"She may be, but she's not worth five hundred thousand. Not to this network."

It went back and forth for several days. I argued with CBS, I argued with Columbia. Finally someone said, "We'll take her at seventy-five thousand, but you have to put your salary in escrow. If she screws up one time, if her mother delays the production for one minute because she doesn't like the lighting or something, it comes out of your pocket."

I took the deal because I had faith in Brooke, but it left me feeling queasy. Had I known what else lay in store, I might have backed off. After the deals were cut between Jay Bernstein Productions, Columbia Studios and CBS Television, I was saddled with three more executive producers. One would not have been unusual, but three? In other words, what was saved on Brooke's fee was being distributed to studio and network henchmen.

After I persuaded Brooke to take the deal, I signed Twiggy, the matchstick English model, in a supporting part. She had reservations— she'd never played a serious role before. "Look," I told her, "if the movie succeeds, it will rejuvenate your career. If it fails, it will be Brooke's fault. You don't have anything to lose."

I did not cast the two detectives. Someone at the network owed favors. As a consequence, I was burdened with Howard "Johnny Fever" Hesseman, a competent actor and former hippie who had evolved into an anti-authority individual full of hatred. He played the chief detective. The junior detective was Ed Marinaro, a good actor and a good guy.

Hesseman turned out to be more of a jerk than any actor I've ever known. Once we arrived on location in Wales, he told the cast they had one of two choices to make. He was the star (in fact, he did get top billing), and the rest of the cast could either eat with him or with me, but the two were not going to mix.

His attitude gave me reason to pause. I did not know his background, nor did I care about it. What I knew was this: I had arrived in Hollywood twenty-eight years earlier with $400 in my pocket. I had worked hard, paid my dues, and now this movie, which CBS had previously turned down, was going into production because of me. Howard Hesseman and a hundred other people were gainfully, if temporarily, employed because of my effort and mine alone. It was a rehash of the first Mike Hammer movie with Kevin Dobson.

The rest of the cast had misgivings about Hesseman's assumed powers. None of them alienated me, but, having to work with Hesseman, they were careful regarding relationships. Ed Marinaro in particular, during a moment when he felt he wasn't being watched by big brother, told me how sorry he was with the way things were going.

It was a test of human nature, which had little to do with the age-old problem of management versus labor. Hesseman was simply devoid of rational thinking. One night after the company had wrapped, my line producer Jeffrey Morton came out of a bathroom to discover he had been left behind without transportation. The only person remaining with a car was Hesseman. When Jeff asked him for a lift, Hesseman retorted, "I don't associate with Bernstein's production people." Jeff had to walk.

Brooke, in contrast, was the epitome of professionalism. She was first to arrive at the set and the last to leave it. She was neither spoiled by stardom, nor arrogant in her behavior. She was a lady of the first order, and her name and public image served precisely the purpose I had anticipated.

Despite Hesseman, whose antics reminded me of a spoiled teenager, we brought the movie in on time and schedule and prepared for its television debut.

After Barbara Corday made me persona non grata at Columbia, I was approached by several producers and studio employees who wanted Barbara out. It wasn't that they felt sorry for me—they were concerned for themselves. They wanted me to join a secret palace coup to get rid of her. I gladly gave them my blessing. The coup was successful, but Barbara ended up replacing Kim LeMasters, who was deposed at CBS. Now I was added to the CBS blacklist. A friend at CBS told me that once Barbara took her chair at the network, I became a noun. I laughed. The cliché was true: I couldn't win for losing.

Hollywood is forever fluid. People come and go; only the institutions remain in place. Barbara Corday's reign at CBS was shortlived. The new executives were open to new ideas. I gave them an old idea: *Mickey Spillane's Mike Hammer*. To my surprise, I got a green light for another two-hour television movie.

Stacy Keach was unavailable, so I cast Rob Estes, who had been in two successful TV series, *Silk Stalkings* and *Melrose Place*. As Velda, we chose a *Playboy* Playmate, Pamela Anderson. It was her first television role. After initial casting, things started falling apart.

I was unhappy with the script. CBS wasn't. We argued. I wanted a rewrite; the money people overrode me. Profit had always been important, but by the 1990s, after most of the studios and networks had been gobbled up by non-industry corporations interested solely in the bottom line—profit had become everything. Quality of product was a distant, secondary goal. I raised hell. The new people at the network called me on the carpet.

"Jay, you're being too difficult," they said. "We don't give a shit about the quality—we need the product. Here's the deal. We're going to give you $250,000 and credit as executive producer. But you can't go within 100 miles of the locations while the movie is being shot. Take it or leave it. Otherwise, *Mike Hammer* is on the shelf."

I took the money.

I never intended Mike Hammer to become a cottage industry. After the Rob Estes–Pamela Anderson fiasco, I thought I would put it to rest. Then, almost ten years to the day the last series went off the air, Stacy Keach called me.

He had met two producers of syndicated programming on a golf course. They wanted to know if *Mike Hammer* was available. I was wary.

Syndicated series were difficult at best—it was all about marketing. Without the benefit of an initial network airing and subsequent studio distribution, the odds were against success.

I met with the producers. Their money came from Europe. They were full of promises. One promise I asked for was up-front distribution contracts in the five major television markets in the United States. They said they could deliver. I was still wary. I called Mickey Spillane. He said, "Let's do it. I need the money."

We did it, or rather they did it. Again I was executive producer, but I never went to the set, not once. Mickey and I stayed home. I got $37,000 per episode for doing nothing. They shot twenty-two segments of *Mike Hammer: Private Eye*. The shows were terrible, produced on the cheap and aired at three o'clock in the morning in the major markets. I took my money and kept my mouth shut, but I wasn't pleased. I had never been in the business solely for money.

Chapter 31

RETIREMENT

When Barbara Corday blacklisted me at Columbia, I was promised a buyout deal for *Houston Knights*. I never received anything except my stipends as executive producer. I figured Columbia owed me, say, $300,000. It was an arbitrary figure. Just for the hell of it, I called my lawyer and told him to send a bill for $600,000. This was ten years after the series ended.

A few days later I received a check for $549,000. It floored me. They would fire an actor because of an accounting error when he was supposed to get a $200 raise (I was aware of just such a case), but they could send me almost $600,000 without debate. I surmised that someone said, "Let's not get into another war with Bernstein."

Whatever; it was time to retire, time to be forgotten.

Of course, I did not retire in the conventional sense. It was not my nature to sit back and watch the parade go by. I continued to consult for hundreds of wannabe actors and I became an advisor on several television documentaries and docudramas, usually unpaid. I produced several biographical documentaries (Alan Ladd, Sammy Davis, Jr., William Holden, Susan Hayward, et al.) because I wanted to make sure their lives and accomplishments were reported honestly. Television documentary-making had already begun its copycat effort to reproduce on film the sleaze of printed tabloid journalism.

I am still haunted by the death of Sammy Davis, Jr. I had been in Palm

Springs when I heard about it on the radio, in 1989. Rather than giving a proper and praiseworthy obituary, the commentator had spent the best part of ten minutes talking about Sammy's flirtation with Satanism, a flirtation that in real time and in real life had been about as long as the radio report. Nothing was said about Sammy's triumphs and achievements. I had become so upset that I got drunk and obnoxious and ended up in jail in the desert in the middle of nowhere. As usual, I had to call Robert Shapiro to get me released.

In 2003 and 2004, NBC produced back-to-back docudramas featuring the television-series experiences of Suzanne Somers and Farrah Fawcett respectively: *Behind the Camera: The Unauthorized Story of Three's Company* and *Behind the Camera: The Unauthorized Story of Charlie's Angels*. I was a consultant on both movies, and given a credit on the second one.

It is difficult for actors to play people who are not only still living but who are still viable commodities, as Suzanne and Farrah certainly were; but the actresses who portrayed them did competent jobs. Wallace Langham, a young actor from Texas, played the Jay Bernstein role in both movies, and I thought very creditably.

Docudramas are seldom totally accurate. Time is often compressed and otherwise dull scenes are embellished for dramatic purposes. I've never had qualms with such changes as long as the storyline sticks to the general truth and the characters are rendered as closely as possible to their true selves. The movie about Suzanne was fairly accurate, except for the time gap between when she fired me and when Alan Hamel got her a job without my help, a pitch job for Thighmaster. I didn't complain, although with the compression of time it appeared that Alan successfully took over her career where I had left off. The real gap was seven years. Seven long years between the final contract I had negotiated for her and his first.

When I saw the rough cut of the movie about Farrah, I thought it was okay, too, although minor liberties had been taken with the truth. Then, about two weeks before it was aired, a friend of mine showed me the final cut, surreptitiously. After my consultation was finished, the producers had added a fifteen-second scene of Jay Bernstein (that is, Wallace

Langham) at the end of the movie. It had me at the corner of Hollywood and Vine accosting young women, saying, "Do you want to be a star? I'll make you a star! Just sign here!" It was not only insulting, but demeaning.

I called the producers and told them I wanted the scene removed. "Not only would I never approach someone that way, but it's misleading to young actresses."

"But it's funny!"

"It may be funny to you, but it's not funny to me."

"Well, we're not cutting it."

Telephone calls went back and forth. It was like a police interrogation. One executive would give me the "nice" treatment, like he was my best friend; the next one would play the tough guy: "If you press this, Jay, you'll never work in this town again!"

I finally referred them to my attorney. They cut the scene.

I bumped into a man at a party who told me that he remembered being in my home a couple of times "in the old days." I did not recall him, but thousands of people had been guests at my home at one time or another. "What I remember most vividly," said the man, "was a beautiful young woman sitting in your Jacuzzi. What happened to her?"

"Oh, she's still there," I told him. "Her name has changed a few times and the color of her hair and eyes, but she's still sitting there, and she's still twenty-five."

The man laughed, unaware that I was serious. With the exception of Susan Hayward, all of my girlfriends through the years had been in their twenties. It wasn't that I didn't like women in their thirties and forties, or even older. I worked with many of them, and was fond of most of them. But I had a fixation on beautiful young women. Hollywood was always about young people, and I suppose I wanted to retain a grip on that age.

A friend asked me, "Why do you always go out with young women?"

"Because their stories are shorter," I answered. But the real reason was because that was my business—making young people into stars.

During the *Mike Hammer–Houston Knights* years, I was making $100,000 a week between the two shows. I had a deal at Paramount for another $10,000 a week, which the studio paid me to make sure Mary Hart didn't get a series on the air. At the same time, I was managing clients like Bruce Boxleitner and William Shatner, from whom I collectively received a half-million dollars a year. It was a great deal of money. I had a limousine and a chauffeur and a huge movie-star home, but all of it, including the money, was nothing more than accoutrements to the Hollywood dream I was living, a dream that came true.

By chance, I saw *The Warriors* on television a couple of nights ago. Michael Beck. Then I ordered a copy of *Streets of Fire*. Michael Paré. It was weird watching those fellows after a lapse of almost twenty years. I watched them play out their roles with admiration, wistfully because they had not become the big stars I thought they would. For a fleeting moment I was tempted to blame myself for their shortcomings. But I didn't. Had they made that publicity junket back in the eighties, their careers might have taken a different course. I don't know what happened to them. I've heard that Paré is still acting, and the last I heard of Beck he was reading John Grisham's novels for Books on Tape.

Most of the stories of my life have a footnote. Twenty-five years after Farrah fired me, I got a call from Richard Barrie, who had engineered my termination with her and whom I had not seen since Farrah and I parted as manager and client. Fabergé no longer existed, although I'm sure Richard and his father came out of its demise as wealthy men.

"Richard, it's been a long, long time," I said without bitterness. "What can I do for you?"

He wanted advice from me regarding his daughter, who hoped to pursue an acting career, which meant she had that age-old dream of becoming a movie star. If I could give them a few minutes, they would fly out from New York. I laughed and told him I would be delighted. The following day Richard, his British wife and their lovely daughter arrived at my doorstep. The would-be actress was nineteen, bright, beautiful and certainly presentable, but she was like 10,000 other wannabes I had interviewed in a forty-five-year career. All I could offer was the truth. It was a tough business; few people succeeded in it. As for me, I was no longer managing talent.

A week later, I got an unexpected call from Farrah. We had seen each other off and on through the years, and had talked infrequently on the telephone, so I wasn't overly surprised. Usually when Farrah called, she had a problem and needed advice.

"Farrah, how are you?" I said. "What can I do for you?"

After a long pause, she got it out: "Jay, will you become my manager again?"

Then I got a call from Suzanne Somers. She wanted me to come to a preview of her autobiographical one-woman play, *The Girl in the White Thunderbird*, before it opened on Broadway. I went—it was presented in a small theater in the Valley—but I had trouble sitting through it. All the deals I had put together for Suzanne were now attributed to Alan Hamel. I grew angry as I sat there. The man next to me, an agent I had known for years, gripped my arm and whispered, "Don't let it get to you, Jay. It's showbiz."

The curtain fell. I didn't go backstage. I went home.

When I received an RSVP invitation to the opening of the play on Broadway, I called Marsha Yanchuck, Suzanne's secretary.

"Marsha, this is Jay. Would you tell Suzanne that I can't respond to the RSVP invitation regarding her play?"

"Why can't you, Jay?"

"How can I respond when I never existed?"

As for Farrah, she will always and forever be my special Angel. Period.

Suzanne, and all my stars for that matter—at the end of the day, I love them deeply with all my heart. How could I not? They are a part of me. I am a part of them. Regardless of personal or industry politics, we all did something very special together indeed. We created magic!

We lived our dreams.

We helped the world.

We changed the world.

We did our jobs.

And we did them very, very well.

Hollywood, a town that devours its young and forgets its old . . . but I'm still smiling.

THIS MEMOIR IS THE RESULT OF A YEARLONG COLLABORATION between Jay Bernstein and me. Jay had wanted to write a history of Hollywood as seen from the inside looking out, interweaving his personal experiences during a period just short of fifty years. I worked daily with him for a solid year, piecing his amazing story together. Then suddenly on April 30, 2006, Jay succumbed to a massive stroke. Fittingly, Farrah Fawcett stayed by Jay's side at the hospital until his final breath on earth.

A few weeks later, a memorial service was held for Jay at Paramount Studios. It played to a packed house at the Paramount Theater, an event Jay would have appreciated, with 500 stars, directors, producers, friends and fans in attendance. In my mind the service reaffirmed that Jay was more than another Hollywood character.

Although Jay had vivid recollections of almost every person he represented, befriended and combated during his career, he was aware that only a handful could be explored in a memoir. Therefore he chose a select few people around whom to weave his story, not all of whom he considered friendly witnesses to the events.

"I'm not interested in other people's viewpoints," he once said to me. "They would be at odds with mine. I want to tell my story of Hollywood as I saw it, as it happened to me, without a Rashomon effect.

"Let's say we take an Australian aborigine to Africa to see his first elephant," he continued. "Before we show him the elephant, however, we blindfold him. Then we put him behind the elephant and take the mask off. All he sees is a big asshole and a tail. Then we put the blindfold back on the aborigine, take him away and ship him home. He doesn't know anything about elephant tusks, trunks and ears, but back among his kin he is nevertheless the resident expert on elephants. Well, the world is replete with aboriginal elephant experts, particularly when it comes to the Hollywood jungle."

Jay thought of himself as a product of television more than of motion pictures, but an interesting fact surfaced during the final stages of assembling his story. His clients were nominated for more than a hundred Oscars and received in excess of forty.

Finally, Jay had wanted to write more thoroughly about certain people who are hardly mentioned in the preceding pages, in particular Stan Moress, Stan Rosenfield, Jon Morton, Gray Frederickson, Michael Mesnick and especially Delmy Tochez, all of whom were close friends or members of his "team" at one time or another, some for much of his adult life.

Alas, he died too soon.

JAY BERNSTEIN was a legendary Hollywood publicist, personal manager, producer and director.

LARRY CORTEZ HAMM was a veteran Hollywood writer and historian, and the ghostwriter of many screenplays, newspaper and magazine articles and autobiographies.

DAVID RUBINI is a writer, producer and a former publicist, television and radio ad executive, and advertising agent who splits his time between Dallas and Los Angeles.

ROGER KARNBAD/CELEBRITYPHOTO.COM

In Loving Memory

JAY BERNSTEIN
1937–2006

LARRY CORTEZ HAMM
1947–2009

Maude Adams	Edd "Kookie" Byrnes	Dennis Day	Eydie Gorme
Nick Adams	James Caan ★ ★	Jimmy Dean	Frank Gorshin
Jack Albertson ★	Michael Callan	John Denver	Lou Gossett, Jr. ★
Lola Albright	Corinne Calvet	John Derek	Curt Gowdy
June Allyson	Art Carney ★	Bruce Dern ★ ★	Lord Lew Grade
Ed Ames	David Carradine	Angie Dickinson	Sheilah Graham
Melissa Sue Anderson	Keith Carradine	Donna Dixon	Lee Grant ★
Pamela Anderson	Barbara Carrera	Kevin Dobson	Kathryn Grayson
Susan Anspach	Jim Carrey	Richard Donner	Jane Greer
Roone Arledge	Lynda Carter	Kirk Douglas ★	Joel Grey ★
Elizabeth Ashley	Angela Cartwright	Michael Douglas ★	Merv Griffin
Frankie Avalon	Veronica Cartwright	Faye Dunaway ★	Andy Griffith
Burt Bacharach	Jack Cassidy	Billy Eckstine	Charles Grodin
Joe Don Baker	Carol Channing	Vince Edwards	Steve Guttenberg
Stanley Baker	Chicago	Samantha Eggar ★ ★	Dan Haggerty
Gene Barry	Lois Chiles	Rob Estes	Larry Hagman
Drew Barrymore	Candy Clark ★ ★	Linda Evans	George Hamilton
Bee Gees	Dick Clark	Fabian	Julie Harris ★ ★
Ed Begley ★	Petula Clark	James Farentino	Richard Harris ★ ★
Tony Bennett	James Clavell	Farrah Fawcett	Mary Hart
Milton Berle	The Clinger Sisters	Francis Faye	Richard Hatch
Carl Betz	James Coburn ★	Norman Fell	Isaac Hayes
Theodore Bikel ★ ★	Dabney Coleman	José Ferrer ★	Dick Haymes
Fred Biletnikoff	Joan Collins	Sally Fields ★	Susan Hayward ★ ★
Linda Blair ★ ★	Chuck Connors	Totie Fields	Joey Heatherton
Robert Blake	Mike Connors	Eddie Fisher	Dwight Hemion
Blood, Sweat & Tears	Robert Conrad	Peter Fonda ★ ★	Catherine Hicks
Sonny Bono	Hans Conried	Glenn Ford	Arthur Hill
Ernest Borgnine ★	Jeff Conaway	Steve Forrest	William Holden ★
Bruce Boxleitner	Tim Conway	Tony Franciosa ★ ★	Hope Holiday
Eileen Brennan	Alex Cord	Aretha Franklin	Earl Holliman
Lloyd Bridges	Bud Cort	Mary Frann	Ron Howard ★
Danielle Brisebois	Howard Cosell	Victor French	Engelbert Humperdinck
May Britt	Bob Crane	Zsa Zsa Gabor	Jeffrey Hunter
James Brolin	Richard Crenna	James Garner ★ ★	Jim Hutton
Foster Brooks	Gary Crosby	Greer Garson ★	Lauren Hutton
Dr. Joyce Brothers	Xavier Cugat	Christopher George	Jill Ireland
Yul Brynner ★	Robert Culp	Lynda Day George	John Ireland
Delta Burke	Vic Damone	Gil Gerard	Michael Jackson
George Burns ★	Mac Davis	Gladys Knight & the Pips	The Jackson Five
Wendell Burton	Patti Davis	Paul Michael Glaser	Carolyn Jones ★ ★
Red Buttons ★	Sammy Davis, Jr.	Bobby Goldsboro	Dean Jones

★ ACADEMY AWARD WINNER   ★ ★ ACADEMY AWARD NOMINEE

Quincy Jones	Patrick McGoohan	Suzanne Pleshette	Elke Sommer
Shirley Jones ★	Ed McMahon	Eleanor Powell	Steven Spielberg ★
Tom Jones	Kristy McNichol	Juliet Prowse	Mickey Spillane
Sam Katzman	Sid Melton	Richard Pryor	Mark Spitz
Robert Kaufman	Don Meredith	Richard Quine	James Stacy
Lainie Kazan	Jason Miller	Martin Rackin	Tommy Steele
Stacy Keach	Robert Ellis Miller	Deborah Raffin	Craig Stevens
George Kennedy ★	Donna Mills	Lou Rawls	Raymond St. Jacques
Eartha Kitt	Sir John Mills ★	Aldo Ray	Sharon Stone ★
Shirley Knight ★	Juliet Mills	Martha Raye	Susan Strasberg
Don Knotts	Martin Milner	Helen Reddy	Sally Struthers
Burt Lancaster ★	Sal Mineo ★	Robert Reed	The Supremes
Michael Landon	Robert Mitchum ★ ★	Debbie Reynolds	Donald Sutherland
Abbe Lane	Ricardo Montalban	Buddy Rich	James Taylor
Robert Lansing	Elizabeth Montgomery	Righteous Brothers	The Temptations
Tom Laughlin	Terry Moore ★ ★	Rodney Allen Rippy	Alan Thicke
Peter Lawford	Vic Morrow	Joan Rivers	Danny Thomas
Steve Lawrence	The Muppets	Cliff Robertson ★	Mel Torme
George Lazenby	Don Murray ★ ★	Smokey Robinson	Claire Trevor ★
Brenda Lee	Jim Nabors	Diana Ross ★ ★	Forrest Tucker
Peggy Lee ★ ★	Ralph Nelson	Katherine Ross ★ ★	Cicely Tyson
The Lennon Sisters	Franco Nero	Richard Roundtree	Robert Urich
Mervyn LeRoy ★	Wayne Newton	Mort Sahl	Lee Van Cleef
Shari Lewis	Warren Oates	Susan Saint James	Casper Van Dien
Ray Liotta	Hugh O'Brian	Emma Samms	Dick Van Dyke
Peggy Lipton	Edmond O'Brien	Dick Sargent	Rachel Ward
Cleavon Little	Arthur O'Connell ★	Telly Savalas	Sela Ward
Rich Little	Tatum O'Neal ★	John Saxon	Dionne Warwick
Joshua Logan ★ ★	Jennifer O'Neill	Gia Scala	Adam West
Herbert Lom	Jack Palance ★	Seals & Crofts	Mae West
Julie London	Michael Paré	George Segal ★ ★	Barry White
Loretta Lynn	Eleanor Parker ★	Peter Sellers ★ ★	Margaret Whiting
Shirley MacLaine ★	Barbara Parkins	William Shatner	Stuart Whitman
Lee Majors	Leslie Parrish	Bobby Sherman	Billy Dee Williams
Jayne Mansfield	Minnie Pearl	Brooke Shields	Paul Williams
Peter Marshall	George Peppard	Henry Silva	Fred Williamson
Dean Martin	Tony Perkins	Melvin Simon	Jonathan Winters
Dewey Martin	Nehemiah Persoff	O.J. Simpson	Shelley Winters ★
Ross Martin	Joanna Pettet	Frank Sinatra ★	David Wolper ★
Tony Martin	Jo Ann Pflug	Alexis Smith	Chuck Woolery
Al Martino	Slim Pickens	Gary Smith	Gig Young ★
Virginia Mayo	Donald Pleasance	Suzanne Somers	Terence Young

★ ACADEMY AWARD WINNER   ★★ ACADEMY AWARD NOMINEE